Susie Murphy is _____ _____ _____ _____ author. She loves historical fiction so much that she often wishes she had been born two hundred years ago. Still, she remains grateful for many aspects of the modern age, including women's suffrage, electric showers and pizza. A Class Forsaken is her third published novel.

ISBN-13: 979-8670498647

www.susiemurphywrites.com

A Class Forsaken

A Matter of Class, Book Three

Susie Murphy

Also by Susie Murphy

A Class Apart
A Class Entwined

For Mam, who has been giving me feedback on my writing since I was eleven years old, and for Dad, who helped me take a crucial step forwards when I needed it. Love and gratitude to you both.

Chapter 1

'Arrah, here's the rain again.'

'I need to get my boy indoors. He's only after getting rid of a cough, the craythur.'

'Jaysus, 'tis coming down hard now. Hurry up, you in front!'

Cormac smiled, even when a fellow hastening past trod on his foot. The Irish accents flowed around him in eddies of urgency and commotion as folk scurried about the pier, intent on dodging the rain whether they were boarding or disembarking. After so many years surrounded by the refined voices of the upper class English, the recognisable brogue of his countrymen stirred within him the joy of homecoming. Granted, he was in Cove, a seaport town in Cork harbour, where the locals had a high-pitched inflection quite different to the flatter accents of the inhabitants of Carlow, but it would not be long before the soil of his native county would be beneath his feet once more.

He put a protective hand on Emily's shoulder, coaxing his daughter to his side to shield her from the heaving crowd.

'Stay close to me, *a stór*,' he said to her, his 'treasure'.

Her eyes, their shade of blue identical to his own, were wide with delight as she gazed about her, enamoured by the sights and sounds, from a donkey and cart clattering by to the scrawny head of a yapping dog poking out from inside its owner's coat.

Beside them, Bridget raised her face and let the rain trickle down her cheeks, like she was being baptised by the Irish skies. Then a large drop landed in her eye and she ducked her head, laughing beneath the rim of her bonnet.

The uncongenial weather could do nothing to dampen their spirits. After their frantic escape from law enforcement in London and a three-day voyage around the south coast of England, they had finally reached Ireland.

Home.

There were many uncertainties ahead, but most would have to wait; their first concern was finding a place to stay for the night. Fortunately, the friend they had made on the voyage had offered assistance in that matter.

Nancy McLoughlin followed behind them, endeavouring to keep control over her gaggle of children. Clutching her baby to her chest, she exclaimed, 'Peggy, hold onto your sister's hand afore she gets lost in the crowd. Put your cap back on, Danny, can't you see it's raining? Tommy, get back here!' she hollered as her eldest darted away from the straggling group.

Cormac neatly seized the boy by the elbow as he ran past. 'Heed your mother,' he chided. 'This is no place to go wandering.'

Nancy caught up to them with the rest of her offspring, the bundles in the two girls' arms their only luggage. Cormac and Bridget each carried a valise.

'Lord in heaven,' Nancy said, her working-class English accent at odds with the Irish voices around them, 'it's bedlam here.' She clipped Tommy about the ear. 'Don't you run off again or your father will hear of it.'

The boy assumed an angelic air of contrition.

'What's the name of the street we're looking for?' Cormac asked Nancy.

'Harbour Row,' she said. 'It looks out over the water so it ain't likely to be far.'

Glancing around the pier, he spotted a ticket seller booth whose occupant was staring out dismally through a sheet of water running off the roof. Skirting the deluge, he asked the ticket seller for directions and the fellow imparted them in a Cork accent so thick that Cormac had to ask him to repeat it twice. Finally grasping enough of the necessary details, he thanked the man and beckoned to the others, leading them away from the thronged pier.

They were looking for McLoughlin's Boarding House on Harbour Row. Nancy's husband was an Irishman whom she had met in London, but in the past year he had returned to his hometown to set up a boarding house with his unmarried sister. Nancy had received word that the enterprise was proving to be a success and she and the children were travelling now to join him. When she had learned on the ship that Cormac, Bridget and Emily would be seeking a night's accommodation after they disembarked, she had pressed them to come to the boarding house too. While they had only a limited amount of money, and most of it had to be saved to purchase a pair of horses for the next stage of their travels, they had decided that one night in a comfortable establishment would be very welcome after three nights spent in a less-than-snug ship's berth.

By the time they reached Harbour Row, the rain had eased to an intermittent spattering of drops. McLoughlin's Boarding House was easy to identify by the sign displayed over its front door proclaiming the name of the proprietor. The doorstep was scrubbed clean, flower boxes full of daffodils adorned the window sills, and the window panes were being wiped dry by a stumpy woman who had to stretch up on her toes with her cloth.

She turned when they approached the doorstep and dropped back to the flats of her feet, giving them a pleasant smile. 'Can I help you? We have some rooms available.'

Nancy said, 'Are you Agnes, Dan's sister?'

The woman's forehead furrowed and then cleared as she looked around at all the children.

'You must be Dan's wife! Bless the Lord, you've arrived

at last!'

After they embraced, she cleaned the last few wet spots from the window with fastidious care and led them all inside. There ensued a furore as chaotic as the pier when Dan McLoughlin appeared from the depths of the house and his children swarmed around him, screaming with excitement. He hoisted his two daughters up into his arms and his two sons clung to his coat but he still managed to lean over and bestow a tender kiss upon Nancy and to touch the tiny fist of the baby he had not yet met.

'I'm so happy to see you all,' he said, his voice deep and thick with emotion.

Once the uproar of reunion had subsided, Nancy gestured to Cormac, Bridget and Emily.

'You have room for some guests? We met on the voyage and they're in need of accommodation for the night.'

Dan nodded genially. 'We've a fine room overlooking the harbour which should do nicely. We'll settle the arrangements shortly but first I must tell ye, children, that ye've arrived just in time. What d'ye think is happening just down the road this very afternoon, and will be gone tomorrow?'

Tommy and Danny offered a few wild guesses before their father declared, 'A circus!'

The children's screams renewed with a vigour even greater than that of greeting the father they had not seen in almost a year.

'I ain't never seen a circus!'

'Can we go?'

'Please, please, please!'

Dan laughed. 'I'll take ye myself!'

Emily turned shining eyes up to Cormac and Bridget. 'Oh, *please!*' she breathed. 'May I go with them?'

Cormac hesitated. While they were now in Ireland, which he considered home, Cove was an unfamiliar town to him and, after their difficulties leaving London, he felt wary of strangers. Was he being too overprotective to not want to let Emily out of his sight?

Nancy watched him waver in indecision. 'She'll be fine. No harm will come to her in Dan's care. And it's a lovely treat.'

He glanced at Bridget and she nodded.

'Very well,' he said, and Emily whooped as loudly as any of the McLoughlin children. 'But you must be on your best behaviour, Emily.'

'I will!' She thrust out her chest with pride.

'We'd better hurry,' Dan said. 'The clown passed by this way not long ago, shouting that it was starting soon. Let's go!'

He disappeared out the front door with Emily and the other children in his wake, like chicks following their mother hen. Nancy shifted her baby from the crook of one elbow to the other.

'A bit of peace will help this poor child nod off, I hope,' she said.

'I'll show you to Dan's room,' Agnes said to her. 'And then I'll book ye in for the night, Mr and Mrs…?'

'McGovern,' Cormac said and Bridget gave him a glowing look.

***

Their room boasted a striking view of the harbour from its window, the departing rain clouds leaving hazy sunshine glimmering on the water's choppy surface. Bridget set down the two valises beneath the window sill and admired the vista while Cormac helped a young lad wedge a small mattress for Emily onto the floor next to the high bed. Agnes made up the mattress with sheets and blankets.

'There's water in the pitcher,' she said, indicating a washstand in the corner. 'And if ye need anything else, don't hesitate to ask.'

She shepherded the lad out of the room before her and

11

pulled the door closed with a precise snap. Bridget surveyed their accommodation: the bed had plain but clean bedcovers and more daffodils stood in a vase on the washstand. She crossed the room to the pitcher; the prospect of washing was appealing after limited opportunities for ablutions aboard the ship.

'I'm a bit tired after the journey,' she said, 'but we really should wash.'

Cormac rubbed his jaw where a fading bruise was still visible, courtesy of his last encounter with Garrett. 'Good idea,' he said absently.

He stepped up to the washstand but, instead of touching the curved handle of the pitcher, his hands went to her waist.

'Do you know what I've noticed?' he murmured, bending his head to her.

She blinked. 'What?'

'We are alone in a bedchamber.'

His lips landed upon hers and he eased her mouth open in a deep kiss. She closed her eyes and leaned into his sturdy chest, disappearing into a blissful daze until he pulled gently away.

'Are you still feeling tired?' he asked.

Her gaze cut to the high bed. 'Not so much.'

He grinned.

They scrambled to remove their clothing and slid naked between the bed's fresh sheets, relishing the feel of soft linen against sensitive skin. Lying on their sides facing one another, she offered her mouth to him once more. He had not shaved since they left London and his stubble scraped her chin with a pleasant roughness. As they kissed, she let her hand rove down the long, smooth arc of his back, feeling the bumps of his spine and the strength in his muscles. She roamed lower and stroked the curve of his buttocks with a possessive triumph. This exceptional specimen of a man was now hers; the ring on her left hand attested to that. It was only a circle made out of thread, but to them it had as much significance as if he had given it to her at the altar before God. He was her husband and she his wife, body and soul. They had no need of a legal marriage contract to know that.

They explored each other's bodies beneath the bedcovers, hungry for satisfaction and too impatient to adopt a more leisurely pace. The sensations were all the more intense given their imposed abstinence on the ship, and it was through only a dim haze of awareness that Bridget heard footsteps coming up the boarding house stairs. As her heartbeat pounded faster, the steps grew louder, making their way along the corridor outside the bedchamber. She strove to smother a gasp but it burst from her just as a groan broke from Cormac's throat. Had the footsteps faltered? She could not be sure and she did not care. She floated down from the pinnacle of ecstasy, feeling as though she had disintegrated and the separated parts of her body were trying to knit themselves back together.

She nestled into Cormac and they lay there, recovering their senses.

'I think someone may have heard us,' she mumbled after a while.

'No matter,' he said, smoothing back a loose lock of her chestnut curls over her shoulder. 'We're as good as married now, are we not?'

She pressed a warm kiss to his chest. 'We are.'

The decadence of going to bed in the afternoon settled upon them, their limbs heavy and languid. Bridget felt a delicious sleepiness steal over her and she relaxed in Cormac's embrace. She slipped deeper towards sleep but an uncomfortable tug drew her back from oblivion. As the realisation came to her, she squirmed in discomfort.

He felt her move and stirred himself. 'What's the matter?' he asked, his speech slurred with tiredness.

'Nothing,' she said, but the word came out in a high pitch that belied her protestation.

He woke more fully and cocked an eyebrow at her.

'It's nothing,' she tried again, but her traitorous body writhed once more and he let out a snort of disbelief. She gave up the pretence. 'It's just — oh, dear God, I can't say it.' She threw her arm over her eyes. 'I need a moment to myself. Would you mind dressing and leaving the room?'

The tension in his body slackened as he understood. 'You don't really need me to leave, do you?' She heard the trace of laughter he was attempting to hold back.

Her cheeks flamed hotter than the sun. 'Yes.'

He settled back in the bed. 'I'm too comfortable to move.'

She flung her arm away in horror. 'You expect me to do it in your presence?'

'Why not?'

'Because—' she spluttered. 'It's private!'

This time he did laugh. 'Considering what we've just been doing, I don't think there's much need left for privacy, do you? Using the chamber pot will be no great revelation at this stage.'

She gaped. 'I can't…' she said weakly.

'You can. Would you prefer if I closed my eyes?'

'I'd rather you close your ears,' she muttered.

He chuckled. 'You'd best get around to it before you wet the sheets.'

Uttering a groan of embarrassment, she slid out of the bed, reached underneath it and pulled out the chamber pot. It was clean and decorated with a pretty willow pattern but she couldn't find it in herself to appreciate it. A folded rag rested neatly in the bottom of the pot. She took it out and, with a mortified glance back at the bed, where he had tactfully turned away on his side, she lowered herself over the pot. She cringed at the tinkle of liquid against ceramic but felt a surge of relief as the pressure on her bladder eased. She hastily wiped herself with the rag, pushed the pot back under the bed, and slithered back under the covers, drawing them completely over her head.

He pulled them back down.

'Why are you so embarrassed?' he asked, grinning.

She scowled; he was taking far too much enjoyment from her discomfiture. 'I cannot think of a less romantic thing in this world than relieving myself in front of you. The passion in our relationship is irretrievable after this.'

He did not bother to credit this with a verbal answer. Instead, he pulled her beneath him, nestled himself at the apex between her thighs, and spent the next several minutes demonstrating to her that her assumption was preposterous.

Sweating and panting, she lay exhausted beside him. 'I believe you have made your point.'

Eyelids already drifting closed, he turned and placed a blind kiss on her cheek. '*A rún mo chroí,*' he whispered, '*go deo.*'

She loved when he spoke his native tongue; the Irish words flowed like honey. And there were no other words she loved to hear more than those.

'Secret of my heart, forever'.

Chapter 2

Emily returned with the McLoughlin family later, full of excited chatter and awed descriptions of dancing dogs, entertaining clowns and two black-skinned performers who executed daredevil feats on the backs of horses.

'I thought they would fall off but honest to goodness they never did!'

She continued to talk nineteen to the dozen, her tone both animated and reverential, as she submitted to a thorough wash in a tin bath – which Cormac had requested after he and Bridget had finally risen from bed – before they all dressed to go down for their evening meal.

The boarding house had a communal dining room which hummed with chattering guests and the clinking of cutlery as Cormac, Bridget and Emily descended the stairs. When they entered the dining room, they spotted Nancy and her swarm of children seated at a long table and joined them there, Emily squeezing beside the two girls, Peggy and Rosie, and exclaiming about the circus performers again.

Cormac and Bridget had barely seated themselves opposite Nancy when Dan McLoughlin entered the dining room, carrying a tray of full glasses. After distributing the drinks among a group of talkative men in the corner, he came over to their long table but, instead of speaking to his wife or children, he dipped his head towards Cormac.

'Mr McGovern,' he said apologetically. 'Could I ask yourself and your wife to step out for a few moments?'

Puzzled, Cormac said, 'Of course.'

He and Bridget followed Dan out of the dining room

and into the hallway beyond, where they found Agnes McLoughlin waiting for them. She folded her arms and glared at them with undisguised disgust.

'Ah, here are our well-respected guests,' she said snidely.

Dan hurried to his sister's side. 'We said we'd be calm and polite, Agnes,' he reminded her nervously, tucking his empty tray under his arm.

'I've no wish to be,' she said. 'These people don't deserve any such consideration.'

Cormac and Bridget exchanged gaping glances.

'Madam,' said Cormac, keeping control of his temper, 'can you explain why you have adopted this unjust attitude towards us?'

'Indeed I can,' she said, looking like she was itching for this confrontation. 'We're decent, God-fearing folk here and don't take kindly to those who'd engage in disgraceful behaviour under our roof.'

Shocked, he could only assume that the footsteps they had heard earlier outside their bedchamber had been hers.

'There has been nothing indecent about our behaviour. We are a lawfully married couple and —'

'Are ye?' she sneered. 'I doubt that, sir, given the evidence before my eyes.' She gestured towards Bridget. 'If that's supposed to be a wedding ring, then I'm a patron saint of Ireland.'

Bridget clasped her left hand inside her right, but everyone had seen the circle of thread, as far from a gold band as it was possible to be.

Cormac set his jaw. 'We have fallen on hard times and were obliged to sell her ring. Thank you for drawing attention to our unfortunate circumstances.'

Dan put a restraining hand on his sister's shoulder. 'We must've been mistaken,' he muttered. 'Let's leave them be.'

She shook him off. 'No,' she said. 'They're having an affair, I'm certain of it. No properly married husband and

17

wife would be fornicating in the middle of the afternoon with such brazen passion as I heard, not if they'd been married long enough to have a daughter of that girl's age.'

Fury and embarrassment rose in Cormac's chest. 'You have been listening at keyholes? What sort of proprietor does that make you?'

'One concerned with the standards of her establishment,' she replied primly. 'This is a boarding house, not a brothel.'

'Miss McLoughlin,' said Bridget in a placating tone, 'I can assure you –'

'Be assured, Mrs McGovern, or whatever your real name might be, I can see the truth of the situation. Judging by the marked similarity in looks between this man and that unfortunate child, 'tis obvious that he's her true parent and you're the offending third party. I'm guessing his fading bruise was inflicted by his abandoned wife when she learned he was deserting her for a hussy with no morals. The fervour of your earlier activities tells me ye've but recently absconded together and hence the dissatisfaction of your wicked choices has yet to settle upon ye. 'Tis only a matter of time before it does though, and then ye'll heartily regret your actions. But know this: God won't hear your pleas for mercy and ye'll never enter his kingdom.'

Outraged, Cormac snapped, 'You have your facts entirely wrong, madam. Do not cast righteous judgement upon us when you are so ignorant of the truth.'

She bristled. 'D'you swear then, *sir*, that a legal marriage contract exists between yourself and this woman?'

She looked like she would not believe it unless she saw it printed in the newspaper. He glanced at Bridget, his shoulders sagging. Lying any further would get them nowhere; the woman was entrenched in her opinions on the situation and, while she had the particulars incorrect, her overall deduction was regrettably accurate.

Still fuming, he said through gritted teeth, 'No, it does

not exist.'

Triumphant, she said, 'Such goings-on will not be tolerated in this house. Ye will remove yourselves at once and never darken our door again.'

Dan cleared his throat. 'Sister, we ought to show some compassion. They'll have difficulty finding another place to stay at this hour, and they've a child to think of.'

Agnes gave an indignant sniff and opened her mouth but Dan cut across her.

'We'll be Christian enough to allow them to stay until morning.' He looked at Cormac. 'But I'll have to ask ye not to return to the dining room with our other guests. We can bring a food tray to your room.'

Compelled to re-establish the upper hand, Agnes said, 'On no account may ye continue to share the same room. We insist that ye pay for another room and sleep apart.'

'Surely that won't be necessary —' Cormac began.

'Those are my terms,' she said with a steely gaze. 'Separate rooms or the front door.'

Humiliated, he gave a jerky nod of surrender.

She pointed to the dining room. 'And fetch your daughter. She mustn't remain among our guests either.'

He could no longer look at Bridget as he turned to do Agnes's bidding. Pushing open the door to the dining room, he heard the shrew snap at her brother, 'This is all thanks to your wife. She's a woeful judge of character to invite such profligates here.'

He couldn't make out Dan's response but hoped he would be kinder to Nancy than Agnes was being. Their companion on the voyage had been instrumental in assisting their escape from London and this was a shameful way to repay her.

'Come, *a stór*,' he said to Emily when he reached the long table. 'We are very lucky to be getting our dinner served upstairs this evening.'

He avoided Nancy's surprised look and guided his daughter away from the table, trying not to think about the stain of disgrace he and Bridget had inadvertently placed upon her.

***

Bridget woke to find herself wedged into one corner of the bed, Emily's arms and legs spread out like a starfish next to her. She rearranged the little girl's limbs into a narrower space and shuffled away from the edge where she herself was in danger of falling out. Thinking far ahead into the future (very, *very* far ahead if Cormac had any say in it), she imagined Emily getting married and sharing a bed with a disgruntled husband who would have to put up with her monopolising all the space.

The curve of her smile disappeared as the altercation from the previous night came flooding back to her. If it was so obvious that she and Cormac were not married, then that cast a great shadow on Emily's legitimacy and eligibility for marriage. Would she be able to find a man willing to overlook the taint of scandal arising from her parents' improper conduct? Bridget experienced a stab of guilt at having prioritised her own desires before her daughter's welfare. But how could she have turned away from Cormac? She could not have. They, and Emily, would have to deal with the consequences and the pertaining dishonour as best they could.

A sharp rap on the door brought her back to the present. She sat up, pulling the bedcovers up around her shoulders. 'Come in.'

Agnes McLoughlin stalked into the room, bearing a tray. 'Breakfast,' she said shortly.

Bridget considered returning the woman's rudeness in kind but opted for a more magnanimous course of action.

'Thank you,' she said as Agnes dropped the tray on a side table with a clatter. It was a paltry affair of porridge and burnt toast. 'Perhaps we could bring it to the other room to share it with — ?'

'No,' Agnes interrupted. 'I wouldn't allow it. In any case, he's not there.'

Startled, Bridget said, 'He's not?'

'My brother tells me that your *paramour*,' she said as though she were referring to a piece of rotten fish, 'left the house more than an hour ago. I can't say where he went.'

Next to Bridget, Emily began to stir.

'Very well,' she said, unwilling to expose her daughter to this woman's vitriol any more than necessary. 'We shall have our breakfast here and then go to the other room to pack, for that is where our valises are,' she added pointedly.

Agnes pursed her lips and left the room.

After the disappointing breakfast fare, which Emily barely nibbled at, they went back to the first room where Cormac had slept alone, and Bridget set about making their preparations for leaving the boarding house. She did not know what their next step would be but assumed that Cormac's absence was due to some purpose in that regard. They had spoken of purchasing two horses to make the journey to Oakleigh swifter and easier; perhaps that was what he was doing.

As she gathered their belongings into one of the valises, Emily pawed through the other.

'I want you to do my hair, Mama,' she said. 'Where is my brush?'

With a hiccup of misgiving, Bridget also searched through the valise in vain. The silver-handled hairbrush had been a gift from Lady Bewley, Cormac's 'aunt' when he had posed as Oliver Davenport, and it was one of the few sentimental items they had brought, along with the wooden watercolour box Cormac had made for his daughter and the little pouch containing the lock of hair belonging to baby James, Bridget's little boy who would remain three months old forever.

'It must be buried deep in the bottom, gooseberry,' she said. 'Here, you can use mine today instead.'

They completed their basic toilette and waited for Cormac to return, Bridget growing more and more anxious as time went on. She felt like a condemned prisoner, knowing that Agnes McLoughlin was somewhere downstairs, counting down the minutes until the filth had removed itself from her pristine environs. Bridget wanted to be gone.

A silent breath of relief escaped her when the bedchamber door opened and Cormac entered. He looked grim but his expression softened as Emily leapt up and ran forwards for a hug. Bridget's own body relaxed as she witnessed this strong reminder that, despite some of the unwelcome consequences of their flight from London, nothing could be more important than that Emily now had a loving father in her life. He embraced her and kissed her golden hair.

'Time for us to get going,' he announced in a bracing manner.

He and Bridget each picked up one of the valises and they headed for the door with Emily. Out in the corridor, they encountered Nancy McLoughlin crossing the landing, only two of her five children hanging off her.

'You're leaving,' she said, her expression serious.

'Farewell to you, Nancy,' said Bridget. 'We are so very sorry for any awkwardness we have caused you and your family. I cannot imagine that relations between you and Agnes are cheerful this morning.'

'They ain't,' Nancy replied, 'but that's down to her behaviour, not yours. Hush, Rosie, let me speak to these people for a few moments.' She patted her chattering daughter absently on the top of her head, then looked back at Bridget and Cormac. 'I knew from the manner of your departure from London that all ain't strictly lawful between you. But I've had enough time to form a sense of your characters. Whatever sins you've committed afore now, I can say that you have a lot more decency in you than that narrow-minded woman. I'm sorry you're being forced to leave in this way and I wish you well on your journey.'

'That is extremely kind of you,' said Cormac. 'But we know what our failings are, and one of them has been to put you in a discomfiting position with your sister-in-law. It was never our intention. Do please accept our apologies.'

She smiled. 'Don't you worry about my sister-in-law. She's shown her colours and I'll learn quickly how to deal with her.'

Thinking that Agnes McLoughlin might have met her match, Bridget followed Cormac and Emily downstairs to endure that woman's final censorious comments upon their ignominious departure from the boarding house.

Outside, Cormac did not lead them towards the boarding house's stables as Bridget had expected, but set off down the street at a brisk walk. She and Emily hastened to catch up but he did not slow his pace until they had reached the end of Harbour Row. There, he halted and turned to her.

'Give me your hand,' he said.

She offered him her right hand but he shook his head.

'Your other one.'

She raised her left hand. He removed her glove and, dipping his own hand into his pocket, slipped a ring onto her finger above the circle of thread. She let out a gasp. No ordinary band of gold, it depicted a love heart clasped within a pair of hands and topped with a crown. The detail in the metalwork was exquisite.

'The goldsmith told me this style has its origins in Galway and that it represents love, friendship and loyalty. I had always intended on getting you a proper ring at some stage but recent circumstances expedited matters. I'm sorry it is not under more romantic conditions that I give it to you. But,' he finished fiercely, 'I'm determined that you'll never have to suffer last night's humiliation again.'

She cupped his cheek. 'We knew that sort of censure was a risk. Everything became a risk when we did what we did. And I wouldn't change my mind for the world.'

The angry lines around his mouth diminished. 'I'm glad you think so. But from now on you are Bridget McGovern, my wife, and you have the ring to prove it. I won't have anyone questioning our morals again.'

She examined the gold ring. 'It must have been expensive...' she said hesitantly.

He sighed. 'We have all paid the price of this ring.' He looked down at Emily. '*A stór*, I have something to tell you. I'm afraid we no longer have your hairbrush. I had to sell it today.'

Emily's face fell. 'But Papa!' she cried. 'Can we not get it back?'

'We can't. You will have to share your mother's hairbrush from now on. She has a very pretty brush too.'

Emily's lip stuck out in a pout and she began to cry. 'I don't *want* to use Mama's hairbrush. I want my own!'

'That's not possible anymore,' he said patiently. 'I'm sorry that you have to suffer this loss. But there is no way to change it now.'

Emily pushed her weeping face into the front of Bridget's dress and wailed. Bridget gave the little girl a comforting squeeze around her shoulders. She knew Cormac had done what he had to do. He looked pained but compressed his lips in resignation.

'We cannot afford to ride to Oakleigh now,' he said over Emily's sobs. 'Even with the sale of the hairbrush, buying the ring has severely depleted our funds. Especially as we had to pay for two rooms last night.' His blue eyes darkened at the humiliating memory. 'And we must save most of what we have left should it be needed to find my family. We shall have to make our way on foot. It will be a more beggarly way of travelling.'

Faltering, she said, 'We have my father's pocket watch. We could...'

He shook his head again. 'Not yet. That has far more emotional significance than a hairbrush received a few weeks ago. We ought to hold onto it, in case we find ourselves in a more dire situation in the future.'

Extricating herself from Emily's grasp, she set her valise on the ground and rummaged through it. She found the pocket watch, slid it out of its protective navy satin cloth, and held it out to him.

'You should carry it. It once belonged to a good man. I'd like to see another good man have it. Consider it my equivalent gift to the ring.'

He accepted it solemnly and traced its circumference. Her father had been an important person to him too. He pocketed the watch with care.

'Come now, Emily, that's enough,' he said.

Emily seemed to recognise the weight of his use of her proper name rather than his usual Irish term of affection and her snuffling ebbed reluctantly.

'We have more adventures ahead of us,' he said. 'Let's face them with bravery.'

He raised Bridget's hand to his lips and kissed the gold ring.

Chapter 3

The weather in March could be unpredictable in Ireland. Sometimes it came like an early summer, banishing the winter with days of gentle sunshine and refreshing breezes.

Not this March.

As a chilly rain whipped at her cheeks, Bridget contemplated the road ahead. A veritable lake of muddy water stretched from one ditch to the other, the biting wind rippling across its surface. The same wind buffeted her back as she took stock of just how wet her feet were about to become. Emily danced along the edge of the flood, splashing the toes of her boots in the water.

'There's no way around,' Cormac said with a resigned air. 'Up you get, *a stór*.'

He put down his valise to hoist Emily up onto his back. She whooped and, pointing up the road, cried, 'Sally forth, brave knight!'

Eyeing Emily's dry ankles with envy, Bridget took hold of both valises and followed Cormac to the verge. She eased one foot after the other into the water, wincing at the cold. The exposed hem of her dress, already damp and mud-spattered, greedily soaked up the watery muck. She shuffled along, the hidden ground beneath varying between a squelching consistency and a shifting bed of stones, and did her best to forget the fact that the going would have been so much easier had they been riding. She tried not to imagine what Madeleine, her frivolous friend from Dublin, would say if she could see her now.

She had been aware beforehand of the path she was

choosing. She had known that there were not going to be any more lavish feasts, ballroom dancing or nights at the theatre, and she had been prepared for a basic, unvaried diet and a good deal of walking. But she had not taken much time to consider how challenging it would be to keep *clean*. The previous evening, she had washed her and Emily's grubby skirts in a stream; the result had been passable but a far cry from the standards she was accustomed to. Then there was the grim reality of having to relieve oneself behind a convenient bush – in retrospect, the chamber pot back at McLoughlin's Boarding House seemed utterly decadent. And they were only drawing to the end of their second full day on the road. The one positive thing to be said was that finding water to drink posed no problem for the rainfall kept the streams fresh and flowing.

She slipped on a loose stone and, with her hands full, barely recovered her balance. She felt the water slosh into her boots and groaned. Cormac turned back to her, Emily's arms tight around his neck.

'I'm fine,' Bridget said, forcing a smile. 'It's just a shame it's not summertime.'

He agreed with a sympathetic nod and faced forwards again, Emily encouraging her steed to race towards freedom. Cormac splashed to the far end of the flood and the pair of them cheered in victory.

'Come, Mama!' Emily exclaimed. 'You're nearly there.'

Fingers aching with the weight of the valises, Bridget nonetheless gained a boost from her daughter's exuberance and struggled onto dry ground with relief. Cormac set Emily down and looked skywards.

'There's no sign of it stopping,' he said. 'I hope we can get shelter again tonight.'

The first two nights, they had been lucky enough to encounter friendly farmers' wives who had permitted them to sleep in their hay barns. Emily had played a significant role in this, charming the women with her

27

bright smile and sweet voice so that they could not refuse her a place to lay her golden head. Could their luck hold out for a third night? As the water soaked into her stockings, Bridget very much hoped so.

Even as she thought this, Cormac added, 'At this rate, we should take a room in an inn if we come upon one,' and it buoyed her up no end. While she strove for equanimity in the face of this challenge, she longed for a warm bed and a cosy hearth, no matter if it meant paying for them.

He took the valises from her and, with the light failing, they walked on through the countryside. Emily's feet started to drag so Cormac distracted her by pointing out the varieties of trees and hedges they passed – a source of continuous wonder to a small girl who had lived all her life in a busy, smoky city – and suggesting names for the hens she was going to look after in the future. She perked up at the mention of her hens and talked at length about how she was going to run the best-organised hen coop in the world.

There continued to be no sign of an inn or any other form of accommodation and, as darkness fell, Bridget worried that they would have to spend the night in the open after all, but then a building came into view in the twilight: a two-storey farmhouse with candlelight glowing from the windows on the lower level. She contained her moan of relief and quickened her pace to catch up with Cormac and Emily, the latter of whom had just announced that she intended to paint a sun on her hen coop so that her hens would always be cheerful.

'That is a very thoughtful idea, gooseberry,' Bridget said and added to Cormac, 'Shall we seek shelter at this farmhouse?'

'Please God they'll take us in,' he said. 'It'll be a miserable night otherwise.'

Before she could respond, they heard the sound of wheels and turned to see a donkey and cart coming towards them out of the gloom. The wheels made a sucking noise as they rolled through the mud and the farmer sitting at the front of the cart leaned over the side and spat, 'If ye get stuck one more time...'

Cormac called out a greeting and the farmer looked up in surprise. He squinted and pulled the cart to a stop next to them.

''Tis bad weather for ye to be on the road at this hour,' he said, pointing a grimy, cracked fingernail at them. 'And with a child and all. I wouldn't be out so late myself only for the wretched wheels on this thing. They'll be the death of me.'

'We've been unlucky with the weather, it's true,' said Cormac. 'With no sign of it letting up, we're hoping to get inside for the night.'

The man harrumphed. 'And I suppose 'tis at my house ye'll be looking for shelter.'

'We certainly don't wish to be an inconvenience.' Cormac glanced up at the darkening sky. 'But if you had shelter to offer, we would be very grateful.'

The man let out another harrumph. He leaned over the side of his cart again, this time to get a better look at Emily.

She stared back without fear and asked, 'Do you have a hen coop?'

The farmer's gaze cut back to Cormac. 'That's an English accent,' he said sharply. 'And you don't sound too Irish yourself, if I'm being honest.'

Bridget kept her own mouth shut as Cormac responded in an even tone, 'Our daughter was raised in London, but my wife and I are as Irish as the day is long.'

The mistrust didn't leave the farmer's face but he gave a grumpy shrug. 'I've got a big family. If 'tis a roof ye want, it'll be one of the outhouses.'

Cormac inclined his head. 'That would be very generous, thank you.'

'Ye can follow me up to the yard so.'

The farmer snapped his reins and, with a great effort on the donkey's part, the wheels of the cart came unstuck from the mud and rolled on up the road. Bridget, Cormac and Emily trudged after, their boots slipping into the ruts the cart tracks had left behind. Bridget felt like pointing out that the farmer could have at least let Emily sit on the cart, given that it was empty, but she bit back the complaint. Beggars could not be choosers and they were lucky he was aiding them at all.

By the time they reached the farmyard, the farmer had already unharnessed the donkey; the abandoned cart lay to one side and the farmer was stamping out of the stables. He jerked his thumb towards a small shed at the far end of the yard.

'Ye can stay in there. Mind ye don't leave a mess behind.'

And with that, he marched up to the front door of his farmhouse, its windows shining invitingly, and disappeared inside.

Cormac led them over to the shed and pushed open the door with his shoulder. It fell back at his touch, tilting inside the shed on one rusted hinge. Peering in, Bridget could just make out a rough floor littered with unwanted farmyard detritus: a broken cart wheel, mounds of torn sacks, a bucket with a cracked base. It stank of mildew and dung.

Emily wrinkled her nose. 'What's that smell?'

Cormac set down the valises and cleared his throat. 'You know, *a stór*, I think this is the perfect time to continue your fun from the ship. Do you remember we were sailing the mighty seas?'

'Yes, we were searching for hidden treasure but the pirates caught up with us.' She swung out her arm in a slicing sword motion. '"Give up your ship," they said, "or walk the plank!"'

'To save our lives, we walked the plank, didn't we? Which is why we are so wet now.' He brushed at the

30

sodden sleeve of his coat, scattering droplets across her face.

She ducked away, giggling. 'We jumped into the sea so the pirates wouldn't take us prisoner!'

Bridget chimed in, 'Luckily, land was in sight and we could swim to shore.'

'But the pirates followed us. They know we found the hidden treasure.' Cormac made a dramatic show of looking over his shoulder before pulling out the pocket watch. 'We must hide it from them tonight so they cannot get their hands on it. Do you think this is a good hiding spot?'

The little girl nodded enthusiastically. 'It's so smelly that they'll never want to search inside.'

'Then that makes it ideal for us. But first, I must scout it out to ensure it's not a trap. Here,' he said, handing the watch to Emily with a solemn bow. 'Take the treasure and guard it with your life.'

She tucked it in close to her chest. 'With my life,' she promised.

He turned back to the shed door. 'And now I bravely enter this unknown realm.' He strode inside.

Emily, round-eyed, gaped up at Bridget. 'Will he be safe, Mama?'

'Your father is the most courageous person I know,' she said, her heart bursting with adoration for him. 'I think he will be fine.'

They heard a shout from the shed. 'Get back, fiend!' There was some banging and another yell, this one of triumph. A few moments later, Cormac reappeared in the doorway, breathing heavily and wiping his forehead.

'The coast is clear,' he panted. 'I discovered one nefarious buccaneer but he will not bother us again. You may bring in the treasure now.'

Gravely, Emily tiptoed inside the shed, still hugging the coveted goods. Bridget followed, breathing through her mouth rather than her nose. The shed was dark and cramped, with just enough floor space for them all to lie down. Cormac bustled over to the corner, gathering some of the torn sacks into a pile and fashioning them into a kind of nest.

'Your bed awaits, *a stór*,' he said with a flourish.

So enamoured by the fantasy, Emily did not seem to care about the decrepit conditions of her surroundings. She snuggled into the mound of sacks, hiding the pocket watch carefully beneath one of them.

'I'll keep it safe, Papa, I promise,' she said as a yawn escaped her.

Bridget took off her cloak and laid it over her daughter, tucking the ends in around her elbows and feet.

'Sleep well, gooseberry,' she said, kissing her forehead and trying to suppress a shiver at the same time.

Emily's eyes fluttered closed and Bridget realised the poor child was so tired that she hadn't even noticed her hunger. Just like in the confrontation with Agnes McLoughlin, a spear of guilt went through her gut. She prayed this beggarly part of their lives would be fleeting.

Cormac pushed the cart wheel and bucket to one side and used the remaining sacks to cover the floor next to Emily's nest. Now that the game was over, Bridget could see the tautness in the line of his jaw. He retrieved the valises from the yard, opened his own, and dug out two shirts which he balled up to make pillows.

'My coat is large enough to cover us both,' he said, not looking at her as he knelt by the makeshift bed.

She didn't say anything, only put a hand on his shoulder. He took it and pressed a kiss to her fingers.

'I will make a better life for us than this, I swear it,' he said.

'I know,' she said. 'We will make it together.'

After he had shoved the shed door shut as tightly as he could, they lay down together on the sacks and he threw his coat over them both. It smelled like him and she breathed it in with pleasure. She tried to doze off, but she could not ignore the fact that her feet felt like two blocks of ice. They had not dried properly after their immersion in the muddy flood and now they were so frozen and uncomfortable that they hardly seemed like parts of her own body. How she longed for the bed warmer that had kept her sheets so cosy in London.

Although she did her best to keep silent, a tiny whimper leaked out of her. She hoped Cormac might have already fallen asleep, but he raised his head.

'What is it?'

'Oh, it's nothing,' she murmured.

He waited.

'It's just…my feet…'

He slid out from under the coat, leaving it wrapped around her, and slithered down their 'bed'. Reaching beneath the end of his coat, he removed the boot and stocking from one of her feet and touched her skin.

He clicked his tongue in sympathy. 'You should have said something sooner.'

He enveloped her foot in both of his hands and she moaned at the sensation. Though his fingers were not unaffected by the cold weather, they were still so much warmer than the temperature of her feet that they felt like a blanket. He briskly rubbed her sole and her instep and her toes until proper feeling began to return, and then he did the same with her other foot. By the time he had finished, she was whimpering again, this time with inarticulate gratitude.

He slipped back beneath the coat. She pressed her back to his front, he wrapped his arms around her, and they drifted off to sleep, undisturbed by pirates.

Chapter 4

They woke to a drizzly dawn, light and raindrops seeping in through the cracks in the shed's walls. Bridget's neck felt stiff as she bent over the nest of sacks to wake Emily. The little girl, spread-eagled across the sacks, roused grudgingly.

'Can I have hot cocoa?' she mumbled, curling into a ball against the cold air inside the shed.

'I'm afraid there's no cocoa here, gooseberry. But instead we have those delicious wild mushrooms your papa found beside the road outside Cove. That kind farmer's wife cooked them for us, do you remember?'

Emily made a face. That was what they had had for breakfast the last two mornings as well. It took a long time to coax her to eat anything at all, and in the end she only managed a couple of bites before pressing her lips shut tight. Bridget cast a look of exasperation towards Cormac.

'Leave her be for now,' he said. 'She'll eat when she's hungry enough.'

They gathered up their belongings, left the sacks stacked in a neat pile in the corner, and emerged from the shed. The farmer was in the yard, kneeling by his cart and examining the spokes of its wheels. A shadow of guilt crossed his expression at their appearance.

'Grand day,' he called over, as the drizzle drifted down from the overcast sky.

'A soft one,' Cormac agreed.

The farmer stood. 'Caught me in a bad mood,' he muttered. 'I should've…could've let ye…'

Cormac shook his head. 'We're very grateful for your

assistance last night. We were glad to get cover from that weather. Thank you.'

The farmer grumbled something unintelligible and coughed. 'Where are ye headed next?'

'We're making our way to Carlow, to the Oakleigh Estate.'

'Carlow?' the farmer barked. 'Ye've a ways to go yet.' He scratched his nose. 'Oakleigh. Why's that ringing a bell for me?'

Bridget frowned. 'Have you heard news from there?'

The man's eyes narrowed; it was the first time she had spoken in his presence. 'Mayhap 'tis nothing. Best be getting on your way now. Safe travels to ye.'

He nodded curtly and strode back to the farmhouse. Bridget and Cormac exchanged mystified looks.

'I'd hoped we might buy some bread and cheese from him,' said Cormac. 'But I think a further request on our part might be beyond his tolerance, whatever's vexing him.'

Shrugging, he took Emily's hand and led them both from the farmyard.

They had not gone far before they ascertained that Emily had not had a restful night's sleep. She started to dawdle while they were still within sight of the farmhouse, and a sulky look settled on her face and would not go away. She had either forgotten or did not care about last night's narrow escape from pirates and no amount of play-acting on Bridget and Cormac's parts could entice her back into the fantasy. She kicked at stones, walked intentionally into puddles her mother told her to avoid, and dragged her heels more and more as the morning wore on into the afternoon. Cormac tried to distract her with an elaborate story about a rabbit that had dashed across their path and must be the king of all rabbits because of the size of its ears, but she was having none of it.

'Why don't you sing us a song, *a stór*?' said Cormac.

'I don't want to.'

'Would you like to ride on my back for a while?'

'No.' She stuck out her lower lip and scuffed the toes of her boots into the mucky road. 'I'm hungry,' she whinged.

'We still have some mushrooms —'

'I don't *want* mushrooms!' She halted. 'I want to stop walking.'

'We have to keep going, *a stór*. I know it's a long journey but at the end of it we'll be able to make our new home. Remember, you'll have a hen coop to look after and you're going to be so busy.' Bridget noted that Cormac was careful not to give any specifics about when or where their journey might end; after all, there was no guarantee or even likelihood that Oakleigh would be their final destination.

Emily scowled. 'I don't want a new home anymore. I want to go back to my old home.' Putting her hands on her hips, she said, 'My first papa wouldn't make me walk this far.'

Bridget felt the accusation keenly. Cormac kept control over his expression, but she was certain it must have cut him very deep.

'I won't tolerate any more complaining, Emily,' he said. 'Sometimes we have to do things that are difficult. I am trying to make it easier for you. You can ride on my back if your feet are tired.'

With a defiant glare, she sat heavily on the ground. 'I'm not going any further,' she declared, her nose in the air.

Expelling an inward groan at the mud which must now cover the backside of Emily's cloak, Bridget said sharply, 'This is not the way you were raised, Emily. You do what you are told when you are told.'

Emily scrunched up her face. 'No!'

Bridget imagined the scene with Garrett standing there instead of Cormac and knew that Emily would never dare to behave this way in his presence. Garrett did not instil love, but he did instil fear. Perhaps Cormac's playful manner towards Emily had some drawbacks.

He stood contemplating their daughter for a few moments, one hand clasping the other wrist.

'Very well, Emily,' he said at last. 'I see we cannot persuade you to go any further. However, we have no time to spare on silly tantrums and your mother and I must continue on regardless. Do you remember the way back to the farmhouse? You can wait for us there, though I expect it will be several weeks before we can return to collect you. Or, if you'd prefer not to wait, you can ask the farmer to write to London to send you back. The choice is yours.'

He sent Bridget a meaningful look and then turned on his heel and walked away up the road, a decisive swing to the valise in his hand. Bridget stared down at Emily's appalled face.

'Mama?' she said tremulously.

Bridget gulped. 'I do love you very much, gooseberry,' she said and planted a quick kiss on Emily's upturned forehead. Then she followed Cormac with her own valise, leaving their daughter sitting in the middle of the road with her mouth agape.

When she caught up to Cormac, he didn't even turn his head. 'Don't look back,' he said. 'We must keep walking until we reach that bend ahead.'

They walked in silence as far as the bend and followed it around until they were out of Emily's sight. There, Cormac stopped, his cheeks red.

'What are we doing?' Bridget asked, hesitant to stoke the fire but anxious to understand.

'She needs to learn. We are travelling the countryside with the clothes on our backs and a few bare belongings. It's a precarious venture so we must be able to rely on her to obey us when necessary. We were lucky in London. If she hadn't played along back on the ship, we wouldn't have made it to Ireland at all. We can't run the risk that she might let us down in a moment of jeopardy.' He swallowed. 'I'm her father, not her playfellow. This will be a crucial lesson for her.'

'What if she goes back to the farmhouse and asks them to write to London?'

He didn't pause. 'She won't. Just give her some time.'

The words were barely out of his mouth when they heard running feet slapping muddy ground.

'Mama?' A sob. 'Papa?'

Emily came dashing around the bend and let out another sob when she saw them standing there. She started to run towards Bridget but Cormac said, 'Wait a moment, Emily.'

She came to a faltering stop, two big tears on her cheeks.

'Do you have something to say?' Cormac asked her.

'I'm s-sorry.'

'What are you sorry for?'

Her lip trembled. 'I'm s-sorry for n-not doing what I was t-told.'

'Do you understand that it's important to do what you're told?'

'Y-yes.'

'And will you do so in the future?'

A loud sniff. 'Yes. I promise.'

'Go give your mother a hug so.'

She ran forwards but encompassed her hug around them both, one hand on each of their waists and her head squashed between their hips. Bridget's valise knocked painfully against her knees.

'Were you really going to leave me?' Emily wept, her voice muffled.

'Of course not, *a stór*.' Cormac took off her bonnet and kissed her crown. 'We adore you.'

She wept harder, pressing her little arms tightly around them.

'I'm sorry,' she whimpered again.

'We have forgotten it already,' said Cormac.

Bridget did a very good impression of the farmer's harrumph. 'Well, I haven't. How are we going to clean that big muddy patch on your bottom?'

They all laughed, though Emily's effort was a bit quivery. Cormac replaced her bonnet, took out his handkerchief and cleaned her runny nose, while Bridget inspected Emily's backside.

'Hmm, it'll do for now, I suppose,' she said, giving the girl's rump a cursory wipe, followed by a light smack. 'Let's be on our way again, shall we?'

Cormac let Emily fold up his handkerchief and tuck it into her own pocket. She obediently stepped into line with them and they set off again, the rain still spitting down. This time when Cormac encouraged a song, Emily obliged by bellowing out *Rain, rain, go away, come again another day*!' over and over and over until Bridget quite regretted Cormac's suggestion. After a few dozen renditions of the rhyme, the little girl thankfully switched to 'Little Robin Redbreast'. She had only recited it seven times when she interrupted herself with a sudden gasp.

'Did you see it?' she cried. 'There was a robin right there!' She ran ahead, chasing the bird as it flitted from hedge to hedge.

Bridget cast a sideways glance at Cormac.

'How are you after that?' she asked.

He blew out his breath. 'Hurt. Infuriated.' He looked away. 'Jealous of that damn bastard.'

'Don't be,' she said, infusing the words with all her sincerity. 'She might have obeyed him but she would never have hugged him afterwards. That kind of fear is not a trait to covet from one's child. A fit of disobedience is a small price to pay for an otherwise unconditional love. You are the luckier party.'

He gazed ahead to where Emily, peering out from under the wet rim of her bonnet, was beckoning them to come catch a glimpse of the robin, and Bridget saw the lines of dissatisfaction melt from his features.

'I know,' he said softly.

They caught up to Emily just as they heard an excitable

neigh and, for the second time in two days, a farmer's cart came trundling up behind them. This one had a pony harnessed to the front and a covered bundle in the bed at the back. The farmer had a head of straggly hair which he pushed away from his brow as he looked upon the travellers. Bridget's instinct was to say nothing and let him carry on, but he stopped of his own accord.

'*Dia duit*,' he addressed Cormac.

'*Dia is Muire duit*,' Cormac returned the Irish greeting.

The farmer nodded his approval. 'Heard talk of some English folk wandering around this area making a nuisance of themselves. Just wanted to make sure you're the right sort.'

Cormac frowned. 'My wife and child have accents that may not be to your taste. If that will offend you, please don't let us delay you on your way.'

The farmer looked chastened. 'I meant no harm. 'Tisn't in my mind to accuse you of anything. Just that 'tis wise to be wary...of late...' He cast a fleeting, inexplicable glance over his shoulder towards the covered bundle in his cart. 'Beg pardon for getting us off on the wrong foot. Hackett's the name.'

'McGovern,' said Cormac.

'Pleased to meet you, Mr McGovern. Where are you and your family off to this fine day?'

Emily snorted at his generous description of the weather and he gave her a broad wink.

Mouth twitching, Cormac said, 'We're on our way to Carlow.'

'Ah, ye've still a good distance to go.'

Emily, who had approached the pony tentatively and was reaching up to touch its nose, looked crestfallen at this.

'Yes, we're aware of that,' said Cormac. 'But the thought of home keeps us going. I'm a Carlow man by birth.'

'Are you now?' Farmer Hackett pulled thoughtfully on one long hank of hair. 'Don't know many folk from

40

Carlow but the wife has an uncle who's a priest over there. D'you know a Father Macken?'

Cormac laughed. 'I do indeed. He baptised me, would you believe.'

'Go away.' Farmer Hackett let out a barking laugh of his own. 'And are ye planning to walk the whole journey or could my Bess help ye along a bit of the way?'

Bridget's heart leapt.

Cormac touched his cap. 'We'd be very grateful for Bess's assistance.'

Emily whispered to the pony, 'Hello, Bess.'

Farmer Hackett grinned. 'Sure, hop in so and we'll see if we can take ye a little further on your journey.'

He jumped down and went around to the back of the cart to push the covered bundle to one side, shooting the travellers a furtive glance as the items beneath made clanking noises. Bridget and Cormac climbed into the back of the cart, stacked the two valises, and pulled Emily up to sit beside them. Farmer Hackett urged Bess forwards and they rolled on up the road. The jolt of movement caused the bundle to jerk towards Bridget's foot and the corner of the covering flapped up, exposing the pointed heads of several pikes. Disturbed by the sight, she nudged Cormac and pointed at them. He looked startled and frowned at the back of the farmer's head but said nothing. Bridget was thankful for the respite from walking, but the inexplicable presence of those weapons made her uncomfortable.

Despite that, the appearance of Farmer Hackett and Bess vastly improved a day that could otherwise have been miserable for the three travellers. Not a mile down the road, a fancy carriage passed them, rattling through the puddles so carelessly that Bridget, Cormac and Emily would have been drenched had they been walking on the verge.

'Toffs think they own the road,' Farmer Hackett muttered from the front of the cart. 'And everything else to boot. Damn thieving Protestants.'

Bridget caught Cormac's glance. The less said about their connection to Oakleigh, the better.

The finest part of the whole encounter was that, upon arriving at Farmer Hackett's farm, he insisted they stay for a meal and his wife fed them the best dinner they had eaten since leaving London: creamy mashed potatoes, succulent chicken, and a rich gravy.

'Can we live here?' Emily asked as she spooned up the last of her gravy-soaked mash.

Mrs Hackett chuckled. 'Ye'd be very welcome, pet, but I expect your ma and da have other plans. Maybe ye'd stay the one night though?'

Bridget smiled; the offer was too tempting to refuse. 'Thank you very much for your hospitality. You are too kind.'

Mrs Hackett and her husband gave them an actual room in the farmhouse (consigning their youngest two to the hearth in the kitchen) and they all had a most satisfying night's sleep, the strife from earlier in the day forgotten.

They departed from the farm the next morning with bread, cheese and scones packed in their valises. Emily called a wistful farewell to Bess and received an exuberant neigh in return. As they turned towards the road, Bridget felt a faint warmth on her face and looked skywards; the watery sun had emerged at last.

Chapter 5

One step after another, one day after the next. Their surroundings remained unfamiliar to Bridget until at last a shadow appeared on the horizon, an indistinct smudge that gained definition as they drew closer. Finally, it clarified into the brown slopes of the Blackstairs Mountains, which lay south of Oakleigh Manor, not far from the limestone quarry where Bridget and Cormac had long ago played as children.

She thought her heart might leap out of her chest. She hadn't set foot on Oakleigh land in seven and a half years. Home. She was nearly home. A lump came to her throat as a thousand memories swarmed for her attention.

She felt Cormac's hand wrap around her own. Looking up, she saw her own emotion reflected in his face, fierce joy tempered by deep sorrow. Was he too recalling the way they had parted back then? The agony of their separation seemed somehow nearer, given their proximity to the location of its occurrence. Her betrayal. His banishment. Her mother's lies. His family's suffering.

Please, she prayed. Please, God, let us find them.

He gazed ahead to the mountains. 'We'll make for the cottage first,' he said. 'It's probably falling down after so many years unoccupied but I want to go there anyway.' His voice caught at the end.

She squeezed his hand. 'I understand,' she said.

They continued on. Later in the day, she began to recognise various landmarks, fields and woods where she had gone riding in her girlhood, sometimes with her father and more often with Cormac. It had been an age of innocence, she realised, when the world had been unsullied in her eyes and there had not yet been any death or loss or pain. She glanced over at Cormac, who was now carrying Emily on his back and bouncing her like she was in a saddle. Emily was laughing at the top of her lungs. She hoped their daughter's age of innocence lasted as long as it could.

This would be Emily's first time to see the place where her parents had grown up. At the end of that fateful summer at Oakleigh, she had been a mere speck inside Bridget, her presence not yet even known. Soon she would learn where she had truly come from.

The further they went into Oakleigh's domain, the more Bridget came to notice that the area was very quiet. There were no signs of men toiling in the fields, no herds of cattle or flocks of sheep, not even any farmers' carts lumbering along the road. Strangely, many of the fields appeared to be untilled. This all seemed unusual to her – springtime was when the countryside ought to be in full revival after the winter – and she was just about to comment upon it when Cormac spoke.

'Time to get down now, *a stór*,' he said to Emily.

They were nearly there.

He lowered Emily to the ground and took one of the valises back from Bridget. Then, with a deep breath, he led them up the lane that would bring them to his family's cottage.

Bridget imagined what they would see: a ramshackle structure with the door hanging off its hinges and its roof caved in. Birds might have set up homes for themselves in its walls and eaves. It would be full of dust and ghosts. Still, it might be habitable enough for them to establish a place to sleep while Cormac made his enquiries. It was unlikely that they would need to stay there for more than a few days.

They followed the familiar curve of the lane, bracing themselves for the sight of the dilapidated cottage. But the building that came into view at the side of the road was not what they expected. The whitewashed walls had not collapsed, nor had the thatched roof fallen in. On the contrary, it stood as solidly as it had seven and a half years ago. The door was intact with the top half of it open and the horse shoe still hung above it. There were hens pecking around in front of it and – the most telltale sign of all – smoke issued from the chimney.

They were still staring at each other in amazement and confusion when the half door opened and someone came out. For one absurd, joyous moment, Bridget thought she saw Maggie McGovern coming towards them.

Then she blinked and came to her senses, recognising the freckles and the woman for who she really was: her mother's lady's maid, Ellen Ryan.

At first, Ellen did not notice that she had visitors. She had come outside to shake a cloth out; a shower of crumbs fell to the ground and the hens waddled over to investigate. She was just turning to go back inside when she caught sight of the three figures standing by the side of the road. Letting out a frightened gasp, she dropped the cloth and her hand flew to her pocket. Then she looked at them again, let out an even louder gasp, and her hand went to cover her mouth which had fallen open in an expression of utter bewilderment.

Bridget offered an apologetic smile. 'Good day, Ellen.'

Ellen gaped, her eyes as wide as dinner plates. 'M-my lady,' she stuttered.

'You do not need to address me like that anymore. I am just Bridget now.' She looked over her shoulder as Cormac and Emily approached her side. 'You know Cormac, of course. And this is our daughter, Emily.'

Ellen looked as though one more surprise would knock her over. 'Your—your daughter?' she said, looking uncertainly at Cormac.

He nodded in confirmation.

At this point, Emily chirped, 'How do you do? May I

45

play with your hens?'

This seemed to wake Ellen from her bemused state. She gave a cracked laugh and said, 'God above, I think I need to sit down. Let's go inside.'

She picked up her cloth and led them into the cottage, Emily glancing back longingly at the hens.

Once indoors, Bridget could see that not much had changed since Cormac's family had lived here. The table was turned a different way and there was no sign of Maggie's spinning wheel, but the rocking chair sat in the corner as it always had and the dresser still stood against the back wall next to the ladder leading up to the loft. A sod of turf burned in the fireplace, emanating the same familiar smell.

Ellen's expression became anxious as she watched Cormac look around. His own face was unreadable, making it impossible to tell how he felt about someone else residing in what had been his family's home for so many years.

'I'm so sorry!' she blurted. 'We'd never have settled here if we expected for one moment you'd return. But we — we thought...' She trailed away awkwardly.

'Who is "we"?' asked Cormac, still betraying nothing.

Ellen coloured. 'Liam Kirwan and I. We married nearly five years ago.'

'Oh, how wonderful!' said Bridget. 'Do you have a family?'

'Two boys. And a third child on the way.'

Bridget noticed the small bump beneath Ellen's dress and they exchanged a glowing look that could only be shared by those who have been expectant mothers. Then they both glanced over at Cormac, whose face broke into a smile.

'That is great news,' he said warmly. 'I am delighted for you.'

Ellen allowed a little relief to show on her freckled features. 'So you're not angry with us? For taking over the cottage?'

'Not for one second. I'm glad it hasn't become a derelict ruin. At least it has continued to be a home for somebody's family.'

The air became palpable with the distinct absence of Maggie McGovern and her daughters and grandson.

The ghosts lingered until Bridget asked, 'Where is Liam?'

'He's out in the woods with the boys, but I'm expecting them home in a short while.'

At that moment, Emily, who had been craning her neck over the half door to look out at the hens, hit her chin off the wooden frame and began to cry. Cormac lifted her up into his arms to comfort her. Ellen stared at the two of them.

'The resemblance is remarkable,' she said, almost to herself.

Imagining that Ellen must be burning with questions, Bridget said, 'We have rather a long tale to tell.'

'I'd be very interested to hear it.'

And so they all sat at the table that Maggie McGovern had once presided over, Ellen and Bridget on one bench and Cormac opposite them with Emily in his lap. In turns, Bridget and Cormac related the events over the last seven and a half years that had brought them to this point, leaving out the murkier parts for the sake of Emily's ears and divulging only what was most necessary for Ellen to understand how they had come to be together again. They did not speak directly of Cormac's impersonation of Oliver Davenport, only hinted at a stroke of fortune that had enabled Cormac to make his way to London.

Ellen listened in silence all the way to the end. When they had finished, she let out a soft breath. 'Ah. That's indeed quite a story.'

'A story of sin,' Bridget said lightly, feeling that this would liberate Ellen to give her honest opinion about what she had just heard.

Ellen shook her head. 'It's not my place to comment on that. But I'm glad you're happy and I'm very pleased to see you. Your appearance is just so unexpected. What's brought you back here?'

Cormac opened his mouth to reply but just then they heard voices and footsteps outside the cottage and Liam, Cormac's old friend and fellow stable hand, appeared at the half door, carrying a small boy on his back. When he pushed open the door, an older boy was revealed by his knees. Liam checked at the sight of his wife's visitors. However, instead of uttering loud exclamations of surprise, he just came in, swung his son down from his back and, in his usual, unassuming manner, extended his hand to Cormac.

'Good to see you,' he said as they shook.

'You too.' Cormac grinned.

The two boys ran to their mother to receive hugs and show her the mushrooms they had picked in the woods. Emily, having perked up at the appearance of other children, looked like she was making her best effort not to regard the mushrooms with distaste. Ellen picked the smaller boy up into her lap.

'This is Aidan,' she said, kissing the top of the boy's head. 'He's two. And this,' she said, putting her arm around the other boy, 'is Liam Óg. He's three and a half years old.'

Bridget smiled at the two boys. They were both a copy of their mother, with freckles splashed across their cheeks and noses. Emily waved shyly at them.

'That's Emily,' Ellen told the boys. 'She really likes our hens. Will you take her outside and introduce them to her?'

Liam Óg responded with a solemn nod, just as one might expect from a 'young' version of Liam, while Aidan slipped down from Ellen's lap and grabbed Emily's hand.

'Come on!' he cried in his high baby voice.

'Stay right in front of the cottage,' Ellen warned.

The three of them ran through the still-open door. Bridget heard the boys naming all the hens and Emily laughing in delight as they ran around after them.

Liam moved to sit at the table with the other adults. He had retained his lanky form from his youth and he folded himself onto the bench next to Cormac.

'How are things up at the manor stables?' Cormac asked companionably. 'Have they made you stable master yet?'

Even as he said this, a strange thought occurred to Bridget: why was Liam at home during the daytime?

Liam's eyebrows shot up and he looked over at Ellen.

'I haven't had a chance to tell them yet,' she said quietly.

'Tell us what?' asked Cormac.

Liam's countenance was grave. 'I don't work on the estate anymore. Nobody does.'

'What?' said Bridget, confused. 'What can you mean by that?'

Liam looked directly at her. 'For me to tell ye what's happened, 'tis necessary to make some less than savoury comments about your mother. Please forgive me for that.' As Bridget struggled to grasp this, he continued, 'I think 'tis fair to say Lady Courcey's never been a popular woman among the tenants on Oakleigh land. Lord Courcey was a kind soul, and Lord Walcott did no harm, but she's always been cold and hard to please. Still, she showed a keen understanding of how to manage the estate and so we were all able to make a decent living.' He rested his forearms on the table. ''Til almost seven years ago. Without warning, she reinstated the tithes and anyone working the land was obliged to take on the burden that Oakleigh had once covered. It was galling for Catholic folk to be forced once again to pay tithes to the Church of Ireland, no church of ours. In addition to that, she started putting up the rents, raising them every single year, and made us all work longer hours in tougher conditions.' He stared down at his hands and went on in a lower voice. 'Life became very difficult for every man, woman and

49

child within reach of her influence. Anyone who couldn't pay what the lady demanded was thrown off the estate. Old Fintan Kelly cried the day he was made to leave. I saw him bawling his eyes out in the courtyard. He'd tended the gardens of the big house for over four decades but that meant nothing to her. She was merciless.'

Bridget listened in mute horror. This could not be true.

'About four years back, several of us crossed over the county border to attend an anti-tithe meeting in Kilkenny. There were thousands at it, and we heard all the news and rumours from other estates and other counties: folk refusing to pay the tithes, clashes with the constabulary, attacks on Church of Ireland property. When we got back to Oakleigh, we held a secret gathering among the tenants, servants and farmers who came from every corner of the estate. We decided it was time to stand up for ourselves and for our families.'

Cormac looked astounded. 'You rebelled?'

Liam's expression was calm. 'We simply refused to pay the tithes and the increased rents. The Church of Ireland sent tithe proctors to collect what they believed they were owed, and Lady Courcey ordered her agent Mr Enright to accompany them to ensure the same for her rents. After many failed attempts, the tithe proctors saw the need to be escorted by members of the constabulary as well. We resisted as peacefully as we could, but some of the confrontations turned nasty.'

At the hardened look in Liam's eyes, Cormac asked, 'Has anyone been hurt?'

'Too many,' said Liam. He reached across the table to Ellen and she laced her fingers with his.

'We live in a constant state of fear,' she told Bridget and Cormac. 'Every day brings the dread of a tithe proctor or a rent collector coming to the door. That was why I got such a fright when you appeared. Before I realised who you were, I thought...' She reached once again for her pocket and withdrew a short knife, small but sharp. 'I keep

50

myself prepared, just in case.'

Bridget stared at the knife. To think that Ellen, once a lady's maid to a baroness, had been reduced to defending herself and her family in such a way. And this was occurring on Oakleigh land, where Bridget could never have imagined anything like this being possible.

She tried to speak but only a croak came out. She cleared her throat weakly. 'And — and my mother knew what was happening?'

Ellen's gaze lowered. 'She did.'

'And she did nothing about it,' said Liam. A glower shadowed his features. 'So last autumn we decided we'd had enough. Between allowing all this to happen to her own tenants and continuing to increase the rents, she was crippling us and our families and we couldn't stand it any longer. At another secret meeting, we agreed to abandon the estate, all of us together. A few stragglers remained behind, fearing the lady too much to rebel, but the majority of us walked away from our positions. Maids, footmen, gardeners, stable hands, we all deserted the manor one morning last September. At the same time, excavation work halted at the quarry and the farmers stopped tending the land. They've continued to look after their livestock but keep moving them and concealing them so the tithe proctors won't seize them from the fields as payment.' He shrugged. 'We hoped Lady Courcey would relent once she realised there was no one left to maintain the estate. But she hasn't given in. She sold the horses from the stables and stopped receiving visitors to the manor. She'd prefer to see the house and land fall into disrepair and decay rather than admit she's been wrong.'

Cormac's brow creased. 'But you are still within the confines of the Oakleigh Estate. Why did she not evict you and everyone else who refused to work for her?'

'On occasion, Mr Enright shows up with a constable at someone's dwelling,' said Liam. 'But she doesn't have the means to carry out widespread evictions on such a scale.

Too few remained to act on her command.'

'Who did remain?'

'Cathy was the only maid who stayed behind,' said Ellen. 'I left the household back when I married Liam so I was gone before all this took place. I think Cathy was too scared to leave but it's my belief she also took pity on Lady Courcey. Mr Buttimer and Mrs Walsh stayed for a while but in the end they left too. I heard they went seeking positions in Dublin. It was an impossible life when the lady was being so unreasonable. Now Cathy's the only one left.' She shook her head sadly. 'It hurts us to see the estate like this. We were always so proud to serve Oakleigh. No one is happy to watch it fall into decline.'

Cormac rubbed his jaw, where a beard had sprouted after so many days on the road. 'How have you managed to survive with no income?'

'We get by,' she said. 'We'd be lost without the potato crop, that's what we eat most days. The winter was hard but now that spring is here it's a little easier. Foraging in the woods usually yields something edible.' She pointed at the mushrooms lying on the tabletop. 'We trade our hens' eggs for cow's milk or flour. And also — please forgive us for this, we did feel so very guilty — we sold your mother's spinning wheel. Everyone's in the same position, and we're all trying to help each other as much as we can. But it's difficult, especially with the two boys.'

There was silence in the cottage as nobody drew attention to the glaring concern: in a few short months, Ellen and Liam would have a third child to feed. What would they do then?

'We're still lucky,' Ellen said into the quietness. 'We have a solid roof over our heads. That's more than some poor families have.'

'I am gladder than ever that you have made a home for yourselves here,' said Cormac. 'In these troubled times, it would have been a waste to let the cottage go uninhabited.'

At this point, Bridget could stay silent no longer. 'Oh, Ellen,' she burst out. 'Why did you not write to me in London and tell me what was happening here? I could have saved you all from this!'

Ellen gazed at her directly. 'Could you have?'

'I—yes, of course—I—' Bridget faltered at the sadness in Ellen's eyes. 'Do you doubt that I would have tried to help you?'

'What would you have done?' Ellen asked, her tone gentle.

Bridget hesitated. She had a stirring vision of herself receiving Ellen's letter of distress, sailing at once to Ireland, travelling to Oakleigh, and forcing her mother to undo all the damage she had done.

Then she re-imagined the scenario with more clarity. Garrett would have refused point-blank to let her go. If she had managed to get away, he would not have permitted her to take Emily with her. And once she had reached Oakleigh, what authority would she have had? She herself had signed the contract conferring guardianship of Oakleigh to her mother. Nothing but her husband's signature could reverse that, and he would never provide it. She only had the power of persuasion and that was tenuous at best, given that the last time she and her mother had spoken in person she had cast her out from Wyndham House in London on the night of Emily's birth and sworn that the lady would never set eyes upon her grandchild. Lady Courcey would not have responded favourably to any of Bridget's demands. In fact, her appearance might well have made matters worse, spurring Lady Courcey to greater ire.

Bridget let out a stifled sob and buried her face in her hands.

'She did this to punish me,' she said, her words muffled against her fingers. 'Because of what I did to her, what I cut from her life. She knew the things I loved most in this world. She could not reach Emily, and she had already inflicted all the harm she could upon Cormac, so she took out her revenge on Oakleigh.'

Which meant all this was Bridget's own fault.

It was too terrible to comprehend. Her mother had committed unspeakable sins in the past but she had never done anything on this scale before. The lady had condemned dozens and dozens of families to appalling hardship and she had done it out of pure spite; there could be no other incentive for such cruel treatment of her tenants. How could she have behaved so callously? Could she not see that she was hurting real human beings? Furthermore, the land had suffered as well; Bridget had seen as much on their way here. The estate to which her father had devoted his life was a mere shadow of what it had once been without its loyal workers to maintain it. It was disgraceful beyond belief.

Utter shame pressed down upon her. How on earth could she face Ellen and Liam when they had suffered so much at her mother's hands and, by extension, her own? But when she raised her gaze to meet theirs, she did not find accusations or blame staring back at her. On the contrary, their expressions were full of sympathy.

'We're sorry to be the ones telling ye this,' said Liam.

'It is I who should be sorry,' she replied. 'I cannot believe what she has done. It is reprehensible.' She turned her head to Cormac. 'To think we were going to pay a visit to her. Sit in her drawing room and drink tea! That is unimaginable after learning this awful news.'

'If that was your purpose in coming here,' said Ellen, 'then I think you should still do so.'

Cormac protested, 'We would not set one foot across that woman's threshold after discovering what she has done to you, to all the people on this estate.'

'It might not be very pleasant,' Ellen admitted, 'but it might still be advisable. I met Cathy a few weeks ago and she told me her ladyship's not well. I'm not certain how serious her condition is but, if you don't visit her while you're here now, it's possible you won't have another occasion in the future.'

Recollecting her mother's allusion to her ill health in her letter before Christmas, Bridget wondered if it was even worse than she had intimated. 'Is she — is she dying?'

'I cannot say. But Cathy said Mr Abbott's been by many times.'

In all her life, Bridget could not recall her mother suffering from any ailment so grave that she had needed frequent visits from the physician. Part of her felt sudden worry for her mother's wellbeing and another part immediately responded with nauseating self-loathing for feeling anything but revulsion for the woman. She lowered her gaze so as not to betray either emotion to the others.

'I have no idea what to do,' she mumbled. It was absurd to even think of paying a social call to Lady Courcey when she had exploited her tenants in such a dreadful way. But how could Bridget stay away when her mother's failing health meant that this might be her last opportunity to see her alive?

'You don't need to decide today,' Ellen said. 'Maybe a good sleep tonight will make things clearer for you in the morning.'

Bridget glanced at Cormac. He shrugged. 'I'll leave the decision up to you. You were the one who wanted to see her in the first place.'

She gave a morose nod.

'So that's why ye came back then?' said Liam. 'To see the lady?'

'Actually, no,' Cormac replied. 'We came back for my family.'

Ellen's jaw dropped. 'Didn't Bridget tell you…?' She was so shocked that she didn't even stumble over her first use of Bridget's name without a title.

'She did. I am aware that they are gone from here, that they were forced to leave after I was, but I want to find

55

them wherever they are now. I know it was a long time ago and that my chances of locating them are slim to none. Be that as it may, I'm holding onto the hope that someone here on the estate will be able to give me some inkling as to where they went.'

'There was never any word of them,' said Ellen, looking wretched. 'They just disappeared.'

'Even so, I still have to try.' His bearded jaw was set with resolve. 'I'm sure you understand. If it were your family, you would do the same.'

'I would. But I don't know where you'd even begin to look for this information.'

'I do,' said Liam. Everyone looked at him in surprise. 'There's another meeting taking place tonight. It's been six months since we turned our backs on the estate, so word's gone out that it's time for the men to come together to discuss the next steps we might take. If you're looking to speak to as many people as possible, that's your chance right there.'

'Thank you,' said Cormac, his shoulders sagging with relief. 'That is more than I could have hoped for.'

'It's a good start,' said Ellen, smiling at her husband. 'We can look after the children here,' she added to Bridget. 'You're of course welcome to stay as long as you wish to.'

'That is very kind of you but I shall be going with Cormac to the meeting.'

Cormac looked at her sharply. 'Are you mad? No, you won't.'

Ellen and Liam said nothing but their expressions showed that they too disagreed with Bridget.

She straightened her back against their united opposition. 'I ought to go,' she said. 'My mother has done a great disservice to these people and this is an opportunity for me to beg their pardon for her conduct. I know that an apology does not put money in their pockets or food on their tables but it is all that is within my power to give and so I want to do it with humility and hope that they can see my good intention.'

'No,' Cormac repeated. 'They'll be an angry group of men. How do you think they'd react to your appearance? You're the daughter of the woman they hate.'

'He's right,' said Liam. 'You wouldn't get a warm welcome.'

She slumped in defeat. 'Very well,' she mumbled. She glanced from Ellen to Liam. 'My thanks to you both for not treating me that way when you saw me.'

'We know you,' said Ellen, 'and we know you're not to blame for what has happened. But you are a stranger to most of them. They wouldn't understand how much Oakleigh means to you.' She patted Bridget's arm. 'We'll wait here with the children. Emily can go to sleep up in the loft with the two boys. I'll make sure she's comf –' She broke off. 'Oh,' she said and, without any explanation, she stood up from the table, went over to the ladder, and disappeared up into the loft.

Bridget and Cormac looked at Liam for enlightenment but he seemed as mystified as they were. Ellen reappeared a few moments later carrying a bundle under her arm. Liam helped her down the ladder and she deposited what she had retrieved from the loft on the table in front of Cormac. It appeared to be a number of letters packaged together with a piece of string.

'I've only remembered them now,' she said, a little breathless. 'They started coming nearly four years ago, not long before Liam Óg was born, but I never opened them because they weren't addressed to us. Were they from you?'

Cormac's expression was bleak. 'They were.'

He untied the string and picked up the first letter. Bridget was able to make out the name 'Maggie McGovern' and the address of the cottage on the faded paper.

'I sent them without a signature. If she had received them, she would have known who they were from. I just wanted to help her and let her know that I was safe.'

He broke the seal on the folded letter, drew out a rolled strip of cloth and unfurled it. A coin fell out and rolled along the tabletop. Ellen caught it before it plunged off the edge.

'You should have opened them,' he said. 'This money would have been a great benefit to you these past few years.'

'It doesn't belong to us,' she said, her eyes round as she stared down at the coin sitting in her palm.

'It doesn't belong to us either,' he replied. 'I want you to have it.'

Liam said haltingly, 'We can't accept it...'

'Listen, every one of these has money in it,' said Cormac, pointing to the stack of letters. 'My mother never received them but I think she would knock our heads together if she saw us all in need and refusing to take what will otherwise go to waste. You have a family to support, and I have a family to find. We can each put the money to good use so let us divide it up and not be stupid about it.'

Bridget's heart swelled at his bracing words; Liam and Ellen too looked almost overcome with emotion.

'Thank you for your generosity,' said Ellen, tears brimming in her eyes. 'It'll be such an enormous help to us.'

'And we can use it to aid the other tenants too,' Liam added.

'That is an admirable thought,' said Cormac, 'only please make sure you do not leave yourselves short.'

He opened the rest of the letters and began separating the money into two piles as Emily, Liam Óg and Aidan came running in from outside.

'Papa, I fed the hens!' Emily exclaimed, looking very pleased with herself.

'Excellent work.' Cormac pulled her to his side in a one-armed hug. 'Do you like it here, *a stór*?'

'Oh, yes, very much!'

'I am glad to hear it, because we plan to stay here for a few days. I need to go somewhere this evening for a little while but you and your mother are going to remain here with Ellen. Will you be on your best behaviour for her?'

Emily raised her chin with determination; she would show Ellen just how well-behaved she could be.

'That's my girl,' said Cormac and plucked at her chin before letting her run off with the two boys again.

As he turned back to the table, he caught Bridget's eye and his face became sober. She was already uneasy about his plan for tonight. What kind of crowd would he meet, and would they be able to give him the information about his family that he so desperately needed?

Chapter 6

'Who's there?' came the whisper from the darkness of the woods. 'Name yourselves!'

Two vague forms loomed from between the tree trunks, coalescing into a pair of sentries carrying pitchforks.

Liam stepped ahead of Cormac, moving forwards with his hands held up loosely.

''Tis Liam Kirwan,' he said in a low voice. 'And this here's Cormac McGovern. He's safe, I can vouch for him.'

One of the sentries gave Cormac an appraising look, before nodding to Liam. 'Go on, then. Nearly everyone's already inside.'

'Thanks, lads.'

Cormac followed Liam past the sentries. Liam had forewarned him of their presence – all of the meetings had to be guarded in this way to prevent any risk of ambush. What was more, no one could arrive via the road; the meeting place could only be approached by way of fields and woods to prevent detection.

They emerged from the woods to face the back end of a barn.

'McKinty Farm,' Liam murmured. 'Mick McKinty is the only farmer around with an outbuilding big enough to hold so many of us.'

Cormac recognised the farmstead; when he had worked at Oakleigh, he had been required now and then to take a horse to McKinty Farm to collect produce for the manor kitchens. And, further back in time, he and Bridget had on more than one occasion visited Farmer McKinty's wife to cajole her until she gave them chunks of delicious cheese to nourish them on their wild jaunts about the estate.

Liam went first, leading Cormac around to the front of the barn. He heaved open the door and several voices greeted him as he entered.

'John,' he said. 'I've brought a friend along — hope you don't mind. I think you'll remember him.'

Liam looked back over his shoulder and Cormac stepped up beside him. Standing in the doorway, his first impression was that of many bodies and bright candlelight. Every available space seemed to be taken up by men sitting or standing and the barn was lit with lanterns set on stools or hanging from brackets on the stone walls. There was a buzz of subdued talking but this came to an abrupt stop at his appearance. For a second or two, he could not distinguish anybody among the sea of faces, but then a familiar one near the front of the assembly swam into view: the wiry stable master at Oakleigh, John Corbett. He let out a shout of surprise and delight and pulled Cormac inside the barn.

'Where in God's name did you spring from?' he exclaimed, slapping Cormac on the back.

Several more men gathered around, their faces alight with astonishment and welcome. It felt like going back in time, to be once again surrounded by the stable hands and gardeners and servants who had formed the constant backdrop to life at Oakleigh. They bestowed further hearty smacks upon his shoulders.

'Welcome back, lad!'

'Jaysus, what a shocker!'

'Didn't think we'd ever see you 'round these parts again.'

'Nor I, but I'm delighted to be in your company once more,' he said, smiling around at them with genuine pleasure.

They looked taken aback, and he realised that he must sound very different to the stable hand they remembered. Belatedly, he wondered whether he ought to have assumed a less formal mode of speech with them, but it would appear patronising if he attempted that now after they had already heard him speak in such a proper manner. In any case, once learned, good pronunciation was difficult to throw off.

'What's your story, lad?' asked John in puzzlement. 'Where've you been all this time?'

'It's quite complicated,' said Cormac. He had no wish to drag up his questionable past in front of every fellow who had walked into the barn that evening. 'I have seen and done a lot of things. But it is good to be home.'

A mixed reaction greeted this comment. There were some murmurs of appreciation but many of the men looked darkly at each other as though to say 'He doesn't know what he's come back to'.

'I've heard,' he hastened to assure them. He hesitated for a moment, imagining what Bridget might think of his next words, then ploughed on. 'I've heard what's happened here on the estate, and I'm glad of it. It's about time we took back control. This isn't their land, it's ours, and it has been for hundreds of years.'

A cheer went up around him, spreading to all corners of the barn. One of the younger men – Denis, Cormac recalled, a footman from the manor – shook his hand with vigour.

He studiously avoided Liam's gaze. Liam was the only one in this barn who knew that Cormac had returned in Bridget's company and he intended for it to stay that way.

'I'm glad you think so,' said a voice beyond the nearest circle of men. ''Cause rumour has it you bedded the English filly that used to live up in the big house and that's why you had to clear off all those years ago.'

Over Denis's shoulder, Cormac spotted two unkempt men lounging on stools with their backs propped against the barn's stone wall. He recognised the one who had spoken as Joseph Hayes, a man he knew mainly by reputation and not much of that was good. The balding fellow next to him was Bernie Cuddihy, the proprietor of The Pikeman, the drinking house in the local village of Ballydarry. Both had once been involved in a skirmish outside The Pikeman involving Bridget; she had been rescued by a pair of constables but the incident had given her a fright. Reputations aside, that alone was reason enough for him to dislike them.

'My business is my own,' he said coolly. 'And why I left is none of yours.'

Joseph flashed a gap-toothed smirk as Cormac turned back to John Corbett.

'Liam has told me what you've been doing,' he said.

'I can't say I'm proud of how events have unfolded,' said John. 'Had things remained bearable, I would've been happy to stay as we were.' He shook his head. 'But she just pushed us too far.'

'It can't have been easy to decide to take action. Are you –'

Cormac broke off as five more people entered the barn. At the front was none other than Mrs Kavanagh, the cook from Oakleigh Manor. She gasped when she spotted Cormac.

'Am I seeing a ghost?' she exclaimed.

She came forwards and enveloped him in a vigorous hug. She had always been a big-bosomed woman and there was still ample flesh surrounding him, but there seemed to be somewhat less of her than he remembered and, when she pulled back, there were dark circles under her eyes. They glistened with emotion and it touched him that his unexpected reappearance could affect her so much.

'Stand aside, Maura, and let the rest of us have our turn,' said a female voice behind Mrs Kavanagh.

The pair behind the cook were Farmer McKinty and his wife. The farmer had a rather vacant look but Mrs McKinty strode forwards and wrapped her arms around Cormac. He felt a little uncomfortable, given that he had never known her as well as Mrs Kavanagh and her embrace felt quite a bit more intimate in the way she pressed her chest so tightly against him.

'Uh, good evening, Mrs McKinty,' he said, drawing back from her as politely as he could.

'Oh, you're all grown up now, you can call me Maisie,' she said with a wink. She had to be fifteen years older than him at least but, though her skin had a hardened quality to it, her face retained a certain prettiness.

Mrs Kavanagh muscled back in, shunting an affronted Maisie out of the way.

'Bless us and save us, it's good to see you,' the cook murmured, pressing her broad hand to Cormac's cheek. 'You were always a decent lad. I hope life has treated you well since we saw you last?'

'I've had my ups and downs,' he admitted. 'But it sounds like you've all suffered a great deal of hardship as well.'

Her expression darkened. She beckoned to the last two people behind her, a woman with a pronounced overbite and a man crumpling his cap in his hands. When they came forwards, Mrs Kavanagh said, 'This is my sister, Kitty, and her husband, Colm Brophy.'

Cormac understood the connection at once. 'You were tenants at Rathglaney?'

'Yes,' said Kitty Brophy, one clipped word with a world of anger contained within it.

Cormac recollected his last summer at Oakleigh and the letter Mrs Kavanagh had received from her sister telling her of the uprising on the Rathglaney Estate, which was just over the county border into Wexford. The riled tenants had attempted to burn down the big house and in the process had injured the landlord in residence, Lord Fitzwilliam. Kitty's son and husband had both been involved and arrested, and her son had later been executed.

'I'm sorry for what happened to you,' said Cormac. 'I

can't imagine you've been able to find much peace.'

Kitty pursed her lips. 'We found revenge. Rathglaney is no more. We didn't fail a second time.'

'We had to try again,' said Colm, crushing his cap even tighter. 'For our boy's sake.'

'Ye were right too,' interposed Joseph Hayes, leaning back with his hands behind his head. 'Ashes was all that place was worth.'

'When Maura said something similar was happening at Oakleigh, we came to help,' said Kitty. 'We weren't the only ones. The two fellows on sentry duty used to be Rathglaney stable hands and friends of our Collie. We knew ye had a just cause to fight for.'

'And they aren't the only ones helping us,' said John. 'Word has spread, 'specially thanks to those anti-tithe meetings. Support's coming from tenants and farmers in other places, even other counties, and many of them have carted over supplies.'

Cormac frowned. 'Supplies?'

'Weapons,' said Denis eagerly. 'Pikes and pitchforks and even a few pistols. I held one.'

With a jolt, Cormac recalled riding in the back of Farmer Hackett's cart next to the covered bundle of pikes. This was larger than he had even realised.

'We bury them under the giant's claw,' Denis continued. 'Just like back in '98.'

Joseph let out a noise of exasperation. 'Arrah, let's spill all our secrets to the goddamn stranger, why don't we?'

'He's right, keep your trap shut,' Bernie Cuddihy barked at Denis.

'Come on, lads,' said John. 'I've known Cormac since he was barely up to my knees. And I knew his da before that. We can trust him.'

'Can we?' said Joseph. 'Has he given us even one scrap of information about where he's been all these years? Or why he's bothered to come back after so long? Or why he's talking so fancy and proper?'

'He's told me and my wife,' said Liam. 'We're satisfied he's the same man he always was.'

'And his mother was the best woman you could ever hope to meet,' said Mrs Kavanagh. 'So shut your gob, Joseph Hayes.'

'Thank you,' said Cormac to those who had come to his defence. Then he raised his voice so as to be heard throughout the barn. 'But Joseph's correct. I haven't told you yet why I'm back. I do have an agenda in coming here tonight.'

Angry muttering broke out on all sides.

'Just hear me out,' he said, even louder. 'Some of you may be aware that my family was evicted from their cottage about seven and a half years ago. My mother, Maggie McGovern, my three younger sisters and my nephew were forced to leave the estate as a result of a transgression on my part. To my deep regret, I only learned of this very recently, at which point I made the immediate decision to come back to Oakleigh to find them. I don't know where they are but I am hoping that there might be someone here on the estate who saw them leave, who could tell me which direction they went, or where they planned to go. Is there anyone here who can help me at all?'

There was a hum of chatter as the men digested this news.

'What did they look like, lad?' somebody called from the back.

'My mother and sisters all had dark hair and grey eyes. My sisters were aged fourteen, twelve and five and my nephew was only a baby, around three months old.'

He held his breath. The men looked around at each other, waiting for someone to speak up and say they had seen them. But no one called out again and, as he let his breath out in disappointment, a boulder formed in the pit of his stomach, heavy and sickening. This had been his most promising chance and already it had amounted to nothing.

'Sorry, lad,' John murmured to him with a sympathetic look, before addressing the room in general. 'Perhaps ye could all mention this to your wives and families when ye go home. Spread the word and see if anyone knows anything.'

Liam added, 'And bring any news ye get to myself or John. We'll make sure it's passed on.'

Cormac nodded his gratitude.

'While I have your undivided attention,' John went on to them all, 'I've got some grave news to impart. Ben Bracken was evicted this morning, along with his elderly mother.'

There were shouts of dismay and outrage. Bernie aimed a furious kick at a stray clump of hay and it went flying in all directions. Farmer McKinty looked vaguely anxious at the commotion and started mumbling to himself. No one paid him any mind.

'They're being accommodated over at Hogan Farm,' said John. 'Ben's ma is quite shook up and wants him by her side, which is why he isn't here himself to tell us the tale. But he told me Mr Enright showed up with three constables to do it.'

'That bugger's got it coming to him,' said Joseph. 'Still doing the bitch's bidding like a little lapdog. Deserves to be tossed in the Sruhawn, if you ask me.'

'Would you mind your language when we've women in the company?' said Denis hotly.

'It's no offence to me,' said Mrs Kavanagh stoutly, while Maisie McKinty offered a pert smile and shot Cormac another wink.

'There you go, you milksop,' said Joseph to Denis. The footman went red to the tips of his ears but Joseph carried on, 'What's going to be done about this?'

John folded his arms. 'We need to be careful how we handle it. Mr Enright's no servant. He mightn't have a title but he's a gentleman, the youngest son in a family from the landed gentry. He's got connections.'

'And haven't we got connections too?' demanded Joseph. 'What about that money? Couldn't we find out who 'tis coming from and put pressure on them to act?'

Cormac raised his eyebrows. 'Money?'

John looked ill at ease. 'We're getting financial help from an unknown source. We don't know who's sending it or why, but every now and then a fresh sum of money arrives. I'll get an anonymous note and find the funds buried under the giant's claw, just like the weapons. That's how we've been able to pay for the supplies coming from other places. And we save the rest to help those who've been evicted.'

Staggered, Cormac said, 'And you have no idea where it's coming from?'

''Tis got to be someone rich,' said Joseph. 'Like I said, 'tis a connection. Can't we get a message to whoever 'tis and say we want that Enright bugger stopped?'

Before anyone could respond, there was a scuffle outside the barn. The door banged open and the two Rathglaney sentries came marching in, grasping a struggling figure between them.

'Let me go!' Bridget exclaimed.

Cormac's heart plummeted to the soles of his feet.

Chapter 7

Dead silence fell. Every pair of eyes in the barn became fixed upon Bridget, who went pale under their stares.

'That's Lady Courcey's daughter,' said Denis in disbelief.

'Found her in the woods,' said one of the sentries to John. 'She was trying to sneak up to the barn.'

'I was not sneaking,' she said indignantly. 'I just lost my bearings in the dark. I knew you were there and I fully intended to announce my presence.'

John cleared his throat. 'Your...presence comes as something of a surprise, m'lady.' He eyed Cormac, who read the questions and the suspicion in the stable master's gaze.

Trying his best to keep a lid on his anger, Cormac extricated himself from the surrounding men and stepped forwards.

'Let her go,' he said to the two sentries.

They looked to John for guidance and, at his nod, reluctantly released their grips on Bridget's upper arms. She straightened her skirts and kneaded one of her shoulders. Cormac went to stand beside her, turning to face the others in the room. His show of support seemed to boost her confidence and she kept her chin up as she too looked around at them all. She made eye contact with Mrs Kavanagh but the cook glanced away quickly.

A resentful hiss rose throughout the barn as the men muttered to one another. Cormac caught snatches of 'What's she doing here?' and 'Why's he with her?' and 'What've they come back for?'

'This doesn't look good, Cormac,' said John.

'No, I know it doesn't,' Cormac replied, resisting the urge to cast a nettled grimace in Bridget's direction.

John sighed. 'Can you explain what's going on here?'

'No need to,' barked Joseph, jumping up from his stool. ''Tis obvious. They're here to spy on our plans and turn us all in. I goddamn told you so!'

He spat on the ground at Bridget's feet.

Enraged, Cormac lunged towards Joseph but Liam pulled him back. John walked right up to Joseph and stared him in the eye, though he was at least half a foot shorter.

'Joseph Hayes, that's no way to treat a woman,' he said calmly. 'Be civilised or you'll be thrown out.'

Joseph glared at John, Cormac and Bridget in turn and then sat back down, scowling. John returned his attention to Bridget, who had shrunk back at Joseph's rudeness.

'Forgive us, m'lady. We haven't given you a proper greeting but you might understand why we have some misgivings. May we ask what's brought you here tonight?'

There was a faint tremor in Bridget's hands. Clasping them together, she said, 'Thank you, John. I do understand why my reception has been less than warm and you require no forgiveness for that. I came here tonight to say something to you all but before I do that I need to make one thing clear. You must not address me as 'my lady' anymore. I am not Miss Muldowney, I am not Lady Wyndham, I no longer belong to the upper classes. I belong to Cormac and therefore I am now simply Bridget.'

This caused quite a stir. A young lady of distinguished social standing had deserted her rich husband in favour of a poor – though admittedly well-spoken – stable hand. It was unheard of. Maisie McKinty looked highly disappointed.

After an awkward pause, John came forwards to shake Cormac's hand but, despite Bridget's protestations, he insisted on calling her, at the very least, 'Miss Bridget'.

There were no echoes of goodwill from any of the other men. From their sceptical expressions, it was clear they thought Bridget was trying to hoodwink them by declaring that she was now 'one of them'.

Mrs Kavanagh seemed to be the only other person who softened a little at Bridget's announcement. She said to her sister in a carrying whisper, 'That pair have been smitten with each other since they were children. Bless them, I'm glad they've found love at last.'

Kitty Brophy snapped her teeth together. 'You think she's telling the truth?' she said, not attempting to keep quiet. 'Open your eyes, for heaven's sake. You can't believe a word English folk say. 'Tis all poison from their mouths.'

Visibly hurt, Bridget said, 'You don't even know me. How can you say such things?'

'I know your kind,' said Kitty, 'and that's enough. Most likely, you've paid that lad to act as your lover — far-fetched to begin with, as if you'd ever stoop to dallying with a Catholic peasant — and he's come here first to extract information on your behalf. I wouldn't trust you as far as I could throw you. *Téigh ar ais go Sasana, a bhitseach!*'

Colm Brophy laid a hand on his wife's elbow but his placating words were lost in a ragged cheer from the gathered men. Joseph and Bernie shouted loudest of all. However, John, Liam and Mrs Kavanagh didn't join in, and Farmer McKinty put his palms flat over his ears at the noise.

Cormac balled his hands into fists but kept his tone even as he said, 'That only goes to show the level of your ignorance of this whole situation, Mrs Brophy. Because Bridget understands exactly what you just said.' He knew her grasp of Irish was somewhat spotty but she couldn't fail to comprehend those words of abuse.

'I do,' said Bridget. 'And I will *not* go back to England.'

That shut them all up pretty quickly.

'You call me English,' she continued, 'but I was born in

71

this country and I deem Ireland to be my home. You cast judgement upon me because of who my mother is, without giving me a chance to show you that I am nothing like her. Will you not offer me that opportunity before you throw me to the wolves?' She turned a beseeching gaze upon John. 'When have I ever given you reason to doubt me?'

He looked abashed. 'You're right,' he said. 'We're not being fair.' When a chorus of grumbles rose up, he put out a shushing hand and carried on, 'We'll let her speak.' He pointed to the Rathglaney sentries. 'You two, go back to your posts.'

They retreated with departing glances of distrust towards Bridget, closing the barn door behind them and shutting out the cool night-time air. Liam fetched a stool and John motioned Bridget to sit. Cormac took up a protective stance at her side, alert to the fact that everyone's gaze was trained keenly upon her and, whether she realised it or not, she was now on trial.

'So,' said John, 'you said you'd something to say to us all?'

'Yes,' she mumbled. Then she cleared her throat and raised her voice so that she could be heard throughout the barn. 'Yes, I have something to say. Cormac and I returned to the estate just today so we have only learned about your plight in the last few hours. Liam has told us how you have suffered. You have been reduced to the most terrible circumstances and my mother's behaviour is unpardonable in this regard. I want you to know how ashamed I am of the way she has treated you and how sorry I am that you have been forced to endure such hardships.'

She stopped speaking. There was a ringing silence as her words hung in the air. Then a gruff voice pierced it.

'That's it?'

Joseph was leaning forwards on his stool. He looked incredulous. 'We've been suffering for years, stretched so tight we're only ever a day away from starvation. Our children are skin and bone, our livelihoods are ruined. Your own damn mother put us in this position. And you've the *gall*,' he spat the word, 'to swan in here and say you're sorry? D'you think that'll fix everything?'

'Cool your temper,' said John in a warning tone.

'What about all the folk we've lost? Ben Bracken's brother got killed when the tithe proctor wouldn't take no for an answer. Bernie here buried both his sisters last year, wasted away to nothing, they were. Fintan Kelly died without a penny to his name or a roof above his head. 'Tis my belief he died of shame, between the humiliation of what that idiot grandson of his did and the way that woman disgraced him. She's got blood on her hands.'

Some of the others made noises of agreement.

Cormac saw a vein pulsing rapidly in Bridget's throat. 'I had no knowledge of or control over most of what you have just said,' she said. 'The one thing I did have a say in was the punishment of Mr Kelly's grandson for his attempted theft at the manor. And I in fact convinced my mother to commute Malachy's punishment from transportation to imprisonment. Only for me, he and his two accomplices would be in Australia now. As for the rest, I am devastated to hear of it. My heart goes out to every single family affected by this atrocity.'

Joseph shot to his feet. 'I don't believe a word she says. Her devil of a mother sent her here to fool us!'

Bridget stood herself, red-faced with indignation. Instead of frightening her, Joseph's fury seemed to have fired her up.

'I'll have you know that I have neither seen nor spoken to my mother in nearly seven years. I received one piece of correspondence from her during all that time in which she gave me no indication that there was a crisis on the estate. I was ignorant of your situation but I do still accept the blame for it. I apologise to you all this evening on behalf of my family name and for the fact that this estate has failed you. However, do not accuse me of siding with my mother in this. She has no inkling that I have even returned to Oakleigh.'

Joseph looked taken aback but, unwilling to acknowledge her innocence, merely muttered something caustic under his breath and sat back down again. Bridget spun around to the room at large and held out her palms in a gesture of helplessness.

'I am sorrier than I can say for what you are going through. I sympathise with every one of you, truly I do. I came here to express that sympathy and to assure you that my mother was inflicting this distress without my knowledge. I wish there were something that I could do to help you, now that I am conscious of the circumstances, but regrettably there is not.'

'Well, I don't know about that,' John said, looking pensive. 'I'm starting to believe your heart's in the right place. So maybe you *can* help us.'

Bridget's brow puckered. 'In what way?'

'Oakleigh is yours, isn't that right?'

'Technically, yes. But when I was twenty-one I signed the guardianship of it over to my mother for as long as she lives. And whenever she passes, it will belong to my husband, Lord Wyndham, because all of my property is his.'

Mrs Kavanagh made a huffing sound at this injustice.

John shrugged. 'What if you reclaim what's yours? Why not step in and take over from Lady Courcey while she still lives?'

'Are you asking me to depose my mother?' Bridget said in disbelief.

'I am.'

Joseph snorted, and Bernie spluttered, 'Are you daft? Why would we replace one English tyrant for another?'

'I don't think that's what would happen,' said John. 'She's Irish at heart, my gut tells me so. She doesn't want to see Oakleigh suffer. She wouldn't force the tithes upon

74

her tenants and she'd be fair in her dealings with rents. She could rescue the estate from her mother and give us back our livelihoods.'

'But it is impossible,' said Bridget. 'I would have no legal grounds upon which to do so.'

'Acts of legality haven't been seen too often in these lands over the past few years,' Liam pointed out.

'Even so, I could not do it.' She looked bewildered.

'You'd manage it a damn sight better than how 'tis being managed now,' said John. 'You could restore Oakleigh to the way it was under your father.'

Her shoulders jerked at the mention of Lord Courcey. She wavered, then said, 'But I don't see how it could be done.' She bit the tip of her tongue as a contemplative look crossed her features. 'Mr Enright has a good knowledge of the law. Perhaps he would know some way around it —'

'Not him,' said Joseph. 'His downfall's coming too, same as your ma. He's just as bad as her.'

Bridget bristled. 'I do find that hard to believe. I recall very clearly when I was last at Oakleigh a discussion between Mr Enright and my mother in which he defended your position most compellingly. He advocated that the tithes should remain an expenditure of the estate and not be forced upon the tenants.'

Bernie sneered. 'Didn't take you long to forget the role you're meant to be playing. That Enright devil's not on our side. He's —'

For the second time that evening, the barn door banged open. The two sentries came sprinting in.

'Constables!' they shouted. 'Coming right now! They're nearly here!'

Every head swivelled towards Bridget.

'This is your doing!' Joseph roared at her.

'It's not!' she cried. 'It's not!'

'There's no time for that now,' said John quickly. 'We can't make it out ourselves but the women need to get away.'

Colm was already shunting Mrs Kavanagh, Kitty and Maisie towards the door.

'Go with them,' Cormac said to Bridget.

'No, I should stay —'

He gripped her wrist tightly. 'Go right now and don't argue.'

Fearful, she stumbled to the door. Mrs Kavanagh took her hand and they disappeared into the night.

'Where will they go?' Cormac asked John urgently.

'Colm knows where our bolthole is in the woods,' John replied. He turned to Farmer McKinty. 'Mick, open the trap door, there's a good lad.'

Making fretful smacking noises with his lips, Farmer McKinty hurried with a lopsided gait towards the back of the barn. The men jumped aside as he bent to brush away a layer of hay from the floor; he dug his finger into a metal ring and pulled at it with a grunt. A section of the floor lifted up, revealing a shallow space beneath. The men pushed the farmer out of the way and started hauling farm tools out of the hole. Cormac gaped at the array of shovels, spades, hammers, axes and pitchforks, all of which in this context became weapons. They were passed around and a shovel found its way into his hands. He tested its weight and balance; it was a larger implement than the slender dagger he used to carry when he was in Cunningham's employ, but it would do fine.

John was issuing orders in a low, purposeful voice, commanding them to hide in the corners, in the shadows, behind haystacks, and checking if everyone was adequately armed. He directed a couple of the men to blow out most of the lanterns, leaving the inside of the barn cloaked in gloom.

'Now, keep your silence,' he whispered and waved them into position, coaxing Farmer McKinty into the furthest corner from the barn's entrance, while he himself pressed his back up against the wall next to the door, his spade ready in his hand.

Cormac crouched behind a haystack next to Denis. The footman clutched an axe, fingers wrapped firmly around its handle. The only trace of his fear was a tiny twitch in the muscle of his jaw.

Cormac let out a long, steadying breath. Heavy footfalls sounded outside and gruff voices called to each other. The constables weren't even trying to be quiet.

Then the shout came: 'We know you're in there! Come out single file, unarmed with your hands raised!'

'Sure thing,' Denis muttered through barely moving lips. 'And let me tell ye where I hid my pot of gold as well.'

After a pause, the command was repeated, louder and more annoyed, but no one inside the barn moved an inch. There were indistinct grumbles which were immediately shushed, and all went quiet. Too quiet.

'Be ready,' Denis mouthed to Cormac.

Cormac gripped his shovel even tighter, straining his ears for any sound.

With an almighty clatter, the barn door burst open and feet thundered inside.

The men erupted from their hiding places and rushed the charging constables, who all carried rifles with bayonets fixed to the muzzles. One of them fired his rifle but the shot went wild and then the men were too close for the rifles to be of any use. As Cormac darted out from behind the haystack, he saw John step up behind the last constable and whack him across the back of the head with the flat side of his spade. The man crumpled.

A constable came hurtling towards Cormac, bayonet aimed straight at his chest. He sidestepped and the blade slid past his arm, half an inch from slicing his sleeve. The constable skidded as he tried to halt his momentum and fell face first into the haystack Cormac had hidden behind. Denis dashed over, dug the butt of his axe into the small of the man's back, and growled, 'Stay right where you are, rat.'

Cormac spun about to see another constable bearing

down on him. Instead of trying to pierce him with his bayonet, the constable swung his rifle out and around. Cormac put up his shovel just in time and the rifle slammed against the shovel's handle, like two swords crossing blades. He took the brunt of the collision and felt the impact all the way up to his shoulders. The constable swung again but Cormac, arms still quivering from the previous blow, couldn't bring up the shovel quickly enough and the rifle connected with his temple. He fell sideways, dropping his shovel and landing hard on his hip. His vision went blurry for a second but it cleared as he rolled onto his back. The constable loomed over him, raising his rifle to stick the bayonet in him.

Cormac kicked out at the constable's legs to trip him, and the fellow toppled over with a muffled 'Oomph!' Booting the rifle out of the constable's grip, he scrambled to his knees and struck him a blow across the face. Spittle flew from the man's mouth. Eyes wide and desperate, he struggled to clamber backwards out of Cormac's reach. Cormac felt around blindly for his shovel but his hand landed on the rifle instead. He picked it up and aimed it at the constable's neck.

'Don't move,' he said, panting like he had just run ten miles.

All around him he heard shouts and expletives and exclamations of pain. There were clashes of metal against wood, fists against flesh, knuckles against teeth. The smell of the earlier rifle shot hung in the air.

It was all over with remarkable swiftness. The constabulary had underestimated the number of bodies inside the barn, the amount of weapons at their disposal, and their ability to act quickly. A few uniformed cowards scuttled out the barn door, but the rest were corralled into a loose clump in the centre of the barn, their own bayonets pointed at them. There were superficial injuries, grazes and bruises and cuts, but no serious wounds on either side of the fray.

John stood with a bloody nose in front of the group as they knelt in a ragged cluster of half a dozen men. Joseph and Bernie went around to each one to tie their hands behind their backs with lengths of rope.

'Make those bonds good and tight,' said John. 'We'll have to move them to another place so they can't be found by anyone who comes back looking. Then we'll bind their feet too and decide what to do with them.' He surveyed the constables. 'Of course, we'll have some questions to ask.'

The first of which had to be obvious.

How had they known where and when this meeting was to take place?

Chapter 8

Cormac and Liam got back to the cottage just as dawn was breaking. In the grey gloom, it seemed like a drowsing creature hunched at the side of the road, exhaling a gentle breath of smoke from its chimney. A lone bird, up earlier than its companions, twittered from its perch on the thatched roof. Part of Cormac wanted to remain outside with the bird rather than confront what lay ahead.

Liam pushed open the door, and the wave of warmth from the smouldering fire was welcome on their chilled skin. Bridget and Ellen sat on opposite sides of the table, a single rushlight between them. It guttered in the draught. On the rafter above the hearth, one of the hens ruffled its feathers, unimpressed.

Bridget's face was taut with anxiety but it broke into relief at the sight of them.

'Oh, thank God,' she exclaimed.

She jumped up and ran to Cormac, throwing her arms around his neck. He gave her a perfunctory squeeze. She frowned as she drew back to look up into his face.

'You're hurt,' she said.

She touched his temple where the rifle had hit him. It was tender and he winced.

'I'm fine,' he replied. 'Where's Emily?'

'She's up in the loft, asleep with the two boys.'

He nodded, even as his stomach clenched. Better to get it over with. 'Will you take a walk with me?'

She looked taken aback. Ellen and Liam tactfully pretended not to be listening. 'Yes, of course…'

He said nothing else, only held the door open for her

and followed her out into the dawn, closing the door softly behind them. She waited and he led her into the woods behind the cottage, the light just strong enough now that they could pick their way without tripping over roots. He remembered an occasion long ago when his older sister, Mary, had brought him into the woods like this; it had meant a significant conversation was imminent. Just like now.

He didn't walk very far, stopping when he came to a clearing in the trees where a brook bubbled unseen in the surrounding undergrowth. He turned as she entered the clearing behind him. A questioning crease had settled between her brows.

Clearing his throat, he tried to keep his tone neutral. 'The constables are locked up in the cellar at Hogan Farm. Farmer Hogan's a bachelor so he's not as concerned as some of the others about getting caught. Tell me what happened after you left the barn. You made it to the bolthole safely?'

'We did. Colm guided us to a cave deep in the woods outside McKinty Farm. I'm surprised you and I never came across it in all our gallivanting, but then again the entrance is well hidden by big tree roots. It was freezing inside it.' She shivered and wrapped her arms around herself; he couldn't tell if it was at the memory of the cave or because of the cold morning air. 'After a few nerve-wracking hours, Denis came to tell us it was safe to leave. He escorted Mrs Kavanagh, Kitty and Maisie back to the farm but said you wanted me to go to the cottage, so Colm accompanied me here.' She paused and the brook gurgled in the stillness. 'Why didn't you want me to go back to the farm?'

He ignored her question. 'Ellen must have been worried by your absence, was she?'

Her lips twisted, as though she had figured out the source of his hostility. 'She knew where I had gone. She didn't agree with my decision but she told me about the barn and the sentries so I could at least be prepared. Needless to say, she did not object to minding Emily.'

He stayed silent. Their breath misted in the space between them.

'Why didn't you want me to go back to the farm?' she asked again.

He gave her an exasperated look. 'Isn't it obvious?'

She narrowed her eyes. 'Not to me.'

'Christ above,' he said. 'Really?'

'Just spit it out,' she snapped. 'This kind of prevarication isn't like you.'

'That's because I'm trying with all my might to control my temper, and it's taking a lot of effort.'

They stared at each other. He felt his rage simmering; he was a pot coming to boil, and she was the open fire. He didn't know which was more perilous.

'Can you truly be so blind to the stupid thing you did last night?' he said very quietly.

She pursed her lips and in that moment he hated the way the action was so reminiscent of Lady Courcey.

'Stupid,' she repeated. 'Do you mean going to the barn to apologise to those men for the harm my mother has caused them and their families? To say on behalf of my family's name that I understand she has let down a generation of tenants by her actions?'

'I mean walking into a barn full of men who detest your mother down to their very bones and thinking that they would welcome your apology.'

'I am not my mother —'

'For God's sake, they don't see that.' He threw his hands up in the air. 'You are not two separate people in their eyes. You are one entity, both representative of a foreign country that has kept them downtrodden for centuries. There was the threat of murder in the way they looked at you.' And there were few times in his life when he had been more scared for her.

'John had convinced them —'

'He had convinced them of nothing. All it took was the arrival of the constables to rip away any trust they had begun to build in you. How you thought you would be able to win them over with a few words of contrition is beyond me.'

Her eyes flashed, her body rigid in the strengthening light. 'I thought no such thing. Do you really believe me to be so dim-witted? I understood exactly what I was walking into. I have never forgotten the warning you gave me that day in Ballydarry, after the incident at The Pikeman. You warned me then what these people can be like. I remembered and I went there anyway. I went in with my eyes wide open, and my nerves trembling because I was terrified, but it was something I knew I had to do, regardless of its futility.'

That gave him pause. He hadn't even considered that her behaviour might not have been a feat of utter foolishness but an act of utmost bravery. As she stood there breathing heavily and glowering at him, his admiration for her soared. However, the consequences of her actions remained unchanged.

Flatly, he said, 'They think you informed the constabulary about the meeting.'

'I didn't.'

'Then who did? How are you going to prove it wasn't you? They're not going to take your word for it.' He strode up to her and took hold of her shoulders, infusing his grip with urgency. 'Until we discover who the actual informant is, you are the one they'll blame. You can't go anywhere near those men now. They'll want to lynch you on the spot.'

When he looked into her eyes, he did not regret the fear he had placed there. She needed to be fearful so that she would be careful.

She gulped. 'I cannot fathom how deep their hatred goes. What Kitty Brophy said to me…'

'She has suffered more than most,' he reminded her.

'Her son was executed for rebelling.'

'But then why rebel?' she said, almost plaintively. She put a hand flat on his chest, like she could extract the answer from his heart. 'When they know the risks they are taking with their lives?'

He let go of her and stepped back. 'What a thing to ask. Because the risks are worth taking. Better to die a free Irishman than suffer decades of misery under English rule.'

'I appreciate that, and I recognise their desire to be free from external control.' She held out her hands, palms up. 'But they need to be realistic. Victory in revolt does not guarantee successful long-term autonomy. How do they plan to manage the land without an overseer of some kind?'

'So you think the current system is best? Lady Courcey should stay right where she is?'

'My mother is not a good example. But my father is. You saw how well the estate thrived under him. What would the people do without that kind of guardianship? Would they just grab what they can and end up fighting among themselves? There has to be some sort of structure in place to maintain stability. Otherwise, everyone and everything will suffer, including the beloved land they covet so much.'

'You're deceiving yourself,' he said witheringly. 'Nothing will be different if they remain under anyone else's thumb. At least if the rebels achieve independence, they will truly own their land again.'

She stamped her foot in the leaf litter; last autumn's leaves crackled like crumpled paper. 'At what cost? Look at the damage they are doing to people's lives and property. Denis told us the constables have been tied up as prisoners. They are no better than animals, on either side. The rebels' intentions are good but their methods are flawed, and you know it.'

'I know no such thing.' He kept going, as though caught

by an irresistible current in a fast-flowing river, the words flooding from his tongue before they had even formed in his mind. 'Are you objecting because you might lose Oakleigh?'

Her jaw dropped. 'How dare you say that! Titles and riches have never held weight with me. If the ambitions of this uprising were in everyone's best interests, I would wholly support it. But I can perceive Oakleigh's worth. Its existence gives this land a strength and a stability which the tenants cannot provide for themselves.'

They glared at one another, both unyielding. Even as he felt sick for quarrelling with her, some innate part of him, bred from countless generations of discontent, could not bend. He may not have been alive during the 1798 rebellion but the memory of it ran in the veins of every Irishman and Irishwoman. How could she not see that their emancipation mattered more than anything else?

Her chest rose and fell with a long, deep breath, her dark brown eyes sadder than he had seen them in a long time.

'How dare you...' she said quietly and turned to walk back the way they had come.

He didn't call after her. He stood alone in the clearing for a minute or two, loathing himself and the situation in which they had found themselves. When they had decided to return to Ireland, becoming enmeshed in an uprising had not been part of their plan. But they had walked right into it and he couldn't see how they could step away from it now.

And yet all of it was a distraction from their true purpose, which itself appeared to be turning into a failure. Despair welled in him as he recalled the silence in the barn that had greeted his plea for news of his family. His mission to find them seemed more unachievable now than it had when he was still in London. In this moment, his mother felt as out of reach from him as the last star fading from the sky.

He whirled to a tree behind him, prepared to take out

his frustration on it, but at the last second his curled fist changed to a flat palm and he pressed his hand lightly to the trunk. He couldn't lose hope. Regardless of what was happening between the tenants and Lady Courcey, he had to remember that his family was what he was here for. He would go into Ballydarry that afternoon and speak to the villagers. His mother had built a connection with the women there from many years of bartering hens' eggs; perhaps one of them might know something. If that yielded nothing, he could make enquiries in the next village up the road, and the one after that, to see if his family's steps could be retraced. The odds were desperately low, but not trying was an impossibility.

Heavy of foot and heart, he followed Bridget's path between the trees. It was by now full daylight and the woods were loud with birdsong. Part of him hoped she had not gone far and that they could reconcile before returning to the cottage, but there was no sign of her.

When he emerged from the woods, he found that the hens had been released outside; they loitered in front of the closed cottage door and he had to step over them to get to it. As he pushed it open, he heard an unexpected male voice. John Corbett stood next to the fireplace, while Liam crouched before it, adding turf to the fire. Ellen and Bridget occupied the same places at the table as they had earlier, but the rushlight had been blown out. The children were still not awake.

'—refusing to tell us where they got their information,' John was saying. There was a faint stain on his upper lip, a remnant of the bloody nose he had acquired in the barn. 'Not one of them has given in, despite our...persuasive efforts.'

Neither Bridget nor Ellen looked happy at the insinuation in that remark, but they didn't comment.

As Cormac shut the door behind him, he glanced at Bridget. She avoided eye contact. He sat on the bench next to Ellen.

Liam stood up from the hearth, wiping turf dust off his hands. 'John's just been filling us in,' he told Cormac. 'The constables won't reveal how they found out about the meeting.'

'Our highest priority has to be to identify the informant in our midst,' said John gravely.

'It wasn't me,' Bridget said at once. 'Please, John, you have to believe me.'

'I do believe you,' he said. 'But I may have a hard time convincing the others of the same. 'Tis easier for them to believe 'tis you than to imagine one of us is a traitor.'

'Do you have any idea who it could be?' asked Cormac.

'Not a notion.' John shook his head. 'It makes no sense why anyone would do it.'

'Maybe they took a bribe,' said Liam. 'Money's a powerful motivator.'

'Maybe. But 'tis hard to think of anyone willing to be a Judas when so much is at stake.' John stepped in front of the hearth and put his hands behind his back to warm them. 'Speaking of money, that's the other reason I came to talk to you. 'Tis been two months since our last "donation" from our anonymous benefactor. I gave what was left of it to Ben Bracken and his ma to tide them over after their eviction. But we can't sit around waiting for another payment, 'cause who knows when it'll run out. Maybe our benefactor will grow bored, or broke. So I want to discuss where we can gather more funds. We've added a nice selection of rifles to our cache, and now we'll need ammunition for them.'

Liam cast a fleeting, awkward look towards Cormac and Bridget before resting his hand on Ellen's shoulder. 'We've recently come into some unexpected money. We might be able to contribute it to the cause.'

Cormac's sick feeling intensified. He had sent that money to help his mother survive; the idea of it being used for weapons was so contrary to its original purpose that he couldn't even pretend to be comfortable with it. He rubbed the back of his neck apprehensively. Bridget too looked unhappy.

Ellen reached up to touch Liam's fingers. 'That money's for our family. How it's used is a decision to be made by both of us without an audience.'

Contrite, Liam dipped his head, and John's hopeful expression faded. Before he could persuade Ellen to reconsider, they heard squawks outside and a loud thump on the door. They all stared at each other in dismay. Ellen pressed her hand to her pocket, while Liam went silently to the dresser, extracting another knife from one of its drawers.

Then a voice called, 'John? You in there?'

John let out an exasperated breath. 'Jaysus, 'tis just young Denis.'

He strode over and swung out the top half of the door.

'Next time announce your name as soon as you knock, lad. Nearly scared us to death.'

Denis was sweating, his face pale. 'Heard you might be here. You need to come right now.'

'What's the matter? Come where?'

'Hogan Farm.'

John stiffened. 'Have the prisoners escaped?'

'No,' said Denis. ''Tis something worse. Mr Enright's there.'

'What for, for Christ's sake? Does he want Ben and his ma living in a hole in the ground?'

'He's not there in his official capacity.' Denis swallowed. 'He...he's been badly hurt.'

'Hurt?' said Liam. 'How?'

Denis's pallor took on a greenish hue. 'You'd just better come see.'

John opened the bottom half of the door to leave. Liam started to put the knife back in the drawer, seemed to think better of it, and tucked it into his boot. Cormac, reminded uneasily of the days in Dublin when he had never walked anywhere without a dagger on his person, felt no inclination to arm himself as he rose to join them.

Bridget stood too, pressing her fingertips to the tabletop. 'I understand if the response to this is no, but I should like to come too, if I may. I wish to speak with Mr Enright and try to reconcile your current account of him with the man I used to know. I still find it difficult to comprehend his present indifference to the tenants' plight when he had previously been their staunch advocate. Not to mention, he might be able to provide some insight into the motives for my mother's behaviour.'

'I don't know if he'll be able for much conversation,' Denis mumbled.

Cormac caught the footman's eye. 'Who else is at Hogan Farm?'

'Paddy Hogan, Ben Bracken and his ma. And two men guarding the prisoners down in the cellar.'

He turned to John, who shrugged and said, 'She's probably safe enough. She'll be with us, which makes the numbers pretty even, given that I can't see old Mrs Bracken posing much of a threat.'

'Are you sure?' Cormac asked Bridget, their recent argument still tingling on his tongue.

She looked at him directly for the first time since he had re-entered the cottage. Her gaze was resolute. 'I'm sure. Let's go.'

Chapter 9

No one spoke all the way to Hogan Farm. They took a circuitous route to avoid encountering any members of the constabulary scouring the main road, and approached the farm from behind up a steep incline. Cormac fought to keep exhaustion at bay; he had not slept in more than twenty-four hours and his hip was aching where he had fallen on it in the barn. He had developed a slight headache at his temple, but that had faded in the fresh March breeze.

Denis gulped as he led them towards the front door of the farmhouse. 'I don't know what to say to prepare ye. Miss Bridget, you might be better off staying out here.'

'I do appreciate your concern,' she said, 'but I'll come in.' She squared her shoulders.

Reluctantly, he ushered them inside. The first thing Cormac registered upon crossing the threshold was the stench of blood. The second was the moans of pain. And the third was the indignity of what lay before his eyes.

Farmer Hogan had a large kitchen table, even though he had no wife to preside over it. A pile of dirty cloths, a couple of spoons and an upturned bowl lay discarded on the floor beside it, looking like they had been thrust aside in a hurry to clear the surface. The farmer, wearing a big coat despite being indoors, was leaning over a trembling body laid out on top.

Bridget gagged and covered her mouth.

Mr Enright had been stripped down to his drawers. Someone had smashed his spectacles and then replaced them on the bridge of his nose, where they perched in a sad mockery of their original function. Angry bruises bloomed on almost every visible piece of his skin. And, the very worst of all, the tips of his fingers and toes were bloody stumps: every one of his nails had been wrenched off.

'Holy Mother of God,' said John.

Cormac struggled against his own gag reflex, a sour taste rising in the back of his throat. Liam put a hand out to the wall to steady himself and Denis kept his eyes averted, having already seen enough earlier. Nobody seemed to want to venture further into the room.

Farmer Hogan came over to them, sticking his hands deep in his coat pockets.

'Glad you could come, John,' he said in a glum voice. ''Tis an awful business.' He glanced back over his shoulder as Mr Enright emitted another weak groan. 'I know he's done wrong but 'tisn't fair to leave him in this shape. I caught one of the McKinty youngsters hanging around, probably hoping for a glimpse of the prisoners, so I sent him off to get his ma. She'd know better than me what to do here.'

'That was the right thing, Paddy, regardless of his sins,' said John. Appalled, he approached the table. He reached out as though to press a comforting hand to the agent's arm, but pulled back before he touched the bruised skin. 'Help's on its way, sir. Hold on as best you can.'

'Is—' Bridget's voice came out so cracked that she had to swallow and try again. 'Is there a blanket we could cover him with? H-he must be frozen.'

Farmer Hogan nodded. He crossed to a door at the other end of the room and called out through it. A distant voice responded. The farmer returned to them and said, 'Ben says he'll bring a blanket down in a minute. He's just getting his ma up. I'll give the poor sod my coat in the meantime.'

He shrugged out of his big coat and John helped him lay it over Mr Enright's brawny torso, careful not to brush against his wounded hands or feet. Cautious though they were, the agent whimpered in pain.

They stepped away from the table, rejoining the others by the door.

'Tell us what happened, Paddy,' said John.

Farmer Hogan raised his hand to scratch his forehead and Cormac spotted the slight tremor in his fingers. 'Well, we finished up down below just before dawn, as you know. Once most of the folk were gone, I went to check on my guests upstairs. Poor Mrs Bracken was shaking like a leaf after all the commotion. Ben said he'd take care of her so I headed for my bed, but I was hardly asleep when I heard this almighty banging on the front door. I came down and opened it, and there was the agent splayed out on the doorstep like a dead rat. I thought he was a goner until he groaned. There was no one else in sight so I don't know who did the banging. Ben helped me bring him in. Denis was still down in the cellar helping to guard the constables, so I sent him running for yourself.'

Before he could say anything else, a brisk knock heralded Maisie McKinty's appearance.

'I debated over whether to come, if I'm honest,' she said by way of greeting, entering with a basket covered in a cloth. 'But I'd better help the poor craythur. Sure, he's not going to be carrying out any more evictions any time soon.' She looked over at the kitchen table. 'Jesus, Mary and Joseph!' she said, putting out a hand on Cormac's arm to catch her balance. She leaned on him as she said, ''Tis worse than I pictured it.'

She gave him a squeeze and a surreptitious wink before detaching herself and going over to the table, removing the cloth to reveal strips of bandages inside the basket. Cormac glanced at Bridget. Her eyebrows were raised; the wink had not been surreptitious enough.

Grimacing, he asked the others, 'Do we have any theories as to who did this?'

'Someone who was enraged enough to be this brutal,'

said John. 'And they must have done it fairly quick last night. Who disappeared after the rumpus in the barn was over? Didn't come with the prisoners here?'

'A fair few,' said Denis, his complexion still pallid. 'We couldn't have all gone traipsing through the woods. But my money's on Joseph Hayes and Bernie Cuddihy. I thought it mighty strange that they, of all people, didn't go with us, and now I'm thinking maybe it was 'cause they had other plans in mind.'

John rubbed the back of his hand across his mouth. 'How could they know where to find him though?'

Maisie called over, 'Sure, didn't he just carry out an eviction yesterday? He had to still be in the area, couldn't have gone much further than the nearest inn suitable for a gentleman. Not too hard to find when there's only one of those for miles around. That Blackcastle place on the road to Tullow, y'know.'

Mr Enright let out an exclamation of pain as she lightly pressed a bandage over one of his fingertips and he began to cry in distressing, choking gasps. A tiny, strangled sound escaped from Bridget's own throat. She slipped past Cormac and tentatively approached the table, leaning close to Mr Enright's ear.

'Mr Enright,' she murmured. 'Can you hear me? It's Bridget, Lady Courcey's daughter.'

The agent squeezed his eyes shut, his broken spectacles quivering with the force of his sobs. Bridget eased them gently off his nose and set them aside. She put a soothing hand on the crown of his head and tried again.

'Mr Enright, do you know who I am? Do you recognise me?'

Eyes still closed, he managed an almost imperceptible nod.

'I can't express how sorry I am that this has happened to you,' she said. 'But I assure you I will do everything in my power to bring your assailants to justice.' She stroked his hair, like she was calming a distraught child. 'Did you know them? Can you identify them for us?'

He sluggishly turned his head to one side and back to the other in his best effort at a shake.

John said, 'I wonder does that mean he didn't recognise them, or did they threaten him not to reveal their identities?'

Bridget bent towards the agent's ear again. 'Did they keep their faces concealed?'

He nodded again, tears leaking down his temples to the tabletop. His mouth worked and he stuttered, 'T-two…'

'There were two of them?' asked Bridget. 'Two people attacked you?'

'Y-yes…'

'Were you at Blackcastle Inn? Was that where they found you?'

He shuddered and at last opened his eyes to look up at her.

Whatever she saw in his expression, it was enough for her to say, 'Just rest for now, Mr Enright. Don't worry about anything except getting better. Maisie will take good care of you.'

'I will, I suppose,' said Maisie indifferently.

Bridget shot her an accusatory glance. 'Try to remember he's a human being first, and an agent second,' she said.

Maisie looked like she was preparing a cutting rejoinder but then the door at the far end of the kitchen opened and a man with weather-beaten skin came through, clutching a blanket and supporting an elderly woman around her hunched shoulders.

'Don't look, Ma,' Ben Bracken said, but she shook him off.

'I will indeed look.' She hobbled over to the table, her back so stooped that she was nearly at Mr Enright's eye level. She regarded him for a beat. 'You got what was coming to you,' she said and turned away.

'Ma,' said Ben, flushing bright red. 'Where's your compassion?'

'He showed none to us when he forced us out of our home.'

'He did,' Ben protested. 'Don't you remember how apologetic he was? He said he would've spared us if he could.'

'Lies,' Mrs Bracken said dismissively. She scanned the room. 'Still free, John Corbett? Heard the constables nearly got ye.'

'We lived to tell the tale,' said John. 'They're tied up below our feet now.'

She snorted. 'Incompetent fools. Even with the right information, they couldn't do their jobs.'

John looked at her sharply. 'The right information?'

Ben said, 'Be quiet, Ma.'

'No good in that anymore,' she said. 'May as well own up. It came to naught in any case.' She smiled sweetly. 'And what harm would they do a little old woman like me?'

Everyone in the room went very still. Even Maisie paused in her attention to Mr Enright's wounds to gape at Mrs Bracken.

Ben pressed the heel of his hand to his forehead. When he dropped it, his leathery features were suffused with shame. 'Please forgive her, John. Yesterday was an upsetting experience. Ma thought they might let us keep our home if she gave them information about the uprising. While I was inside trying to plead with Mr Enright, she went out to the constables and told them about the meeting. But then they evicted us anyway. She made me stay with her here last night so that I wouldn't get caught up in the raid. And she didn't tell me the truth until this morning. Otherwise, I swear I would've warned ye.'

By the time he had finished, his words were barely audible. She, on the other hand, laughed loudly.

'Do what ye want with me. Sure, what have I got left now? This foolhardy rebellion's robbed me of one son's life and the other son's ability to earn wages and put food on our table. My daughter's gone for years, seeing the city as a better option than this godforsaken place. And that scoundrel there has robbed me of my final wish to die in the home where my parents and grandparents and great-grandparents on my mother's side all lived and died. The whole damned lot of ye can rot in hell.'

Her wrinkled face was a mask of bitterness and grief. Without waiting for their response, she shuffled back out the way she had come in.

Ben lowered his gaze. 'John, I'm so sorry.'

John grimaced. 'She's been hard done by so I can't say I blame her. I don't appreciate the way she handled it but that's neither here nor there now. At least we came out on the winning side of the raid.'

Shoulders slumped, Ben approached the table holding out the blanket. Bridget took it from him and, with Maisie's help, removed Farmer Hogan's big coat and replaced it with the blanket, tucking it around Mr Enright's battered torso and legs using slow, careful movements. Even so, he uttered incoherent ejaculations of pain. Maisie made soft, crooning noises that verged on mocking in tone. Cormac saw Bridget's jaw tighten.

John folded his arms. 'Well, now we've identified our informant, our next step is to establish who's responsible for this abomination. We need to track down Joseph and Bernie and find out whether it was them that did this.'

'If it was, they'll have gone to hide out somewhere,' said Liam. 'They won't go anyplace obvious like The Pikeman.'

'We'll put the word out for folk to start asking around,' said John. 'See if anyone's come across them since last night. We should send someone up to Blackcastle Inn as well.'

'If it's not too much to ask,' said Cormac, 'could you get them to mention my family as well? I intend to make my own enquiries in Ballydarry this afternoon, but the more people spreading the word, the better.'

'True,' John agreed. 'We'll do that.'

Cormac paused, then surprised himself by hurrying on, 'We might not be able to stay around to help with the uprising. I do recognise the importance of what you're doing but I have to prioritise the search for my family.'

Denis in particular looked dismayed but John gave a disappointed nod. ''Tis the reason ye came back in the first place. Ye've got to put them first.'

'Strikes me as unpatriotic,' muttered Maisie as she finished bandaging one of Mr Enright's hands and moved on to the other.

Bridget glared at her before saying pointedly, 'Thank you for understanding, John.' She betrayed no hint that her and Cormac's most recent private conversation had constituted a blazing argument about their involvement in the uprising.

Next to her, Ben said, 'I don't follow.'

'I'm looking for my family,' Cormac told him. 'They disappeared from the estate about seven and a half years ago and I'm desperately trying to locate them now.'

'I'm sorry to hear that,' said Ben. 'Who went missing?'

'My mother,' said Cormac, his heart cracking a little bit more every time he gave this description, 'and my three sisters, who all had dark hair, and —'

'Did they have a baby with them?' Ben interrupted.

Cormac stood stock-still. 'They did. My nephew. He would have been about three months old.'

Incredibly, Ben said, 'I think I remember them.'

Into the stunned silence, Cormac said, 'You do?' His pulse raced.

'If I recall rightly, there was a woman, two or three girls and a small baby, I couldn't tell if it was a girl or boy.'

'When was this? Where did you see them? Please tell me everything you know,' Cormac begged.

Everyone in the room was now gawking at Ben, who took a few reluctant steps forwards. Self-conscious, he fidgeted with the sleeve of his shirt, pinching the material as he spoke.

'As Ma mentioned, I've a sister who lives in Dublin. She went there years ago looking for work and got a maid's position in one of them fancy townhouses. We were fierce close as children so I've always tried to visit her as often as I can, about every ten months or so. Until he died, my brother looked after our ma and my work here while I was gone. But 'tis harder to get away now that 'tis just me and Ma. When I do go, I travel up to the city with my donkey and cart so's I can bring bits and pieces to Annie and sometimes I make room in my cart for other travellers who cross my path, 'specially if the folk are going a long way.'

'And you made room for my family?' asked Cormac, daring to hope.

''Tis very likely. It was a long time ago and there've been many different faces over the years. But those ones stood out for me.'

'Why?'

'They were all so sad,' was Ben's simple answer. 'I was already several miles away from Oakleigh when I passed them. They were just sitting at the side of the road. It looked like they'd given up, like they couldn't go a single step further. But I don't think it was out of exhaustion. I think it was out of hopelessness.'

Cormac's chest constricted painfully. He knew what that feeling was like and he would not wish it upon anyone, least of all his poor, innocent family.

'I took pity on them,' Ben continued. He had created a stiff peak on his sleeve with all the pinching and he flattened it back down. 'They weren't heading anywhere in particular so I convinced them to get on the cart and come to Dublin with me. At least they'd have a chance in the city as opposed to staying where they were.'

'And they went with you?' pressed Cormac. 'All the way to Dublin? Where did you bring them to?'

Ben shifted from one foot to the other. 'I brought them as far into the city as I could and set them down on a street with lodgings on it. My memory's a bit shaky but the name of the lodgings was O'Meara's or O'Hara's, something like that. That was the last I saw of them 'cause I had to leave them then and go to my sister. It was the best I could do.'

'It was far more than you were obligated to do,' said Cormac, relief flooding through him. It had been so unlikely but here was a solid lead on his family's whereabouts. He wanted to kiss the man's boots with gratitude. 'Thank you very much for your kindness to them and for your help to me. I am indebted to you.'

He went over to shake Ben's hand, wringing it with vigour.

'Good luck with your search,' said Ben. 'I hope you find them.'

Behind him, Maisie shook out another strip of bandage from her basket. 'I guess this means you'll be running out on us as fast as your legs can carry you,' she said sourly.

'That's no concern of yours, Maisie,' Liam said in quiet admonishment. 'And you can't make him feel guilty for it.'

She huffed, cast a resentful glance in Cormac's direction, and returned her attention to Mr Enright's supine form.

Bridget stepped away from the table to come to Cormac's side. 'We may not go immediately. We have some things we need to discuss first.'

When he caught her eye, her gaze said 'not here'.

'As do we,' said John. ''Tis time we begin our own search to see if we can root out that slippery pair.'

He, Liam and Denis held a quick discussion and decided that John would make his way to Blackcastle Inn as he was the only one who owned a horse, while Liam and Denis would start spreading the word among the tenants about seeking out Joseph Hayes and Bernie Cuddihy, or anyone else liable to have carried out the vicious beating on Mr Enright.

John turned to Farmer Hogan. 'Can we leave him here with you, Paddy?'

The farmer bobbed his head. 'Myself and Ben will try to get him upstairs into a bed as soon as he's able for it.'

'Best pick a room with a lock so Ma can't get in and finish him off,' said Ben, seemingly in jest, though no one laughed.

With a final word of heartfelt thanks to Ben, Cormac and Bridget followed John, Liam and Denis to the door. Outside, they all took deep breaths to clear the reek of Mr Enright's blood from their noses.

'I've never seen anything like it,' said Denis weakly.

'I hope you never will again,' said John, squeezing the younger man's shoulder. He looked at Cormac and Bridget. 'Will we see ye again before ye leave?'

'You will,' promised Bridget.

They parted, setting off in various directions from the farmhouse. Cormac and Bridget followed the route they had taken to get there, descending the slope at the back of the farmhouse. It fell away towards a wide meadow, with a stretch of woodland on the horizon. As they entered the meadow, the tall grass nearly up to their knees, Bridget slid her left hand into Cormac's right.

'Can you believe it?' she said, her eyes shining with hopefulness. 'What good fortune that Ben was here.'

'It was an extraordinary stroke of luck,' he said. 'Now we know they made it all the way to Dublin and there will be no need to search every village, town and country lane between here and there. And we even have a place to begin our search in the city, if we can find those lodgings. We've been tremendously fortunate, which is a far cry from where I thought we were when the sun rose this morning.'

A loaded silence fell as their altercation at dawn billowed up again between them. He was the one to break it.

'I'm sorry for our quarrel.' He rubbed his thumb over her knuckles, grazing the circles of thread and gold on her ring finger.

'I'm sorry too,' she replied at once.

'I must especially apologise for accusing you of not wanting to lose Oakleigh.' He hung his head. 'I know your concerns were based on more selfless motivations than that.'

She waved her free hand as though banishing his apology among the blades of grass. 'I understand you meant no ill intent. But what you said in the farmhouse...about not staying to help with the uprising after all...'

He sighed. 'I feel so torn about it,' he admitted. 'On the one hand, I want the tenants to prevail. The land is theirs and they have every right to try to take it back. But on the other hand, I have to concede the point you made earlier: their methods are misguided. Could they be depended upon to rule themselves with good judgement? It is a matter of profound concern that some of them would deem this attack on Mr Enright a suitable path to take.' He swallowed. 'Dear God, that poor man's injuries. You wouldn't do it to a dog, let alone a human being.'

'It was truly appalling,' she said with a shudder.

'Perhaps we should rethink our level of involvement here, particularly now that we have a promising lead on the whereabouts of my family. All things considered, we are probably better off departing as soon as possible.'

She hesitated. 'Might I suggest one last contribution to the cause ahead of our departure? I believe it is imperative that I visit my mother before we leave.'

She waited nervously for his reaction but he didn't make any protestation.

Encouraged, she went on, 'It would not be a social call but an intercession on behalf of the people she has crushed. I cannot stand idly by when I am the only one in a position to reason with her. If she will receive me at the manor, I might be able to communicate the harm that she is causing and convince her to stop her destructive behaviour. There is no one else here who would have any

101

hope of achieving this and so I must try, for their sakes. Surely, you see that I must.'

'I do see,' he said, knowing she was absolutely right. 'I agree with you and I think we should pay her a visit without delay.'

'You don't have to come,' she said, looking surprised. 'I do not expect you to –'

'I wouldn't dream of leaving you to face her alone,' he interrupted. 'I will be there to support you in this duty.'

She offered him a small smile but her expression was troubled. He comprehended that his presence could very well do more harm than good but there wasn't even the slightest possibility that he was going to let her call upon Lady Courcey without him by her side. The lady might say anything to get Bridget in her clutches again and, if she attempted to do it, he had to be there to prevent it. He did not want to offend Bridget by articulating out loud that she did not have the power to resist Lady Courcey by herself, but she knew as well as he did that the lady's best skill was manipulating others to suit her own ends and Bridget had proven herself all too susceptible in the past.

'Ought we to invite Ellen to come too?' she asked. 'My mother once exhibited a fondness towards her in her own limited way.'

'We can certainly ask her,' he said, 'although she may feel obliged to refuse out of loyalty to Liam.' He glanced up at the sky. 'There's time today. We should visit Lady Courcey this afternoon. And tomorrow we can continue our journey to Dublin.'

They reached the woodland at the far end of the meadow. As they slipped in among the trees, Cormac became pensive, contemplating the knowledge that Ben had given him. His family had managed to reach Dublin following their eviction from the estate. That meant they had been in the city at the same time as him; it was a wonder and a shame that their paths had never crossed. Were they still there now? He allowed himself the tiniest

102

measure of optimism. Their mission was not as desperate as it had seemed an hour ago.

But coupled with that optimism was a quiver of worry. Following his family's tracks to Dublin meant returning to Cunningham's territory. He had thieved from the money lender the last time he had set foot in the city; he thoroughly hoped he would not encounter him this time.

Bridget squeezed his hand, rousing him from his thoughts.

'I feel I must broach the issue of Maisie McKinty,' she said. 'Does she have an attraction towards you?'

'I think she does,' he said, wincing. 'Borne out of boredom, I would hazard. From what I can gather, her husband is a bit simple.'

'She seems to have become rather embittered since the days she used to give us hunks of cheese. I find her to be quite an unlikeable woman now.'

'As do I.'

'Good,' said Bridget. After a beat, she added, 'But her behaviour did get me wondering. Did you...that is, have you ever...been with anyone else besides me?'

She peeked up at him sideways through her eyelashes and then looked away into the trees.

He baulked. He hadn't anticipated the question and didn't know how best to respond. Thomasina swam into his mind: long, black hair and bulging breasts, brazen and sultry and disinclined to take no for an answer. He couldn't imagine Bridget would take too kindly to the idea of him sharing a bed with a whore.

So, to preserve their newly restored peace, he lied.

'No,' he said. 'There was no one else.'

She didn't look back at him but he saw the corner of her mouth turn up.

They walked on through the woods, choosing an alternative meandering route to the one they had taken to get to Hogan Farm, just to err on the side of caution.

He yawned. 'I'm worn out. Can I suggest some food and

103

a nap at the cottage before we go to the manor?'

'Oh, yes, please. I could nearly sleep standing up.'

As they navigated a dense thicket of trees further on, he misjudged the distance to one trunk and bumped his hip against it. A hiss escaped his teeth.

'What is it?' she asked as he let go of her hand and touched the sore spot.

'Just my damn hip. I fell on it last night during the raid. Feels like I've got a big bruise there.' Remembering the extent of Mr Enright's contusions, he said guiltily, 'It's nothing to complain about.'

'Are you sure? Do you want me to take a look at it?'

He faltered. When he peered at her, her expression was innocent apart from the mischievous glint in her eye.

'I don't know. Do you think it requires an examination?'

'Possibly. To make certain you haven't acquired a serious injury, of course.'

'Well, in that case...'

He stood still and opened his arms wide to invite her appraisal. When she stepped into his embrace, however, her concentration focused not on his hip but on a sensitive area of skin on his throat which appeared very receptive to the caress of her lips.

'I thought you were tired,' he murmured.

'I thought you were too.'

He tilted up her chin so that her lips landed on his own and they kissed deeply. He slid his hands into her hair; since they had left London, she could no longer style it in the latest fashion and now her loose curls tumbled untamed down her neck, as they used to when she had been a free-spirited girl roaming around Oakleigh with a wild boy at her side. He dug deep into the chestnut-coloured mane, feeling the shape of her skull beneath his fingers. Some things about her were still unknown to him. He craved the day when every contour of her, even the curve of her skull, was as familiar to him as the lips he was kissing now.

Those lips continued to revere his mouth, accompanied by a tongue that was equally assiduous in its attentions. Even as she kissed him with such ardour, her hands acted separately, opening the buttons of his coat and gliding inside. Her nimble fingers found the buttons of his waistcoat and unfastened them one by one. Pushing the waistcoat aside, she tugged at his shirt until she had liberated the front of it from his trousers. She reached up inside it, fondling his abdomen and chest. Then, very deliberately, she touched a fingertip to one of his nipples.

He gasped into her mouth. She didn't release him, only pressed her lips harder against his and caressed his nipple with unrelenting, excruciating single-mindedness. It grew more and more sensitive, while the other ached for similar consideration. Her tongue and her finger moved in unison, stroking until he was nearly undone on the spot.

Shuddering with need, he grappled for her skirts, jerking them up past her knees and thighs. The woods surrounding them were deserted but a battalion could have been congregated there watching them and he wouldn't have cared. Lips still joined, he shifted their positions so her back was to the tree he had collided with. With her skirts bundled about her waist, he lifted her up against the trunk, and she slung her unoccupied arm about his neck and locked her legs around his hips. If it hurt, he didn't notice. All he could focus on was that merciless fingertip. He skimmed his own fingers inside her drawers over her inner thighs and higher, and it became her turn to breathe her pleasure into his mouth. Her legs tightened their grip and, at last, her hand moved to address his other nipple.

He sensed her urgency and desire for forgiveness, for they were the same as his own. It had felt unnatural to fight with her the way they had; not even in their childhood had they quarrelled often, having seen eye to eye on most matters. This, then, was their act of contrition.

Bless me, Father, for I have sinned, he thought. And then for several minutes all capacity for rational thought escaped him.

Chapter 10

Bridget rubbed her eyes and suppressed a yawn, before climbing down the ladder from the loft to the ground floor of the cottage. Cormac had already risen from their much-needed nap and was seated at the table, scrubbing at the hem of his coat with a bristly brush. His shaving things were laid out on the tabletop and his cheeks and chin were already smooth. She felt a small pang of regret; she had been partial to his rough stubble and the arousing sensation of it upon her skin.

She sat on the bench next to him and leaned in to rub her jaw against his. As her skin glided over the silky smoothness, she revised her opinion: both variations were highly pleasing.

His cheek moved as he smiled briefly but he didn't stop scouring his coat hem, brushing away the mud that had crusted there after so many days on the road.

'I ought to do my own too,' she said.

'Already done,' he said and jerked his chin towards the other side of the table where her cloak was spread out on the opposite bench, hem spotless.

He bent his head back to his task and she watched him work, making sharp strokes with the brush. His mouth was a thin line. She could only guess at the strain that was mounting in him right now – he was about to face the woman who had scattered and devastated his family. She hoped he would be able to control his temper. If he got very angry with Lady Courcey, she would take offence and be far less willing to engage with them.

A gust of air swirled into the room as Ellen came

through the door with Liam Óg, Aidan and Emily in tow. All four of them looked windswept while Emily, beaming, carried a bucket full of water.

'We went to the well,' she announced to her parents, 'and I pulled up the bucket!'

'Well done,' Bridget said, and she and Ellen laughed at her unintended pun.

Cormac said nothing, only cast the bucket a dark glance as Emily handed it to Ellen along with its coiled rope. Bridget thought it likely that the bucket was the same one the McGoverns had used when they lived in the cottage, but the rope had to be newer, given that the original one lay rotting in the woods beneath the tree branch where Cormac's sister Mary had taken her own life. Bridget touched his shoulder in silent acknowledgement of that tragedy, then drew Emily towards her to neaten her hair and present the hem of her cloak for her father's eagle-eyed inspection.

Ellen had offered to take care of Emily while Bridget and Cormac went to visit Lady Courcey but Bridget had declined for two reasons. In the first place, she was eager to show Emily around the home in which she had grown up, while Emily was excited at the prospect of seeing her mother's bedchamber and the orchard and the stables. Bridget's second motive was the slim possibility that the sight of her grandchild might soften Lady Courcey more than any logical argument her daughter could present to her. It meant breaking the vow she had made on the night of Emily's birth that Lady Courcey would never set eyes on the child, but Bridget was prepared to maximise any advantage that would help make her mother see sense.

Cormac set the brush on the table and stood, shrugging into his coat. He held his body awkwardly as though his hip was paining him. Guiltily, Bridget recalled their exertions in the woods; if truth be told, her own back was rather sore. Still, she felt no urge to repent.

'We should go now,' said Cormac, with the air of one

108

preparing for battle.

'I'm sorry I can't go with you,' said Ellen with true sincerity. She had refused their offer to come; as Cormac had suspected, her past service to the lady did not outweigh her lifetime commitment to honour her husband.

'We understand,' said Bridget. 'I do hope we'll return with positive news.'

'I hope so too,' Ellen replied, her expression nonetheless troubled.

Bridget swung on her cloak and she, Cormac and Emily departed from the cottage.

They embarked upon the route that Bridget and Cormac had trodden hundreds of times in their youth, up the lane and across the fields towards the manor house. The wind had picked up by a considerable degree since that morning; the tops of the trees bent sideways under fierce gusts and the leaves fluttered madly in the hedgerows. Emily kept laughing every time Cormac's cap threatened to blow away on him. He laughed too for her sake but otherwise he remained tight-lipped.

As they crossed Oakleigh property, they perceived further signs of the revolt that had left the land abandoned. Crop fields lay uncultivated, weeds grew unchecked, and the hedges were ragged as though they had not been trimmed in a long time. There was a distinct air of disuse about the place. In the field containing the giant's claw, they surveyed the three-pronged rock formation with unease. Were there weapons buried beneath it right now? The wind blew furious ripples across the sea of grass, as if it were the giant's laboured breathing. Bridget grasped Emily's hand and they hurried on.

They reached the last field, the Gorteen; a single crow rose up from the turf and wheeled away into the sky, cawing loudly. Shutting the gate to the Gorteen behind them, they proceeded into the manor grounds. All was eerily quiet. They passed the empty paddock and the stables to enter the cobbled courtyard, where they got their first close-up view of the house. Bridget inhaled sharply. The red-bricked manor was in a sorry state. The windows were grimy and the ivy, which had previously been an elegant adornment, had been allowed to spread uncontrolled over the walls and now encroached on every shutter and window sill.

Cormac approached the stables and pulled open the double doors. One of the doors flew out of his grip as the wind caught it and it banged sorrowfully against the wall. Inside, they gazed around in dismay. Dirty straw was strewn everywhere on the ground. A saddle had been discarded in front of one of the stalls and never picked up. The silence was deafening with the absence of stamping hooves, whinnies and snorts, men's voices calling to each other or murmuring to the horses. Cormac rested his palm on the half door of a stall, his posture slumped. With a wrench of sadness, Bridget wondered what had happened to her white mare, Bonny.

A rat scurried across the space and darted out of sight. She yelped and hauled Emily back outside. Cormac followed, closing the double doors on their memories. Heart swelling with sorrow, Bridget turned away and her glance alighted on the orchard door, its green paint peeling. She walked towards it with a sense of dread. Pushing it open, she stepped through to a wilderness that was both like and unlike the orchard she had known. The brush underfoot was a mess of rotten apples that had fallen the previous autumn and had since disintegrated into mulch. The spring daffodils had bloomed as usual but there had been no gardener to prune them back so now they hung limp and dying from their stems. However, the apple trees still stood as strong and verdant as ever and she was thankful that they at least had withstood the widespread neglect that had befallen the estate.

'Do you think our oak tree has survived?' Cormac

muttered behind her.

'I would like to think that not even my mother could defeat our mighty oak tree,' she said.

Her gaze fell upon Emily peering wide-eyed around the orchard and she suddenly regretted bringing her along to witness this scene of desolation which fell so far below the high expectations she had given the little girl.

'Is this really where you grew up, Mama?' Emily asked in a small voice.

'Yes, but I am afraid it has not been looked after very well. Come, let us go visit Grandmama now. She won't be expecting us so our appearance will give her quite a surprise.'

They returned to the courtyard, staring up once again at the dismal-looking manor house.

'I think we should go in through the kitchens,' said Bridget. 'I would not feel comfortable entering by the front door.'

She crossed the cobbles and tried the latch on the kitchen door, which opened with a groan. The kitchens were dark and empty but there were signs that someone had been there not too long ago: a dim glow emanated from a pile of embers in the hearth, some dirty dishes were stacked on a bench, and a meagre amount of white flour lay abandoned on the tabletop. Bridget conjured up an image in her mind of Mrs Kavanagh presiding over this space, giving orders left, right and centre to the kitchen maids, and beaming with satisfaction when everything ran smoothly in her domain. She felt her throat tighten and hastened to get through the kitchens. There were two inner doors, one opening onto the servants' staircase and the other providing access above stairs into the back of the manor's entrance hall. She chose the latter, making for the narrow stairs beyond and leading Cormac and Emily up the steps.

They emerged into the expansive entrance hall. This looked much the same as it always had except that a thick layer of dust lay over every surface, from the handrails on the mahogany staircase to the framed paintings on the walls. They had taken no more than half a dozen steps into the hall when at last they heard sounds of movement from the floor above.

A girl came into view at the top of the grand staircase. Bridget recognised her as the scullery maid, Cathy, whom she had met on Lady Courcey's sole visit to Wyndham House at the time of Emily's birth. There were stains on her apron and straggly bits of knotted brown hair escaped from underneath her maid's cap. She was carrying a bucket and a mop and looked stressed as she descended the stairs in a hurry.

She had almost reached the bottom when she caught sight of Bridget, Cormac and Emily. Letting out a strangled shriek, she dropped her cleaning paraphernalia and clutched the banister to keep her balance. The bucket and mop clattered down the last few steps into the hall; fortunately, the bucket was almost empty and only a spatter of water wet the floor. Bridget heard a muffled call from somewhere nearby but disregarded it.

'Good afternoon, Cathy. Do you remember me? You served your mistress at my house in London several years ago. My name is Bridget and I am Lady Courcey's daughter.'

Cathy curtseyed awkwardly on the stairs but seemed unable to utter a word. Cormac stepped forwards and picked up the bucket and mop. Holding them out to the girl, he said, 'You are obviously busy at work. Are you keeping this whole house by yourself?'

She took the bucket and mop, nodding. 'I try to do the best I can but I'm not able to keep up with it all.'

'I am not surprised,' said Bridget. 'This house is designed to be kept by a staff of dozens and you are only one person. How do you even attempt to manage it?'

Cathy's face lifted a little to be receiving some pity. 'I devote my time to one main chore each day and do as much of it as possible. Today I'm mopping all the floors.

112

Yesterday I washed all the dirty dishes but they're already piling up again.' She looked dejected. 'I can never complete a task 'cause there's just too much to do and the day is never long enough. And I have to stop whenever her ladyship calls. Sometimes 'tis hours before I can get back to my work.'

Bridget shook her head. 'You cannot keep going like this or you will wear yourself out.'

'Forgive me but my mistress says it must be done and I'm the only one left to do it.' Cathy cast her gaze down to the floor.

It was another black mark against Lady Courcey to be working this poor girl like a slave.

Frowning, Bridget said, 'We came here to see your mistress. Can you please announce our presence and ask if she is prepared to receive us now?'

'Right away, m'lady,' Cathy said, even though Bridget had purposely omitted any title when introducing herself. Scuttling down the last few steps, the maid placed the mop into the bucket and leaned it against the newel of the stairs. Then she crossed the entrance hall to the door into the drawing room, knocked softly and entered.

Bridget heard a faint voice demand, 'Did you not hear me call? What was that clatter I heard?'

'Beg pardon, m'lady,' came Cathy's reply. Her voice had become high-pitched. 'I dropped my mop and bucket. I didn't mean to disturb you. Your ladyship, you've got visitors. Your daughter's here to see you and she's with a man and a little girl. Shall I send them in?'

Total silence greeted the maid's words but Lady Courcey must have waved or nodded her acquiescence for Cathy reappeared in the hall and declared that her ladyship would see them now. Bridget and Cormac exchanged apprehensive glances as they approached the drawing room. Bridget did not fear her mother anymore but she had no expectation that this would be a pleasant encounter. How badly would the lady react to their appearance?

Chapter 11

Bridget crossed the threshold first. The air smelled dank. The meagre light struggling through the filthy windows suffused the drawing room with a grey pallor and the lack of a fire in the hearth only added to the dreariness. Despite the gloom, Bridget's gaze was drawn at once to the figure seated in a wingback chair next to the unlit fireplace. Ellen's forewarning ought to have prepared her but she was still caught off guard. She couldn't help it; she gasped out loud.

Her mother was unrecognisable. She seemed to have aged thirty years since they had last met. She sat hunched in the chair, her thin, bony wrists poking out of the sleeves of her dress. Grey streaks snaked through her chestnut hair and the hair on her scalp seemed sparser as though some of it had fallen out, but it was pulled back from her face so that her features stood out. Her cheeks were hollow, her eyelids drooped, and her lips, which had always been a narrow line of severity, now seemed pressed together in a pale grimace of pain. She appeared shrunken, insect-like, the merest shadow of her former dominating self.

Lady Courcey raised her eyebrows sardonically at the shocked gasp Bridget had been unable to stifle. Then her expression brightened as small footsteps followed Bridget into the room and Emily appeared at her side. The poor thing looked terrified at the sight of her grandmother and once again Bridget wished that she had left Emily back at the cottage with Ellen and her two boys. Lady Courcey opened her mouth to speak but shut it with a snap as her eyes focused on the third arrival; Cormac had just materialised in the doorway. The lady began to glower.

Undeterred, Cormac took off his cap, strode into the drawing room and sat on a sofa opposite the empty hearth. He beckoned to Emily and she scampered onto the seat beside him, wriggling under his arm for safety. Lady Courcey watched without comment, her gaze upon Cormac, her lip curling in distaste. Bridget moved to a wingback chair on the other side of the fireplace and lowered herself onto it, stunned at the terrible transformation that had come upon her mother.

'Mother, are you very unwell?' she breathed.

She had expected her mother's voice to have succumbed to the change as well, to be weak and husky, scarcely audible, but it remained as sharp as ever.

'Clearly, I am in the best of health.'

Bridget bit her tongue. 'In your letter before Christmas you said you had been poorly but you gave no indication of the magnitude of your ill health. What sickness is this?'

'Mr Abbott does not know,' Lady Courcey said, looking away. 'He has performed a myriad of degrading tests and suspects it is some sort of foul internal growth, but he cannot be sure.'

'Are you in a lot of pain?'

'Constant and excruciating.'

Bridget glanced at Cormac; he was distracting Emily with a counting game on her fingers, but his head was tilted as he listened intently to the conversation.

Hesitant, she asked, 'Is it...fatal?'

Lady Courcey shrugged. 'In all likelihood.'

Bridget stared, dumbfounded. How could her mother be so blasé about her own demise?

'Why on earth did you not tell me sooner?' she said in exasperation. 'Or place a greater emphasis on the extent of your suffering? You wanted us to make amends. That is what you wrote in your letter. Do you not think that telling me you were gravely ill would have been the best

116

motivation for reconciliation?'

'I did not seek your pity,' said Lady Courcey with a faint sneer; it looked about all she could manage with her strength so depleted. 'I merely hoped I had divulged enough to encourage you to invite me to London. All I desired was to see you one last time.'

Staggered, Bridget said, 'Surely you would not have been able to travel so far in this condition?'

'I would have done it had you asked it of me.'

'But why not invite me to Oakleigh instead?'

Baldly, Lady Courcey said, 'I did not want you to see what had happened here until after I was gone.'

Anger flared up inside Bridget. That was as good as an admission of guilt and it all but confirmed that her mother's reprehensible actions had been premeditated. Most of her compassion leaked away in an instant; perhaps this affliction was God's righteous retribution.

'Before we speak of that,' she said coolly, 'I assume you have noticed that we are not alone in the room?'

Lady Courcey narrowed her eyes at Cormac, whose shoulders tensed even as he tapped out a pattern on Emily's fingertips. Then she returned her gaze to Bridget. 'I had detected an unpleasant odour in the air, yes.'

Cormac let out a mirthless laugh.

Emily paused the counting game to whisper, 'What is funny, Papa?'

Lady Courcey's face blazed with outrage. '*Papa*?' she said with a revolted look.

'Yes,' said Bridget firmly. 'You may not wish to hear this but Cormac is —'

'I have already heard it,' Lady Courcey interrupted. 'I received a letter from your husband two days ago which detailed your unfaithfulness and lunacy.'

Nonplussed, Bridget said, 'Garrett wrote to you?' Had they travelled to Oakleigh on horseback, they might have arrived before this letter.

'He did. He suspected you might come here and he

wished for me to be informed of certain recent events in advance of your arrival.'

Bridget folded her arms. 'Does he believe you can persuade me to return to him? Because that will never happen.'

Lady Courcey laughed as humourlessly as Cormac had done. 'He has no desire for that to happen. Do you think he wants you back after your humiliating conduct? His language in reference to you was quite explicit — he despises you. As he should, given the way you have mistreated him.'

'I am sure he presented himself very well as the innocent victim,' said Bridget.

'He *is* the innocent victim. You are the one who committed adultery and ran away with a miscreant, leaving him wifeless and childless.'

'He conveniently omitted the truth then,' Cormac remarked.

It was the first time he had spoken since entering the drawing room. Lady Courcey's brows drew together in surprise at his refined accent but she refused to look at him, choosing instead to address Bridget.

'Please inform the swine present in the room that I have no wish to converse with it directly.'

'Mother!' Bridget rebuked, disgusted by the lady's blatant rudeness.

'It's fine,' said Cormac, though his eyes burned with resentment. 'That kind of response is nothing more than what I have come to expect from you, Lady Courcey, although it brings into question how you think you can merit the title of "lady".' Before she could react to this insult, he went on, 'I shall continue speaking anyway. You cannot avoid listening, unless you leave the room. Your precious son-in-law was selective with the information he provided to you. He failed to mention his personal transgressions, such as his own acts of adultery and the fact that he fathered an illegitimate son ever before he and

Bridget were married. These things do not cast him in as favourable a light as the role of abandoned husband so I can see why he left them out in his correspondence to you. But perhaps, in view of such facts, you might be obliged to revise your assertion of him as an "innocent victim".'

Lady Courcey stared up at the ceiling as she said to no one in particular, 'How lies may be construed as facts is beyond me.'

'I speak no lies,' said Cormac in a low voice. 'I would not make this up for sport. The illegitimate child was my own nephew and Garrett's actions drove my older sister to suicide.'

There was utter silence, apart from the sound of the wind whistling down the chimney. Emily's eyes were wide as she tried in vain to follow the grown-ups' conversation.

'So you see he is in truth a blackguard,' said Bridget into the quietness. 'When his horrendous secret came to light, there was no possible way I could have remained with him.'

'Do not fool yourself,' snapped Lady Courcey. 'You would have deserted him even if he were an angel from on high. All you ever wanted was that good-for-nothing boy and all you have done is dragged yourself into the mud. I hope you are satisfied.'

'I am satisfied,' Bridget said softly. 'I have found love, which is a difficult thing to achieve in our world. Very few are fortunate enough to experience the joy that comes from sharing true love with another. Cormac and I are two of the lucky ones. And I believe you and my father were also blessed in this regard.'

Lady Courcey's expression darkened further. 'I have no inclination to discuss your father.'

'Well, maybe you should. You have pushed him out of your thoughts for far too long. Don't you remember how he used to make you feel? I was in awe of him because he was the only person who could get you to laugh or smile

119

or sing. You were so different in his presence.'

'I do not want to hear this,' said Lady Courcey, her voice shaking.

'You must have been a decent person once,' Bridget persisted, ignoring her mother's protest. 'How else could he have fallen in love with you? And you loved him. You weren't a perfect human being when I was a child but you would never have been capable then of what you have done since. What changed? What caused you to degenerate to such a degree?'

'He *died*,' her mother hissed. 'You have no conception of what it is like to lose someone so vital to you.'

'I *do*!' Bridget hurled back. She pointed at Cormac. 'I lost him! For years, I feared him to be dead. Not to mention, the death of your husband was the death of my father. How dare you intimate that my grief was so much less than yours? He left us both!' She sprang to her feet, driven by rage and sorrow as she recalled the pouch of fine, dark hair tucked away in her valise. 'What is more, my baby boy perished when he had only begun to live. So don't you dare say that I do not understand grief. I know what it is like to feel as though my very heart has been ripped out of me.' Her voice splintered and her chest heaved with emotion.

Lady Courcey flinched and a look of genuine compassion rippled across her haggard features. 'James was a tragic loss. Lord Wyndham wrote to me several months after it happened. I shed many tears for your little son.'

Bridget wanted to believe her but she could not reconcile the idea of her mother weeping over the death of one child while inflicting suffering upon the lives of so many. Shaking her head, she sat back down, her breath slowing as she regained control of herself. Ruefully, she realised her earlier worries had been misplaced as she had been the one to lose her temper in front of Lady Courcey, and not Cormac. He looked like he was yearning to embrace her

120

but he stayed beside Emily, stroking their daughter's hair. She looked alarmed at her mother's sudden outburst.

Bridget faced Lady Courcey again. 'I understand that Papa's death was a devastating blow to you,' she said earnestly. 'You had a sincere connection with him, one you both knew was true right down to your very souls. Can you not see that that is what I have with Cormac? We felt it even when we were children but we were forced down separate paths. We were unlucky because, unlike you and my father, we came from different social classes and it was not acceptable for us to pursue a life together. But look at all the obstacles that were placed in our way and yet we still managed to come back to each other. Our connection could not be broken. Please tell me that you follow what I am saying, that you have a glimmer of comprehension as to why I have behaved so wildly. I could not resist the connection, just like you and Papa could not resist it.'

Lady Courcey contemplated her daughter as though she were seeing her for the very first time. Then she fixed her gaze upon Cormac, searching his face, perhaps seeking what it was that Bridget saw. Cormac remained silent and unmoving under her stare. At last, she lifted up her thin arm, pressed her fingertips to her forehead, and sighed.

'I am sorry,' she muttered. 'I know what you are begging of me and I cannot do it. You have wilfully lowered yourself to a level of abject poverty and no amount of love can excuse that.'

'Perhaps someday you will be able to understand,' said Bridget, deflated.

'Doubtful, given that my days are numbered,' said Lady Courcey.

Bridget gave her a slit-eyed look. 'Is that what has prompted your appalling behaviour? Aside from your desire to take revenge on me, you knew you were dying so why not demolish it all before you go? After all, you would never have to face the consequences.'

Lady Courcey glanced shiftily to the side and did not respond.

'Come, Mother. We have skirted around this but now we really must address it. Our purpose in coming here today was to speak about the estate.'

Lady Courcey nodded. 'How very astute of Lord Wyndham,' she said, more to herself than to her daughter.

'What do you mean by that?' asked Bridget, frowning.

'Did you not wonder what his letter was about, given that it was not a plea for you to be sent back to him?' Lady Courcey smoothed out her skirts with her cadaverous hands. 'He anticipated that you and the scrounger would try to seize the estate for your own.'

'He's mistaken—' Bridget began hotly but her mother cut her off.

'He wished for me to communicate a number of things to you but I shall summarise for it was quite a lengthy letter. First and foremost, he wanted me to remind you that Oakleigh is legally his, as stated in the papers held by Webb & Brereton in Dublin. He is still your husband in the eyes of the law and everything you once owned belongs to him. On no account may a stable hand ever believe he has a claim to this property. However, having established that, he has no immediate inclination to visit and is happy for me to continue my guardianship here.'

Bridget curled her fingers into fists. 'And is he as ignorant as I was of the deplorable state of affairs on the estate?'

'He is.'

At least it was one small point in Garrett's favour that he had not been complicit in Lady Courcey's crimes. But Bridget had few other reasons to think favourably towards him as her mother carried on.

'Your marriage will stand. You will find it impossible to sue for divorce as he has kept his extra-marital conduct discreet and you have no evidence of extreme cruelty or desertion on his part. While he is entitled to seek a divorce from you and could achieve it by the passage of a private act through Parliament, he has decided not to pursue this. He refuses to allow you the expediency of remarrying which means you and that reprobate will have to face the censure and degradation of living in sin. Should he find a suitable match for himself in the future, then and only then might he consider it.' Lady Courcey bared her teeth like a snake. 'And he would like you to remember that he could appeal for the restitution of his conjugal rights any time he pleases and force you to return to him. You may never rest easy in your adultery.'

Bridget imagined being commanded by a court to take up residence in Wyndham House again. Hearing Garrett's heavy footsteps on the stairs, permitting him access to her bedchamber, her bed, her body. Her skin crawled. She was in a separate country from him but now she wondered if it was far enough.

Lady Courcey said serenely, 'I must applaud Lord Wyndham on his perceptiveness and his management of this disgraceful situation. While it severs my daughter from her birthright, better that than to risk a common stable hand getting its dirty paws on such a prize.'

'I sure as hell don't want it,' said Cormac.

A small whisper came from his side. 'Papa, you said a bad word.'

'I know, *a stór*, I'm sorry. I won't say it again.' He looked straight at Lady Courcey, bristling with anger. 'I do not want Oakleigh. Garrett was wrong about our reason for coming back. Putting that aside, we are here today to confront you about your mishandling of the estate. You are running it into the ground and destroying your tenants' livelihoods in the process. We have seen firsthand the effects of your actions. You need to stop this folly before you ruin these people and the land entirely.'

Lady Courcey looked like she was about to retort directly to Cormac but she caught herself in time.

'What is the meaning of this?' she demanded to Bridget,

her nostrils flaring. A faint spot of colour appeared high on her gaunt cheeks. 'What makes him think he is entitled to speak to me in such a way? He cannot come in here and tell me how to manage the estate!'

'At the rate you are going, there will soon be nothing left to manage,' Cormac interjected.

Bridget added her voice to his. 'He speaks the truth, Mother. You reinstated the tithes and raised the rents and treated the tenants so cruelly that they all deserted their positions last autumn. You cannot deny this for there is not a sinner to be seen working anywhere around the estate and the land is desolate.'

'I make no attempt to deny it.'

'But why do it? The estate had been thriving under your care. Why did you allow it to deteriorate and drive everyone away?' Bridget swallowed. 'Was it in retaliation for the way I spurned you? Were you taking your revenge on me?'

Lady Courcey did not reply but she cast a look of longing towards Emily and then glanced away, her eyes hardening.

Bridget felt the burden of her guilt more than ever, but she pressed on. 'Do you not see the pain that you have caused? You forced the people into this situation and now they are struggling to survive. They were dependent upon you. Are you going to pretend that you have not failed them?'

'Tenants must follow the commands of their superiors. If they do not, then they deserve to suffer.'

Baffled, Bridget said, 'Could no one else talk any sense into you? Mr Enright, or even Uncle Stuart?'

'Mr Enright endeavoured many times to convince me to see the error of my ways, and he threatened to write to Lord Wyndham about what was happening. But he capitulated quickly when I threatened him with exposure. I knew of his secret proclivities and they would not have been well received by his genteel family.' She offered no further elucidation on this but Bridget thought the accusation must have been very serious to induce Mr Enright to preside unwillingly over all those tithe collections and evictions. 'As for my brother, he visited two years ago and, when he saw the state of affairs, he beseeched me to revise my attitude. I told him to keep his nose out. I have not heard from him since. But then, for all I know, he may be dead or, if not, close to it. The last time I saw him, he was the size of an ox and he said his heart was failing.' She smirked. 'Incurable illness or no, I am still certain to outlive him.'

Bridget grimaced. 'I wish one of them had been able to make you see reason. The tenants are human beings, and you are responsible for their welfare. How can you treat them so unjustly? Think of Ellen Ryan, or Ellen Kirwan as she is now. She was a faithful servant to you for many years. Are you happy for her to be trodden into the ground just like everyone else?'

Lady Courcey looked startled. 'Ellen chose to leave my employment a long time ago. She has nothing to do with this.'

'On the contrary, she married a stable hand from the estate and he was compelled to leave his position along with everyone else. She is as deeply involved in this as any other tenant's wife. Ellen and Liam have two small boys under the age of four and she is pregnant with a third child. Her greatest worry is how to feed them all and her greatest fear is that her children will not survive to adulthood. You put those trials upon her. That is how you chose to repay her for her years of constant loyalty.'

There was another long silence; the tension in the drawing room was palpable. Bridget studied her mother. Was there the faintest indication of a conscience behind the lady's sunken eyes?

'It changes everything when you can put a familiar face upon what you have done,' said Bridget softly.

Still Lady Courcey did not respond. She avoided

Bridget's gaze and seemed intent upon straightening out a stubborn crease in her dress. When at last she raised her face again, Bridget could see that it was etched with pain.

'I am tired,' she muttered. 'I need to rest now.'

Disappointed, Bridget got to her feet. 'I beg you to consider the things we have said, to see the truth in them. Will you promise to do that?'

'And what do you wish me to do with the truth?' Lady Courcey bit out, though her voice was becoming weaker.

'I think that should be very obvious. Relax your iron grip on the rents, remove the yoke of the tithes from the tenants, and let Oakleigh flourish once more. The people will come back, I know they will. They love this land; most of the families have worked on the estate for generations. If you treat them fairly, then I am in no doubt that they will all return: the stable hands, the gardeners, the maids, even Mr Buttimer, Mrs Walsh and Mrs Kavanagh. Don't you miss them?'

Lady Courcey contemplated for a moment and then confessed, 'Cathy *is* a terrible cook.'

'She has been kinder to you than you deserve,' Bridget said, but her tone was not harsh.

She moved towards the door; Cormac and Emily stood and followed her, Cormac donning his cap once more. Lady Courcey spoke behind them.

'I shall summon Cathy and get her to prepare your bedchamber for you and the girl.' Of course the invitation did not extend to Cormac.

Bridget turned back, her jaw set in irritation. 'We shall not stay at the manor. We are going to return to the cottage where we are welcome as a family.'

Lady Courcey scowled, then sighed. 'Will you call again tomorrow?'

Before Bridget could reply, Cormac said, 'We are leaving tomorrow. You will not see us again.'

Lady Courcey looked shocked. 'You are leaving the estate already?' she asked Bridget over Cormac's shoulder.

'But you have only just returned. We require more time to get reacquainted. Did you think you would resolve all the problems in one visit?'

Again, Cormac answered before Bridget could speak. 'We did not come back to the estate for the purpose of getting reacquainted with you, nor even to petition you on behalf of the tenants. Our true purpose was to search for my family. We have obtained some enlightening information as to their possible whereabouts and hence we journey on towards Dublin tomorrow morning. We cannot delay.'

'Your—your family?' faltered Lady Courcey, finally speaking to Cormac himself.

'Yes, my family. Do you remember them? You might recall that you dismissed my sisters from their employment and evicted my mother from her cottage, when they had done nothing wrong and had nowhere else to go. It was seven and a half years ago but I am confident you have not forgotten.'

Lady Courcey opened her mouth but no words came out. Cormac clenched his fists.

'If you were a decent human being, you would be feeling remorse right now. But I know that is too much to hope for. You punished my family because punishing me was not enough to satisfy you. And you waited until after I was gone so they would have no one to defend their right to remain. I only became aware of what happened to them in the last few weeks. It is the reason why we returned to Ireland, why we came back to Oakleigh, and why we leave for Dublin tomorrow. We are going to try to find the broken pieces of my family and put them back together again.'

Lady Courcey's expression was indiscernible. Then she said, 'If I begged for your forgiveness, would you give it, I wonder?'

'No,' he said without hesitation. 'Your crime is too great. How could I ever forgive an act that was committed so

127

maliciously on a basis that was so unjustified?'

'You loathe me,' Lady Courcey observed. It was impossible to tell whether her mouth was twisted in regret or irony.

'I do. I see no reason to lie about it, for you have never hidden your abhorrence of me. And your hatred seems to know no bounds. Your granddaughter has been in your presence for the past half an hour and you have made no effort to greet or even acknowledge her, because you know that she is my offspring and not Garrett's. It speaks volumes that you are willing to forego an opportunity to meet this wonderful little girl solely on account of her blood connection to me. She also has a blood connection to you, if you cared enough to recognise that.'

Bridget winced. Lady Courcey's gaze travelled down from Cormac's disdainful countenance to the diminutive figure half hidden behind his back. She stretched out a shaky arm.

'Come here, child.'

Emily's response was to conceal herself totally from view. Bridget went to her side and bent down.

'Will you go to her, gooseberry?'

Emily nibbled her lip, looking dubious at the notion of approaching the terrifying creature that was supposed to be her grandmother.

'Do not be afraid. I will go with you.'

She drew Emily out from Cormac's protective shadow and, with a reassuring glance at his doubtful face, led her over to her mother's wingback chair. Lady Courcey reached out again and took one of Emily's hands; the girl's other hand remained clutched in Bridget's. They regarded each other for a moment or two.

'Do you know who I am?' Lady Courcey asked.

Emily nodded. 'You're my grandmama.'

'That is correct. How old are you?'

'I will be seven in May.'

'My goodness, such a big girl. Did you have a governess

in London?'

'Yes, Miss Davison.'

'And what did she teach you?'

'She taught me how to read and write and count. She knows so many things about history and geography. She can even speak French. But she is not very good at art.'

'Indeed. And are you good at art?'

'I am. I like to draw and paint and I love mixing colours.'

'Do you have a favourite colour?'

'Yes, pink. I can make pink by mixing red and white. But I like how mixing blue and yellow makes green too.'

What happened next made Bridget gape with amazement. Lady Courcey smiled and pulled Emily into a hug. Emily did not let go of her mother's hand but neither did she resist her grandmother's gesture. When Lady Courcey released Emily, there was a wetness glistening in her eyes.

'You are a pet,' she said. Then she looked up at Bridget. 'Please come back tomorrow so that I may see my granddaughter again.'

'Well…perhaps we can delay our departure for one more day,' Bridget said and looked over her shoulder at Cormac. He gave a jerk of his head which she took to indicate his reluctant acquiescence.

Lady Courcey looked pleased. 'Until tomorrow, then.'

And with that, Bridget, Cormac and Emily left the drawing room. They went back across the entrance hall and descended the narrow stairs to the kitchens. There they found a harassed Cathy in the middle of preparing an inelegant-looking dish for Lady Courcey's dinner.

'Let us help you,' said Bridget compassionately. 'Three pairs of hands are better than one.'

Cormac assisted by stoking up the fire, while Bridget unearthed a plate and some cutlery and wiped them with a cloth. Even as Cathy vigorously stirred a pot over the hearth, a chime came from the row of servant bells. Shooting the others a resigned look, she set down her

129

wooden spoon.

'I'd best go see to her ladyship,' she said. 'Thanks to ye both for helping.'

They said goodbye to the careworn maid as she departed from the kitchens. Cormac moved the pot so that it wouldn't burn while she was gone and then he, Bridget and Emily went back outside. The wind still blew fiercely, whipping at their hair and clothes as soon as they stepped into the courtyard.

On a whim, Bridget led the others back into the orchard, following the winding path until they reached the clearing at the centre where the mighty oak tree still stood, proud and tall. She let out a soundless breath of relief. The initials that she and Cormac had scratched into the trunk when they were twelve were worn but still legible. He took her hand and they gazed together at the place they had always called theirs.

'This is where your father and I met for the very first time,' Bridget said to Emily.

Emily's eyes lit up. 'How did it happen?'

Cormac grinned. 'I was hiding in this tree when your mother appeared below me, so I dropped an acorn on her head.'

'Were you angry with him, Mama?'

'A little, but not for long. He was a very interesting boy. He showed me how to climb this tree.'

Emily turned her shining face to Cormac. 'Will you show me, Papa? Please?'

He lifted her and swung her up into the tree, settling her securely in a fork between two branches.

'There you are, your highness,' he said, bowing. 'Would you care for some company?' he added and climbed lithely onto the branch next to her.

She giggled. 'You should come up too, Mama!'

Despite her skirts, Bridget did not hesitate. Within a few moments, she was nestled on the other side of Emily.

'I have not forgotten what you taught me,' she said with

a grin at Cormac.

He smiled back and then they fell silent for a minute or two. They were sheltered from the wind here but they could hear it gusting through the crown of the tree. Emily started humming tunelessly to herself, her gaze following the track of a ladybird as it crawled along her branch.

At last, Bridget said, 'What did you think of her?'

Cormac removed his cap and ran his hand through his hair. 'I saw what I expected to see. She is the exact same as she ever was.'

Bridget's teeth trapped the tip of her tongue. 'I thought so too but towards the end she seemed…different. Did you detect the barest hint of a possibility that she might be able to change?'

'She might be able to change, but she is not willing to. Not even her sickness and impending demise can provide her with enough incentive to make peace and bury her prejudices before she dies.'

Bridget felt her eyes prick with tears.

'I'm sorry,' he said at once. 'I didn't mean to be flippant about her death.'

A teardrop slipped down her cheek and she dashed it away. 'It's dreadful that I should even feel this way. She is nothing short of monstrous. But I still hope that she will try to amend her ways. You don't think it's conceivable?'

'I just think she is too set in her ways at this stage,' he said, his tone gentle. 'Sometimes a person gets to a point where they cannot comprehend any alternatives.'

She sighed. 'I understand your reasoning. But I do believe we made an impact on her today, despite the horrible, insulting things she said. She was visibly shaken when I told her how Ellen and her family are suffering. She always liked Ellen and would never have intended to hurt her this way.'

'And yet she was already aware of the suffering she had inflicted upon hundreds of others and it had caused her no unease up to now. The pain for each person is the same whether or not she knows the individual.'

'I know but she would not see it like that. She cannot relate to a nameless face but she can relate to the loyal girl who helped her dress every day for so many years.'

He shrugged. 'Maybe so. Is it enough to sway her? I don't know.'

'But what about when she spoke to...' Bridget glanced down at their daughter perched between them. 'Her whole demeanour altered. That was unmistakable.' She shifted position on the branch to face Cormac more fully. 'I think I may have done great damage the day I told her she would never know her grandchild. She would have been unsullied in the baby's eyes and perhaps it would have been a way for us to start anew and for her to redeem herself. I denied her that opportunity and cast her out to nurse her grievances alone and in bitterness.' Bridget gulped. 'I wonder might circumstances have transpired differently at Oakleigh had I permitted their acquaintance? Her longing just now was quite palpable.'

'It was a softer side to her than we are accustomed to seeing,' he admitted. 'Do you think she will let her guard down like that again?'

'I would like to believe so. It was brief but it was a sign that she is not beyond redemption. I am hopeful that tomorrow we shall have a warmer reception and better luck with our appeal. After all, who can resist our sweet Emily's charms for very long?'

Emily looked up and the ladybird, which she had managed to coax onto her finger, flew away.

'Are you talking about me?' she said, wide-eyed.

'Only about how wonderful you are.' Bridget kissed the top of her head. 'We are going to visit Grandmama again tomorrow, if that is acceptable to your royal highness?'

Emily thought about it and nodded. 'Her hug was strange,' she commented and said nothing more.

They stayed a little longer where they were, savouring the nostalgia, and then they climbed down from the oak tree and made their way back to the cottage. Bridget did not know what the next day's meeting would bring but she hoped that the situation would be resolved, one way or another.

Chapter 12

'Cormac! Cormac, wake up!'

Cormac jerked awake as someone violently shook his shoulders. He tried to get his bearings; it was pitch black but he knew that he was lying in the loft beneath the eaves of his family's cottage. There were other warm bodies near him in the darkness: Bridget and Emily. In another corner of the loft, Ellen and her two boys were nestled together like a set of three spoons. It was Liam who had woken him.

'What's the matter?' Cormac demanded as everyone in the loft began to stir. Liam was making no attempt to keep quiet.

'You've got to get up now,' he said with such authority that Cormac scrambled to rise at once. 'Bridget needs to come too.'

'Come where?'

'Outside, right away. Ellen, *a ghrá*, take care of the children.' With no further explanation, Liam disappeared down the ladder to the lower floor of the cottage.

Cormac turned to Bridget. She was only an indistinct form in the dark but he could tell she was already alert.

'What's happening?' she asked.

'I have no idea,' he said, pulling on his boots and coat and shoving his cap in his coat pocket. 'Come down below when you're ready and be quick. It sounds urgent.'

He clambered down the ladder, ignoring Ellen's own sleepy enquiry. Liam was not in the dim room below, where the embers in the fireplace had smouldered into a heap of cold ash; it had to be the very heart of night.

Cormac hurried out the open door and found Liam standing in front of the cottage, looking intently at the distant sky. He followed his gaze and saw an orange glow on the horizon. It illuminated what appeared to be a thick bank of clouds hanging low in the air.

'Myself and Denis met up with John after he got back from Blackcastle Inn,' Liam said without turning his head. 'We were about to go our separate ways when we saw it.'

Cormac squinted to better focus on the unusual glow. He realised with sudden clarity that what he had mistaken for clouds was in fact a wide column of smoke. With a jolt, he understood what he was seeing just as Bridget appeared behind them.

'Why did you wake us up?' she said as she swung her cloak around her shoulders. She had not brought her bonnet. Her gaze travelled past them to the strangely-lit sky. 'What is that?'

Liam made eye contact with Cormac. 'There's only one structure in that direction that could burn with so much smoke.'

Bridget stared. 'What does he mean?' she asked Cormac.

He hesitated. 'He means that the manor is on fire.'

Her eyes widened. Without a word, she picked up her skirts and tore up the lane. Cormac and Liam hastened to follow her, leaving Ellen uttering an exclamation of alarm in the doorway behind them.

The three of them raced towards the manor house, not speaking, only running as fast as they could. For most of the way they did not have a clear line of sight to what lay ahead, but once they reached the Gorteen they had the same uninterrupted view that Cormac had had when he was only five and got his very first glimpse of the big house.

Bridget gasped and Cormac swore. Liam said nothing but his face was full of shock. The manor, which should have been impossible to see in the dark night, was lit by angry orange flames engulfing one half of the building.

The wind that had been gusting so strongly earlier that day had not abated and was only adding to the conflagration, fanning the flames and blowing the thick smoke skywards. The fire was immense; already it looked like it was out of control. Bridget's childhood home was burning to the ground.

They had stopped out of sheer amazement and horror, but now they hurtled forwards again across the length of the Gorteen. Cormac heard Bridget's laboured breathing; she was clutching her side in pain but she did not slow her pace, pushing onwards towards the fiery structure. They were close enough now to hear the roar of the flames which billowed out the windows and licked hungrily at the roof.

At last, they reached the manor grounds. Panting for breath, they sprinted into the courtyard to find nearly a dozen men congregated there – Cormac recognised most of them from the meeting in Farmer McKinty's barn, along with Ben Bracken as well. A lone horse stood tethered to the door of the stables, its eyes rolling in fear. The men were staring up at the raging fire with an air of futility; empty buckets and pails lay scattered at their feet. All their heads turned as Cormac, Bridget and Liam dashed up behind them. John Corbett, face ashen, darted out from the middle of the group, Denis on his heels.

'We tried to quench it,' John exclaimed over the howl of the blaze, 'but it'd already spread too far by the time we came upon it. The whole east wing's on fire –'tis becoming an inferno. There's no way of stopping it now.'

'How the hell did it start?' Cormac demanded.

'We've no clue,' said Denis, and the other men shook their heads behind him. Ben was rubbing his brow in bewilderment. A suspicious part of Cormac wondered fleetingly whether any of them might have set it deliberately, but he perceived the genuine dismay in their features.

Bridget looked around the courtyard. 'Where is my

136

mother? Is she safe?'

John lowered his gaze. 'Her ladyship hasn't come out of the house.'

In that moment, Cormac saw fury on his lover's face as he had never seen it before.

'Do you mean no one went inside to save her?' she screamed.

Not one of the men could bring himself to look at her.

'The fire grew at a fierce rate,' John tried, staring at his boots. 'It was too dangerous...'

Bridget had turned away from him before he had finished speaking. 'Cormac!' she cried. 'My mother!'

He quailed. There was a desperate plea in her eyes that he did not want to acknowledge. Her hands reached out impulsively to him. He glanced at the flames surging out of the windows above them. Was she really asking him to do this? Enter a burning house to save the life of a woman who had caused him and his family so much harm? He did not know if he had it in him to be so selfless. Bridget knew how much he despised Lady Courcey.

But when had he ever been able to refuse Bridget anything?

He dug his cap out of his coat pocket and jammed it on his head.

'Cormac, you can't,' said John, aghast. ''Tis suicide.'

'The fire seems to be concentrated in one half of the house so far,' Cormac said levelly. 'Lady Courcey may well be alive in the other half which means there might still be a chance to rescue her before it is too late.' He turned to Bridget. 'Where is your mother's bedchamber? If she has made no attempt to escape from the house, then it could be that she is still asleep and unaware that the building is ablaze.'

The expression on Bridget's face was a tortured mixture of extreme guilt and utter gratefulness. 'It is past my own bedchamber on the first floor, the second last room on the west wing corridor. What a mercy the fire started in the east wing!'

Lucky for him.

'I'll be back as soon as I can,' he said and gave her a brief kiss, hoping it would not be their last.

'Be safe,' she choked and added as a frantic afterthought, 'Cathy is in there too!'

He nodded and turned away. Paying no heed to the other men who called to him to come back, he entered the burning manor house by the door to the kitchens. Fear mounted in him with every step.

Wisps of smoke wafted about the kitchen space but there were no flames in sight. He took a breath and the smoky air scratched at his throat. He picked up a discarded cloth from the kitchen table – it looked like the one Bridget had used mere hours ago – and soaked it in a basin of dirty water sitting next to it. Disregarding the foul odour from the old water, he tied the cloth around his nose and mouth and left the kitchens via the inner door leading above stairs.

When he reached the entrance hall, he got a further glimpse of the terrifying extent of the fire. The east wing of the manor was destroyed. The doors to the library and dining room hung off their hinges and both rooms were consumed by flames. He could only presume that the bedchambers above were in a similar state. The west wing, which included the drawing room and the ballroom, did appear to be as yet unscathed but it would not be long before the fire devoured its way in that direction, as it was already rippling into the entrance hall from the ruined library. He ran for the mahogany staircase, taking the steps three at a time.

At the top of the staircase, he paused and looked left and right. The east wing corridor was lit up with flames bursting from the upstairs rooms; the blistering heat of the blaze gusted up the hallway towards him. Sweating, he started making his way down the west wing corridor which was darker but still clogged with suffocating smoke. The cloth he had tied around his face was already drying out and, as its effectiveness decreased, so the harmfulness of the smoke increased. He began coughing so hard that he had to crouch down for a few moments to breathe in the clearer air close to the floor. Eyes watering and still bending low, he scuttled on to the second last door in the corridor. It was ajar. He gave a loud knock – why was he bothering with manners at a time like this? – and pushed it open.

The bedchamber was empty. The bed looked as though it had been slept in that night but Lady Courcey was nowhere to be seen. His heart sank; how was he supposed to find her now? For one second, he considered ending his search right there and simply telling Bridget that he had been too late. But then her pleading eyes swam into his mind and he knew he would never again be able to face her with honesty if he did not make every effort to save her mother now.

Exhaling in exasperation, he was about to leave the bedchamber when his gaze landed on a little table by the bedside. A pitcher and basin sat on top of it. He hurried over and found that the pitcher was blessedly full of water. Ripping the cloth from his face, he once again saturated it before tying it back on. The effect was immediate and it became easier to breathe. Thankful for this small relief, he exited the room with renewed vigour.

Back in the corridor, he stared down its length and instantly dismissed the rooms at the far end in the east wing; if Lady Courcey was in any of those, she was already dead. The fire had crept further along the corridor almost to the top of the staircase. Soon his escape route would be cut off. Panic rising in him, he dashed to the door nearest to the staircase and opened it. He found himself in Bridget's old bedchamber, recognising the burgundy curtains on the bed and the sheepskin rug at its foot; this room too was empty. He spared half a glance for the dressing table where a number of girlish items – a hairbrush, a jewellery box, a brooch in the shape of a flower – lay scattered on its surface, before he hastened back into the hallway.

Tongues of flame were blackening the newel of the staircase. The fire had raced up the wallpapered walls and now stretched greedily along the ceiling towards the west wing. He ran for the furthest door on the corridor and at last found what he was looking for. In this room, which turned out to be yet another bedchamber, he discovered Lady Courcey seated in a state of serenity on the bed, wearing only her nightdress and clutching a small object in her hands. It appeared to be a smoking pipe. Other things were strewn on the bedcover beside her: a man's hat, a long coat, and a riding whip.

He checked in the doorway, startled to come upon such a calm scene in the midst of the tumult. He looked around; were they in what might once have been Lord Courcey's bedchamber?

Then he came to his senses, darted forwards, pulled the cloth down from his nose and mouth, and panted, 'Lady Courcey! It's time to go!'

She looked up in mild surprise. She blinked at him but made no move to rise. Instead, she looked down at the pipe again.

'He never went anywhere without his pipe,' she murmured to herself. 'He was not a smoker but it belonged to his father and to his father before him. He just always kept it close.'

Cormac stared at the lady. Had she gone mad? He glanced over his shoulder and saw the bright glow through the doorway. They did not have much time before the fire reached it and blocked their way out.

Heart hammering, he approached the bed and said very clearly, 'The manor is on fire. We need to get out at once.'

She picked up the riding whip and cradled it in her emaciated arms. 'He loved that horse so much. It was almost as dear to him as his daughter. I should never have

140

had it killed.'

Cormac shifted uneasily. He had no desire to watch this decaying woman take inventory of her dead husband's belongings, especially when it would not please her to know that the man's pocket watch was now in his own possession.

She reached out and stroked the collar of the long coat. 'He was wearing this the very first day I met him —'

Cormac lost patience. 'Constance!' he bellowed.

This at last provoked a reaction. Her face snapped upwards and she looked affronted by his familiar use of her name.

'What?' she said, the single word loaded with resentment.

'Has it escaped your notice that there is a fire burning outside your door?' He flung out an arm behind him. 'You cannot stay here any longer. It is time to leave. Right now!' he added loudly as the lady still did not get to her feet.

She regarded him with vague curiosity. 'Why are you here?'

'Isn't it obvious?' he spluttered. 'I'm here to get you out!'

'Why?' she persisted. 'You do not care if I die.'

He looked at her and she looked back. They both knew that what she said was true.

'But Bridget does,' he finally answered.

'So you are willing to risk your own life in order to save mine, even though you loathe me down to the very marrow of my bones? And all because Bridget wishes it?'

'"Willing" is a strong word but that is what I am doing, yes.'

He heard crackling and looked around to see that the fire was licking the door jamb. Smoke glided into the room with it and he coughed.

'Please —' he said hoarsely.

'That was an exceedingly stupid thing to do.'

He glared at her. Her predilection to disparage him could not be restrained even when they were both in

141

mortal danger.

Then she said, 'But it is also a mark of such loyalty and love that I cannot comprehend its vastness. What you have done tonight proves that you would do anything for my daughter. I cannot say that you are a better man than Lord Wyndham but I am certain he would never walk into a burning house to rescue his mother-in-law. I have misjudged you.'

Cormac's jaw dropped. He was so taken aback that he could not say a word.

'Having said that,' she went on wryly, 'you have wasted your efforts. I am not leaving this room.'

He shook his head to clear the fog from his brain. 'What do you mean? There's still time.'

Even as he said it, he sensed a rising heat at his back and doubted the truth of his words.

'Not for me.' Her tone was matter-of-fact. 'The sand in my hourglass has trickled away to nothing. And if my alternative is to shrivel into a diseased corpse in a matter of weeks or months, then dying tonight is by far the better option.'

'But Bridget wants you to live,' he said in desperation. A line of flame whispered along the ceiling, while fear thrummed in his veins.

'Thankfully, she has no choice in the matter. I do not know how this conflagration has come about but I am going to seize the opportunity with both hands. I am tired of waiting to die.'

He sagged in defeat. 'What will I tell her?'

'Tell her whatever you want. You can paint my name as blackly as you wish. I shall not be there to defend myself. Say that I went to my death cursing her name. Or say that I dropped to my knees and begged for forgiveness. The possibilities are endless; you have the power to shape my daughter's thoughts with as much or as little bias as you desire.'

She glanced above her where the flame was beginning to

142

flicker at the canopy of the four-poster bed.

'I suggest you leave now,' she said, 'unless you wish to share a fiery grave with me.'

He most certainly did not wish that.

'Goodbye, then,' he said awkwardly and turned away from her.

'Cormac,' she said. Was it the first time she had ever spoken his name? He looked back and saw that her cheeks had become red from the overpowering heat in the room; she appeared more human now at the moment of her death than the pale, insect-like creature they had visited only that afternoon.

'Yes?' he said.

She stared him straight in the eye. 'That little girl is a treasure. I was careless with my own. Make sure you look after yours.'

'I will,' he replied.

Turning back to the door again, he found that it was now encircled with flames. He pulled the cloth up over his face even though it was as dry as paper once more. Shrugging out of his coat, he swung it over his head and back. He did not look at Lady Courcey as he ran forwards and leapt through the doorway.

As soon as he landed in the corridor, he knew he was in trouble. The fire now blazed in every direction, consuming the west wing as viciously as it had the east wing. It was crucial that he get out of the house right now. He looked towards the staircase and saw that the fire had reached the steps; he had to assume that the way down to the entrance hall below was not a safe course of escape. He needed to find another way out.

That was when he remembered the servants' staircase – it wound up through the house from the kitchens and could provide him with an alternative route back to the ground. He had climbed that narrow stairs up to the second floor many years ago when he had visited Bridget on her sickbed after she had been caught out in the thunderstorm. Recalling the heavy rain that had fallen during that storm and longing for a single drop of it now to soothe his dry, parched throat, he scanned the opposite wall of the corridor in search of the first floor servants' door. He spotted it set discreetly into the wall and, relieved, he rushed to it.

The stairwell beyond was congested with smoke but there were no flames in sight. He shut the door behind him and checked his coat to make sure it had not caught fire. Wheezing, he struggled down the stairs, his thoughts growing hazy. All he could concentrate on was taking one step at a time and breathing as shallowly as possible. He got to the bottom of the stairs and blearily reached for the latch on the door to the kitchens.

Instant and searing pain made him withdraw his hand at once and snapped his mind back to attention. Eyes smarting, he examined his fingers and found them raw and blistered. The latch on the door was red-hot and, with his senses back in focus, he could hear the snarl of the fire burning on the other side of it. With despairing clarity, he realised the blaze had spread to the kitchens, cutting off his passage to outside. The courtyard, where fresh air and Bridget waited, was a mere thirty feet away from him but it might as well have been in Cove for all he could do to reach it.

In that moment, his fear escalated into blind terror. Dropping his coat, he crouched down and put his arms over his head. He did not want to die, not yet, not like this. He imagined the excruciating agony of burning to death – probably what he was feeling in his fingers but on every inch of his skin and a hundred times worse. Lady Courcey may have chosen it as her form of departure from this world but he emphatically did not want to follow suit. His instinct was to shout for help, even though the gesture would be futile.

And then, bizarrely, he heard someone scream, 'Help! Help me!'

It was not Lady Courcey. It sounded like the voice was coming from further up the servants' stairwell. With a jolt of guilt, he remembered Cathy.

He sprang to his feet, seized his coat and ran up the stairs, shouting, 'Cathy, I'm coming!'

He met the maid halfway up; she was descending from the servants' quarters at the top of the house. She wore boots and had put on a cloak over her nightdress. She looked scared out of her wits and her face was streaked with tears but she appeared to be unharmed.

'What're we going to do?' she wept.

He made an instantaneous decision. 'This stairs is a dead end,' he said. 'We're going to go down the main staircase instead.'

He prayed that it wouldn't be completely blocked or they would perish inside this house. Tearing the cloth from his face, he tied it across Cathy's nose and mouth.

'Come with me,' he said and grabbed her hand with his unhurt one.

He pulled her to the servants' door leading back into the first floor corridor. He wrapped his coat around his other hand and gingerly eased open the door. A cloud of smoke billowed into the stairwell and he put his elbow up to his mouth. The fire raged along the corridor but he judged that there was enough space to get through. There would have to be.

'Take off your cloak and do this,' he called to Cathy over the clamour of the fire and demonstrated swinging his coat over his head and shoulders. She copied him, her face peeking out nervously from the folds of the cloak.

'Now we're going to run as fast as we can to the stairs.'

She shrank away but he dragged her mercilessly through the gap in the door. As he did so, he thought he heard a fit of coughing coming from the last bedchamber in the corridor. He didn't stop; it was too late for the lady now.

The heat seemed to have doubled in its intensity and the

145

smoke was so irritating on his eyes that he had to narrow them to slits. He dashed along the corridor, coming to a halt when he reached the top of the mahogany staircase. The banisters were ablaze but between them the fire surged only in pockets down the flight of steps. If they could avoid the worst sections and make it down to the entrance hall, they might be safe. He squinted around to make sure Cathy had followed him; she was at his side but her terrified eyes above the strip of cloth were focused on something behind him. He spun about to see most of the floor in the east wing disintegrating and disappearing into the rooms below. The thunder of the collapsing floor was deafening.

'Hurry!' he hollered at Cathy, tucking his coat more securely around him. It wasn't much protection but it was better than nothing. 'Down the staircase now. Don't stop for any reason!'

They hastened down the stairs as swiftly as they dared. He led the way, sweating and fighting to catch his breath. He sidestepped the pockets of fire, picking out the safest path to the bottom. But the last few steps blazed across from edge to edge.

'We have to jump!' he yelled to Cathy. 'I'll go first and then I'll catch you.'

He didn't give her a chance to argue. He leapt over the flaming steps and crashed onto the floor of the entrance hall, his knees buckling. Regaining his balance, he turned and held out his arms. Eyes wide and fearful, Cathy bent her knees and jumped, but not far enough. Her booted feet landed on the bottom step and, stumbling, she let out a high-pitched screech of pain. He wrenched her out of the fire but the damage was done; the hem of her nightdress was alight. He threw his coat around her legs and rolled with her across the floor of the hall, his cap falling off as he did so. The flames were quenched but she still shrieked. When he pulled the coat away, the burns showed up on her legs in angry, red blisters.

He winced but there was no time to lose; his priority was to establish their escape route. He leapt to his feet and hurtled to the front door. It was locked and Cathy was in no condition to tell him where the key might be. He whirled around and sprinted over to the drawing room. Rather than risk burning his hand again, he rushed at the drawing room door and heaved his whole body weight against it. Weakened by the fire, it gave way more easily than he had expected and he fell into the room.

More fire. Every object in the room was ablaze, including Bridget's magnificent grand piano. He did not stop to think. He lifted the piano stool into the air and threw it at one of the windows. It smashed through the glass and a huge gust of air came blasting into the drawing room, sending the flames into flurries. He ran back out to the entrance hall where Cathy was curled up in agony on the floor. He hauled her to her feet, ignoring her screams, and lifted her up into his arms, leaving his coat and her cloak behind. Carrying her into the drawing room and over to the window, he hoisted her through the jagged gap and she fell to the ground on the other side. He climbed out himself, scraping his skin on broken glass in the process, and landed with a thud on the gravel below. Knowing that they still needed to put some distance between themselves and the burning house, he forced Cathy to crawl with him across the ground until they were a good forty feet from the building. It was only then that he judged they were safe and he collapsed in exhaustion.

He breathed in a deep lungful of cool air and started coughing and spluttering. He heard Cathy choking too and glanced over to see her on her hands and knees, retching onto the gravel. Her legs looked swollen and raw. That kind of injury would take weeks to heal. He was lucky that his blistered hand was the worst thing that had happened to him.

He rolled over onto his back and lay there, his body still wracked by hacking coughs. Through a haze of pain and fatigue, he perceived shouts and running footsteps on the gravel.

'They're here! I told ye I heard breaking glass!'

In the next instant, he heard Bridget's voice screaming his name and felt her hands clutching at his face. For a moment he couldn't place the contrasting sensations of rough and smooth against his cheek; then he blurrily realised it was the two rings he had given her. That day in Cove when he had slid the gold ring into place above the thread ring on her finger seemed a lifetime ago.

'Oh, Cormac!' she sobbed. 'I am so, so sorry! As soon as you walked into the house, I regretted letting you go. I never should have asked you to do such a thing. I was terrified I was going to lose you forever. But you're alive, thank goodness you're alive!'

She wrapped her arms around him and held him tight. But something was strange; she seemed far away from him and his vision was going dim. As he slipped into unconsciousness, he heard her calling to him but he couldn't answer.

Chapter 13

Bridget's heart seized as Cormac's head lolled away from her.

'Cormac!' she cried. 'Dear God, *no*!'

She became vaguely aware of the sound of hooves and wheels crunching gravel behind her but she had no thought in her mind other than her lover lying lifeless in her arms. She screamed his name again and violently shook his shoulders. He remained slack and unresponsive. She cradled him and wailed, unable to accept it as true.

Several pairs of boots came into her line of sight and a gruff voice said, 'Let him go, madam. We are taking him into custody.'

She gazed up to see four members of the constabulary, uniformed, armed and steely-eyed, staring down at her.

'P-pardon?' she stammered.

'Release him at once. He's our prisoner. And so is that girl there.'

She gaped. The only thing she understood was that they wanted to take Cormac away from her, so she pulled him closer to her chest. Footsteps came stamping up beside her.

'What's the meaning of this?' John Corbett demanded.

A younger constable answered him. 'This fellow here is a criminal. We saw him escaping from the house, and the girl too. Arson's a hanging offence.'

The enthusiasm with which he announced this stirred a memory in Bridget's mind. She considered the constable more closely. He was a man in his twenties now but she remembered him when he had still been a novice and had threatened the men who'd intimidated her outside The Pikeman with a slight waver in his voice. Almost eight years later, Constable Tierney showed no signs of trepidation as he held his rifle and bayonet at ease, poised to use them at the merest hint of resistance.

She glanced at the first constable who had spoken and recognised Constable Quirke. Even eight years ago, he had seemed weary of his role – now he looked downright surfeited. He turned his jaded gaze towards John as the stable master clicked his tongue in protestation.

'Arrah, you've got it all wrong,' he said. 'The chap went into the house to save the lives of the inhabitants. He had nothing to do with starting the fire.'

Constable Tierney shrugged. 'We'll leave that for the magistrate to decide. Get him to the wagon, boys.'

The third and fourth constables swung their rifles over their shoulders so their hands were free to seize Cormac. Beyond them, a horse-drawn wagon stood waiting.

'No!' Bridget snapped. 'You're not taking him anywhere.'

'You have no say in the matter, madam,' said Constable Quirke, though his eyes looked confused, as though he was struggling to place her. Of course, it would be difficult for him to match the well-dressed Miss Muldowney he had met long ago with the woman now before him, when she was not clothed in the fashions of the upper classes and clutched a criminal so fiercely to her.

'I think—' She gulped and sobbed, 'I think he's dead!' Tears spilled down her cheeks as she voiced the greatest fear she had ever known.

'What?' John exclaimed. He dropped to his knees beside her and felt Cormac's neck for a pulse. After a tense moment or two, his shoulders visibly relaxed and he let out a breath. 'You craythur, don't you worry. He's not dead, just passed out. He must've taken in a fierce amount of smoke.'

The air escaped her lungs in a shuddering gasp and she

wept all the harder. 'Thank heaven,' she whimpered and kissed Cormac's sooty forehead.

John frowned. 'He doesn't look good though. The sooner Liam gets back, the better.'

She wiped the back of her hand across her face, nodding. As soon as Cormac had entered the burning house to search for Lady Courcey, Liam had jumped on John's horse and ridden to seek out the nearest physician, anticipating with good sense that medical help would be needed on the scene. She prayed he would get back to them with all possible speed.

Constable Tierney huffed. 'If he's alive, he's coming with us.'

John stood and folded his arms. 'I'm telling ye, ye've got the wrong man. There are near a dozen men over there who'll confirm he was one of the last to arrive here tonight.'

The other men from the courtyard were hovering at a distance, their postures wary; they looked ready to bolt at a second's notice. After all, barely twenty-four hours ago they had been complicit in an illegal meeting of rebels and the incarceration of some of these constables' comrades-in-arms. Denis was the only one who had come near – he was kneeling over Cathy and looked as white as a ghost, even with the glow cast from the burning building.

Constable Quirke scratched his nose tiredly. 'If not him, then who? A fire this big doesn't start by accident. There's foul play behind this.'

'We don't know how it happened,' said John. 'But you're welcome to stay and search the grounds if you think the perpetrators might still be nearby admiring their handiwork.'

Constable Quirke narrowed his eyes. 'And who might you be to be offering a welcome such as that? You're acting like a person in charge around here and that strikes me as mighty suspect, given what's been happening at Oakleigh this past while.' He stepped closer to John, staring at him intently.

To John's credit, he did not recoil at the constable's approach. Coolly, he said, 'I'm only a concerned parishioner who came running when I thought I could be of service. Like right now, I'm going to help this young lady bring her man to a place where he can recover from his injuries.'

He gestured to Denis, who shuffled over, his expression guarded.

'Give me a hand, lad,' John said, and he put a gentle palm on Bridget's shoulder. Sniffing, she released her grip on Cormac and allowed John and Denis to lift him between them.

'Where to?' asked the footman.

'The stables,' said John. 'They're not joined to the house so there's no danger of them catching fire too.' He whistled to the men clustered nearby. 'Will one of ye bring the girl?'

Ben Bracken detached himself from the group and jogged over to Cathy. He bent down and murmured, 'I've got you, pet.'

She moaned when he moved her and he took care not to jostle her as he straightened up with her securely in his grasp.

Paying no heed to the four constables, who watched them with blatant distrust, John, Denis and Ben carried the two invalids around the corner of the house and back to the courtyard. Great billows of smoke poured off the building and swirled around them in the night air. Numbly, Bridget realised that her mother had not made it out of the house.

One of the other men opened the double doors of the stables to let them through, and there ensued a flurry of activity as old mounds of straw were fashioned into makeshift beds for the patients. They laid Cormac out in one stall and Cathy in another and rooted around in the loft above for any discarded rushlights or blankets they could find. Ben discovered the abandoned saddle Bridget and Cormac had seen the previous day and used it to prop up Cathy's thighs so her blistered legs would not touch the straw.

Bridget lingered by Cormac's side, subtly but undeniably ignored by the men. John was the only one who continued to acknowledge her; the rest acted like she was a shadow in the corner of the stable stall. She understood why and did not blame them. There was no question but that she deserved their censure.

She knelt next to Cormac, her skirts and cloak spreading out around her. As her gaze roved over his body for signs of injury, she noticed the burns on his fingers. She squeezed her eyes shut, sick with shame.

What she had done had been inexcusable to the point of insanity. What on earth could she have been thinking to ask him to put his life in such danger? In a moment of the most extreme selfishness, she had begged for his help and thus placed him in an impossible situation: if he acquiesced, his own life would hang in the balance, but if he refused, she would hold him responsible for her mother's death. He could only have given her one answer to her request, and that answer had almost cost him his life and might have left Emily without a father.

Had he perished, she was sure the men's attitude towards her would have been far more vocal. But by providence or his own innate luck he still lived and so they confined their reproach to a discreet disregard for her presence. However, any respect they might have held for her was lost – she had shown herself willing to risk the life of a good man for the sake of an evil woman. She was hardly any better than her ruthless mother. She hung her head in disgrace. There was just one good thing that could be said about the whole debacle: at least Cathy had been saved, which meant only one soul had died inside the house, and not two.

Bridget clutched the folds of her cloak as hard as she

could, her knuckles protesting against the strain. Her mother was gone. The burning house was her tomb and she was now beyond all redemption. Only Bridget and Cormac knew there had been the faintest hope that the lady might be open to change. To everyone else, she remained a hardhearted tyrant and that was the final memory they would retain of her forever. They were probably glad she was dead.

Bridget did not cry. Yes, there was sadness but above all there was emptiness. Now she had lost both her father and her mother and she had been unable to say a proper goodbye to either one. She felt unfinished, like she could never be quite whole again.

Someone gave an almighty shout outside the stables and her eyes flew open. Had the physician arrived? She struggled to her feet, hampered by her skirts, and dashed out of the stall, but in the courtyard she found only Denis. His arms were outstretched, his face tilted up to the sky.

'Rain!' he cried. ''Tis raining!'

A few more men joined them, cheering. John Corbett clapped his hands in relief and Ben Bracken flung his cap into the air. Bridget looked upwards. Thick clouds had gathered above the plumes of smoke and drops spattered her forehead. If it strengthened and lasted long enough, it would douse the raging fire in the manor.

Too late.

Shoulders leaden, she turned to go back into the stables, but a movement by the orchard wall caught her eye. Three male figures were gathered before the peeling door – had they come through it or had they just congregated near it? They crossed the cobbles, two of the figures pushing the third in front of them. When the light of the fire fell upon their features, she recognised them as Joseph Hayes and Bernie Cuddihy, shoving Farmer McKinty ahead of them. The farmer was crying.

'John!' Joseph called out, his posture full of swagger. 'We've got him.'

John stalked forwards, scowling. 'We've been looking for the pair of ye. Where've ye been this past day?'

'Never mind that,' said Bernie. 'Wait 'til we tell ye what we saw.' He smacked Farmer McKinty on the back. ''Tis better to own up now, Mick. They might go easier on you if you do.'

The farmer blubbered but didn't say anything. Joseph shook his head in exaggerated disappointment.

'Ah, Mick. We're trying to help you here.' He held out his hands, palms up, to the other men who had crowded close. 'I'm sorry to be the one telling ye this but we caught him in the act. It was too late to stop him but we're both witnesses to the truth.'

'What're you on about?' John said impatiently.

Joseph elbowed the farmer. 'Tell them. Tell them it was you started the fire.'

Bridget felt something unpleasant sprout in the pit of her stomach as the rain began to come down more heavily. She didn't like leaving Cormac unattended for so long, but she couldn't turn her back on what was happening.

Farmer McKinty snivelled, his nose running. 'I d-did it,' he managed to get out, rubbing at his eyes like a child.

Denis stared, mouth open. 'Mick started it?' he said disbelievingly to the other two.

'Saw him with my own eyes,' said Bernie. He motioned to John with a loud sigh. 'I guess you'll be wanting to send for the constabulary.'

John's jaw tautened. Then, to Bridget's surprise, he swivelled in her direction and said to her in a confidential tone, 'M'lady? What's your opinion on this?'

She blinked. Why had he relapsed to that formal address again? She had been happy to tolerate 'Miss Bridget'.

When she said nothing, he prompted, 'What d'you want to do, m'lady?'

'What do *I* want?' she said. 'Surely I have no say?'

'They're your tenants. They're under your orders.'

'My—' she began and stopped. She goggled at John as

155

realisation dawned. 'You mean…?'

His countenance softened at her sheer astonishment. 'You're the lady of the big house now.'

She stood frozen. He was correct. With Lady Courcey's death, her contracted guardianship of the estate had come to an end, and thus responsibility for it had reverted back to the title-holder. Her daughter. Garrett could lay claim to Oakleigh in legal terms, but he was in London, while Bridget was standing right here on the land that her father had always intended to be hers.

A wave of powerful emotion surged up inside her as the restraints her mother and Garrett had long imposed upon her fell away. She had a duty here, and she intended to carry it out to the best of her ability.

She cast a cold eye towards Farmer McKinty. His cheeks were soaked with tears and raindrops. Then she looked past him to Joseph and Bernie.

'You claim you saw this man set the fire?' she said.

They both nodded confidently.

'Then where have you been all this time while others were making efforts to quench it?'

Bernie's answer came at once. 'He ran away from us. We had to catch him and bring him back.'

'And what were you doing on the manor grounds in the first place, and at such a late hour?'

'Hunting rabbits,' Joseph chimed in. 'We saw one run under the gate at the Gorteen, so we followed it. Caught Mick red-handed.' His expression was smug, like he knew their story was watertight.

'I see,' said Bridget. 'And where were you last night?'

'At the barn, with everyone else,' said Joseph, his eyes wide and innocent. 'You saw us there.'

'Yes, but you were not present later at Hogan Farm. Where did you go after the meeting?'

'Hunting.' He crossed his arms. ''Tis how we spend many nights. We've got families to feed and that's no easy task these days, thanks to your damn mother.'

156

'Indeed. And did you go hunting before or after you paid a visit to Blackcastle Inn?'

He narrowed his gaze. 'We were nowhere near Blackcastle Inn.'

She feigned surprise. 'Oh, how very strange. Because Mr Enright can identify both of you as having been there before dawn.'

'He can't have,' said Bernie, indignant. 'Sure, we were wearing—'

Joseph jabbed Bernie in the ribs and he snapped his mouth shut, going red in the face.

Bridget drew herself up. 'As of this moment, I refuse to believe a single word that comes out of your mouths. And I hold you accountable for the destruction that has occurred here tonight.'

Joseph sneered. 'You've got no proof! You can't—'

The rest of his words were swallowed in a clatter of hooves on cobbles. Bridget's heart leapt as Liam, angel that he was, came riding into the courtyard accompanied by a bearded man on another horse; she recognised him as Mr Abbott, her mother's physician who had tended Bridget herself when she contracted a fever after the thunderstorm. Behind them came a third male rider whose face was not familiar to her.

Liam slid from his horse, panting. 'We got back as quick as we could. Thank God 'tis raining now. Is everyone safe?' He looked around, taking in the hostile stance of the assembled group and the still-weeping farmer at the centre. 'What's going on here?'

Bridget decided that she had no time for the criminals right now. 'Ben, could you and some of the others escort these men into the harness room in the stables and stand guard over them? I shall deal with them presently. Please be sure to treat Farmer McKinty with kindness. And perhaps, John, you could find the constables on the grounds and alert them to this new development in the situation.'

'I can do that,' said John, his expression grim but approving.

Joseph's jaw fell open, while Bernie said weakly, 'There are constables already here? We thought we'd be long gone before…'

Bridget did not deign to respond. Ben and the others didn't look very happy about taking her orders but they led Joseph, Bernie and Farmer McKinty away, disregarding the protests from the first two and gently steering the stumbling farmer through the stable doors. John left the courtyard at a trot to seek out the constables, while Bridget returned her attention to Liam and the physician, who had also dismounted from his horse.

'Thank you for coming at this late hour, Mr Abbott, I am so grateful.'

The physician detached a black medical case from his saddle. 'Lady Courcey has been a regular patient of mine for several years. This is not my first night-time visit to her. Her waning health has been a sad sight to behold, but I shall do what I can to help.'

Bridget bowed her head. 'I'm afraid my mother is beyond your help, sir. She did not escape the conflagration.'

Liam inhaled sharply. 'What about —'

She gave him a reassuring nod, even though she felt far from reassured herself now that she had spent several minutes absent from Cormac's side. What if his condition had worsened in the meantime? She addressed Mr Abbott with a rising sense of urgency. 'While my mother cannot be saved, there are two other victims of the fire who would gladly receive your attention.'

He knit his brows. 'Who? Lady Courcey was the only upper class resident in the house.'

It maddened her that this could be an impediment but she kept a tight rein on her temper. 'That is true,' she said, 'but would you deny your assistance to two lower class individuals just because of the circumstances of their

158

birth?'

He let out a huff. 'This is highly irregular. I do not tend servants and suchlike.'

'I appeal to your Christian goodness, sir,' she said, ignoring the rain that was growing into a downpour and drenching her bare head. 'Please, only you can provide the care they desperately need.'

Touchily, he said, 'Oh, very well. Direct me to them.' He snapped his fingers at Denis, who still lingered nearby. 'You there, look after my horse.'

Despite being a footman and not a stable hand, Denis took hold of the reins.

'Speaking of Christian goodness, this is Father Macken,' Liam interjected, waving over the third man who had descended from his horse with the difficulty of a person suffering from stiff joints. 'I thought it best to seek him out too…in case the last rites might be needed…'

Bridget swallowed. 'I sincerely hope that will not be the case, but thank you, Father, for coming. Perhaps you could bless them with a swift recovery?'

'I shall appeal to the Lord Jesus and the Blessed Virgin Mary to watch over them,' Father Macken said in a wavering voice.

He was advanced in years, with sagging jowls and wrinkles around his eyes and mouth. By his name, Bridget knew him to be the priest at St Mary's Catholic Church in Ballydarry. She had never attended Mass there but Cormac had brought her inside the empty church on a number of occasions. She was glad Liam had thought to summon the priest, but she made no mention of the soul lost within the manor house; Lady Courcey had not been a Roman Catholic.

She led Mr Abbott and Father Macken into the stables and pointed out the two stalls where Cormac and Cathy lay. Though she knew Cathy's legs were badly burnt, she directed the physician to Cormac's stall first because at least the maid was awake, while Cormac's lapse into unconsciousness was an increasing source of worry. When she tried to follow Mr Abbott into the stall, he made an irritable gesture at her.

'Don't crowd me,' he said. 'I need time and space to examine him. Leave me be for now.'

Anxious, she said, 'Will you tell me if he awakens?'

He let the half door of the stall swing shut without answering her.

As she turned away in frustration, she remembered the trembling, disfigured form of Mr Enright lying on Farmer Hogan's kitchen table. She resolved that, after the physician had finished examining Cormac and Cathy, she would attempt to persuade him to visit Hogan Farm. He would have less grounds for objection, given that Mr Enright was a member of the landed gentry.

Because Mr Abbott clearly had no desire for company, she guided Father Macken to Cathy's stall instead. She did not follow him in, but she heard the maid's soft whimpers and the old priest's comforting murmurs.

The clip-clop of hooves drew her attention back to the stable doors, where Liam and Denis were bringing the three horses in out of the rain. Denis averted his gaze from her, blushing but determined to follow the lead of the majority in shunning her. Too ashamed to keep her head up, she trained her eyes on the compacted earth beneath her feet until they had passed her by, leading the animals into stalls at the further end of the stables, away from the improvised hospital wing.

When she looked up again, her gaze fell upon the closed door of the harness room. Ben and two others stood outside it. Steeling herself, she crossed the central aisle of the stables.

'Ben, could I please ask you to accompany me inside?' she asked, forcing her voice not to quiver. She had to maintain a facade of composure in order to confront this next challenge.

His expression was grim but he took off his cap and

stepped aside to let her through.

The harness room was bare of any articles that might have marked its original function; the pegs, hooks and racks along the walls were empty of halters, reins and saddles. All the room contained was three men clustered in the far corner, two of them leaning in an intimidating fashion over the third.

'You heard me, Mick,' said Joseph in a growl. 'You've got to convince them it was you.'

Farmer McKinty was on his hunkers, his hands close to his head like he was afraid they might hit him. Joseph and Bernie jumped back as Bridget entered, followed by Ben who stood near the door, ready to intervene if the two men proved difficult.

'Mick's got something to say –' Joseph began at once but Bridget silenced him with a glare. She strode over to the farmer and squatted next to him. He had scrunched his eyes shut and mucus coated his lip and chin. She fished inside her pocket, praying for a handkerchief, and found one.

'Shall we clean you up?' she said gently.

When he opened his eyes, he made weak smacking noises with his lips and moaned fretfully. She doubted his ability to understand her intention, so she wiped his face for him, then folded the handkerchief and tucked it into his fist.

'You just rest there for a little while,' she said and patted him on the shoulder before rising again.

She faced Joseph and Bernie with her shoulders back; at least here she was not the most contemptible person present.

'You have committed a terrible crime,' she said.

'It wasn't us,' Bernie insisted.

She bestowed a withering look upon him. 'Please dispense with the denials. Not for one second can I believe that Farmer McKinty acted of his own free will. You may have set the fire yourselves or you may have coerced him into doing it, but either way you are the culpable ones.'

Bernie threw a glower of resentment in Joseph's direction. Mutinous, Joseph shrugged and scoffed, 'Arrah, there's worse in this world than what we did.'

'Indeed?' said Bridget. 'Worse than murder?'

He blinked, and Bernie repeated, 'Murder?'

'Yes.'

'We didn't kill anybody,' said Joseph, his forehead creased in confusion.

'And yet my mother is dead,' she said with surprising calmness.

His eyes bulged. 'The lady's dead?' He shot an accusing look over at Ben. 'You didn't tell us that!'

Ben scratched his nose and stared ahead, saying nothing.

Joseph whirled back to Bridget, his expression more panicky. 'We didn't know she'd died. We didn't mean for that to happen.'

She gave a contemptuous snort. 'You expect me to believe that?'

''Tis the truth!' he said, his voice rising in pitch as he realised the enormity of the charge being laid against them. 'I swear 'tis the truth!'

'Honest to God, 'tis!' said Bernie earnestly.

Bridget folded her arms. 'So you are saying that you set fire to the manor with the belief that you were not putting anyone's lives in danger?'

Joseph wiped his sweaty hands on his unkempt clothes. 'We wanted to scare her. The big house is a symbol of her wealth and power. We wanted to damage it so she'd realise she wasn't untouchable. But there should've been plenty of time for her to escape. Why didn't she get out of the house?'

Bridget wanted to know the answer to that question too. But that was a conversation she must have with Cormac, not with Joseph Hayes.

'My mother still had one maid working for her. The servants' sleeping quarters were on the topmost floor. Do

162

you think the girl had a decent chance of escape?'

'Did she die too?' Bernie asked hollowly.

'She was saved. No thanks to you.'

They both stared at the floor. In the silence, Farmer McKinty's whimpers became audible; he was rocking on his haunches in the corner and sucking on the edge of Bridget's handkerchief. She hoped it was a clean edge.

Regarding Joseph and Bernie with revulsion, she carried on, 'And now to your other crime. The appalling attack on the land agent, Mr Enright.'

She waited for them to protest but neither of them said anything. Her stomach turned. Their silence may as well have been a confession. Knowing with certainty that the two men before her had instigated that vile atrocity made her want to flee from the room, as though their very presence was poisonous, but she stood her ground and, when she spoke, her voice was quiet and controlled.

'I cannot fathom the depraved mind that could do that to another human being. No man, no matter how despicable you deem him to be, deserves such disfigurement, indignity or pain.' She let her hands drop to her sides. 'Answer me this: did you go directly to Blackcastle Inn after the raid on the barn?'

Joseph gave a tiny jerk of his head.

'And where did you conceal yourselves afterwards? Men went searching for you but you were nowhere to be found.'

'We got Mick to hide us in his barn,' muttered Bernie. 'Figured it was the last place anyone would think to look.'

She pursed her lips. 'The way you have abused that poor man is deplorable. Your wickedness knows no bounds.'

Her blood was boiling but she strained to preserve her cool exterior. She clasped her hands before her. 'The assault on Mr Enright alone would be enough to condemn you. But coupling that with what has transpired here tonight…' She took a breath. 'I have no choice but to exact punishment with a severity proportional to the offences

163

you have committed. And I believe nothing less than transportation will be appropriate.'

Joseph's gaze snapped up, his eyes full of scorn. 'You? What power do *you* have here?'

'Have you so soon forgotten my mother's passing? With her death, the responsibility for Oakleigh has come into my keeping. It is my duty to pass judgement upon you, or at least to communicate it to those who will carry it out.' She bared her teeth. 'Did you know that, as the land agent, Mr Enright serves as the local magistrate on behalf of the Courcey title? He would have the authority to reason with me to have your sentence commuted. But I don't think he is likely to plead for leniency in this case, do you?'

Joseph's lip curled. She saw in his face the exact moment when he realised the ghastly future which now lay before him. Without warning, he lunged for her, his hands stretching for her throat. Ben leapt forwards but he was not quick enough. Bridget felt Joseph's fingers close around her neck.

In the next instant, they were ripped away and Joseph was lying flat on his back, grunting as the wind was knocked out of him. Farmer McKinty stood over him, breathing heavily, the handkerchief still in his grasp. Ben hauled Joseph to his feet and shoved him into the furthest corner of the room from Bridget. He dragged Bernie away from her too, but the fellow showed no resistance, cowering away from Ben's threatening fist.

Before Bridget could recover her breath, footfalls pounded outside the harness room and John appeared at the door, flanked by Constables Quirke and Tierney.

'That's them,' John said, pointing at Joseph and Bernie.

The constables aimed their rifles in the direction of the pair of men. Joseph and Bernie exchanged glances of misery and defeat. In the absence of their bravado, they appeared small and weak, as insignificant as mice.

Bridget stepped forwards and addressed them for the last time. 'You are no longer welcome on Oakleigh land.

164

However, your families may remain and I will ensure that that they are looked after.'

Joseph opened his mouth but she turned on her heel and left without another word.

She felt a potent energy thrumming in her veins as she strode through the stables and out into the rain, desiring solitude. She sucked in the cool, damp air. The feeling of power was intoxicating.

And that scared her.

Chapter 14

It was an hour or two past dawn and the rain had stopped falling. The light was grey, the air was cold, and the manor house was a smoking ruin. The skeleton of the outer red-bricked walls still stood forlornly in the weak daylight, but the building's elegant innards had been demolished. There was no hope of salvage. Oakleigh Manor was no more.

Ash floated in the air, settling on the cobbles of the courtyard and in Bridget's hair. She lingered next to the gaping frame where the kitchen door had once hung and touched her palm to the blackened bricks, the carcass of a great creature with its entrails mangled.

Mrs Kavanagh and her sister stood nearby. The cook was weeping copiously, her hands pressed to her face.

'I don't know why you're so upset,' Kitty Brophy said, her tone snide. 'This is a *good thing.*'

The woman did not understand. She couldn't see that Mrs Kavanagh was not grieving for a pile of charred debris, but for the loss of a place called home. No matter the terrible developments of recent years, Oakleigh had for so long held them all in its bosom. It had been the seat of the Courcey title but more importantly the seat of their affections. It had been a cherished refuge and the beating heart of this land. And now it was gone.

'M'lady?' said a man's voice.

Bridget looked around, wiping her cheeks. John was crossing the cobbles towards her, his expression neither friendly nor unfriendly as he approached.

'Yes?' she said.

'He's awake.'

Her stomach flipped sickeningly. She of course wanted Cormac to be awake but she dreaded facing him after what she had put him through. She took in a trembling breath.

'Will he see me now?'

'He asked for you,' said John, betraying no hint of what Cormac's disposition had been when he had made the request.

She followed John back to the stables where a couple of men loitered inside by the doors. Their features hardened at the sight of her; she suffered their silent condemnation without complaint. John held open the half door of Cormac's stall for her and she edged inside.

Fresh rushlights had been lit and placed on a bench along one wall. By their light, she discerned Mr Abbott leaning over Cormac on the makeshift straw bed. Her heart jumped into her mouth. He was lying on his back with his eyes closed but they fluttered open when she came in. His burnt hand was wrapped in a loose bandage and there were jagged cuts on his other hand – apart from that he appeared to be physically sound. However, it was a shock to hear him speak.

'Bridget,' he said in a scratchy whisper. He winced but forced out, 'You're safe? John told me about the constables…'

His voice was unrecognisable as his own, a husky croak far removed from his usual, smooth tones. He must have inhaled a great deal of smoke to bring about such a stark alteration. She felt even worse than she had before entering the stall.

'Never mind me,' she said wretchedly. 'How are you feeling?'

His answer was lost in a fit of coughing. Mr Abbott gave him a mechanical pat on the shoulder and moved aside to make room for Bridget in the tight space.

'Don't let him talk for long,' he warned her. He put a roll of bandages into his medical case, closed it with a snap, and exited the stall. John let the half door swing shut and Bridget and Cormac were left alone.

She knelt beside the straw bed and gazed at her injured lover. His hair was caked with soot and his eyelids looked heavy, as if it were an effort for him to keep them open. Guilt gnawed at her insides but she could not bring herself to speak. If she opened her mouth to ask for forgiveness, she was liable to dissolve into floods of tears. So she just rested her hand on his unbound one and did not say anything.

He, too, was silent for a long time. Then he said hoarsely, 'Is Cathy in a bad way?'

'She's sleeping,' said Bridget. 'Mr Abbott gave her laudanum for the pain. Her burns are severe but he said she will heal.'

'That's good to hear.' He took his hand away to rub his eyes. When he dropped it again, he did not place it back with hers but instead let it fall to his lap. She felt a hiccup of unease.

There was a rap on the half door and they looked up to see Father Macken there. He raised his arm in an apologetic wave.

'I've been by already,' he said. 'But I heard you'd woken.'

Cormac struggled to sit up. 'Come in, Father,' he rasped.

The priest entered the stall. The disturbance in the night had taken its toll on the elderly man and his posture was stooped with tiredness.

'Liam Kirwan feared the last rites might be needed,' he said, 'but I'm glad that wasn't the case.'

'You and me both,' said Cormac. A shadow crossed his face and, in a brief moment of uncharacteristic antagonism, he added in a mutter, 'Pity my sister never got them.'

Bridget comprehended what he meant and, had their hands still been clasped, she would have squeezed his now. It had been Father Macken himself who had denied

168

Mary the sacrament of the last rites because she had intentionally ended her own life.

The priest did not appear to have heard Cormac's bitter words. 'By all accounts you acted bravely last night,' he said. 'God bless you for your efforts to save the maid.'

Cormac let out a sigh, the exertion of ill will too great to sustain. 'Thank you, Father.'

Father Macken looked in Bridget's direction. 'My condolences on the loss of your mother,' he said, somewhat stiffly. 'Have you sent word to St Canice's?'

She shook her head. St Canice's was the Church of Ireland establishment in Ballydarry and her father was interred in the graveyard there. Of course her mother would wish to be buried alongside him. But no one had yet gone into the rubble to retrieve her body...or what remained of it.

'I can go by there on my way back to the village,' said Father Macken. 'I'll let them know their services are needed.'

'I would greatly appreciate that,' she said.

Cormac cleared his throat, the sound as rough as nails. 'Father, I've just remembered. We met your niece and her husband on our journey here and they told us to send you their regards.'

He glanced at Bridget and she took over in the telling of how they had encountered Farmer Hackett and been so well received by him and his wife at their farm.

Father Macken beamed. 'Well now, isn't that lovely to hear? I know we're not meant to have favourites, be they children or nieces and nephews, but she was always mine.' The end of his sentence was nearly swallowed in the yawn he tried, and failed, to suppress.

The corner of Cormac's mouth lifted. 'Go away home to your bed, Father. Thank you again for coming and for your prayers.'

The priest made the sign of the cross and backed out of the stall, yawning even more widely.

After he was gone, Bridget realised she had been grateful for his interruption. Now she and Cormac were by themselves again and a dense cloud of tension rose in the air between them.

He looked down at his bandage, picking at it with his fingernails. 'Do you want me to tell you what happened with your mother?'

She stiffened. After a beat, she said, 'Yes.'

'She said that I could lie,' he muttered, almost to himself. 'She said that I could give you whatever version of events I wanted. But I think the truth is best in the long run.' He looked up at Bridget with red-rimmed eyes irritated by the smoke. 'Your mother chose to die last night. She had an opportunity to escape but she did not take it. It was her wish to depart this life and she fulfilled that wish.'

Bridget was unable to respond for several seconds. 'I d-don't understand.'

'I found her. She was upstairs in your father's bedchamber and she had his things about her. She knew the house was on fire but made no move to flee. I tried to convince her to come with me but she refused.' He rubbed the back of his hand across his forehead, smearing the soot there. 'In the end I had to leave her. There was no way of changing her mind.'

Bridget tried to swallow but her throat was too dry. Could it be true? Had her mother's demise in the fire been a deliberate act?

'I know this must be hard for you to hear,' he said, his voice little more than a croak, 'but she was aware that she was not going to live for much longer and she decided that sooner was better than later.'

Bridget felt dazed. Yesterday her mother had seemed intent upon seeing her granddaughter again; there had been a sense of purpose in her manner. But mere hours later she had given up on life altogether.

'Did she—did she say anything to you? Did she have any message for me?'

170

He was about to speak when he was overcome by another bout of coughing. She looked around anxiously for a cup of water but there was none. The fit passed and, wheezing and eyes watering, he was able to reply, 'There was no message. She just told me to look after Emily better than she had looked after you.' He paused. 'She also said that she had misjudged me.'

Bridget's heart lifted. Was that a sign that her mother had repented? Had she at last, in her dying moments, accepted Cormac for who he was? Perhaps she had even begged his forgiveness for what she had done to his family.

'I would not give too much weight to that,' he rasped, as if he had read her mind. 'It was not a scene of lamentation and reconciliation. She was still your mother through and through, unremorseful to the end.'

Bridget was disappointed. He could have let her hold on to that tiny shred of consolation. But then she remembered that she did not deserve any such solace to her conscience.

It was time to make her apology, insufficient though it would be.

'Cormac, I am so awfully sorry.' Tentatively, she reached out and laid a gentle hand on his arm. He did not react to her touch. 'What I did to you was unpardonable. I had no right to ask you to put your life at such risk but I was frightened for my mother and I knew you would not say no. I took advantage of you and abused our bond of love and trust.' Self-loathing clawed at her throat. Tears filled her eyes but she tried to hold them back. 'I cannot ask for your forgiveness because I know I am not worthy of it, but I swear in my disgrace that I will endeavour to earn it over time by any means within my grasp.' A single tear escaped, making its lonely way down her cheek. 'I realise that this is poor comfort for how much you have suffered but please let me know if there is anything I can do to begin making things right again between us.'

For several long moments, he stared into his lap. When

171

he looked up, his countenance told her that he agreed with everything she had said, but his words were not harsh.

'Just please do not ask me to do something like that again,' he murmured.

'I promise,' she said, eyes lowered.

Neither of them said anything else. There was no need for him to reproach her further for she knew full well the magnitude of her wrongdoing. She considered asking him about how he had saved Cathy and escaped from the fire, but then she remembered the physician's caution to avoid letting him talk too much. She swallowed her questions and the silence stretched between them until they heard another light knock. This time it was Liam standing beyond the half door of the stall.

'I brought a visitor,' he said and held open the door to reveal Emily in front of him.

Her fretful expression cleared at the sight of her parents. Bridget stood up and stepped away as Cormac lay back and held out his arms. Emily slipped into them, laying herself on the straw next to her father and hugging him like she had not seen him in a year. No words were necessary. Bridget felt sad and a little bit excluded; she and Cormac had not shared a similar exchange of affection. She reminded herself that she could not expect that yet – he would let her know when he was ready for such intimacy again.

Liam started to leave the stall but she caught his eye and motioned for him to stay. He stepped inside and she joined him near the door.

'How is Ellen?' she asked, keeping her voice quiet.

'She's fine now, but she was sick with worry while we were gone. I wasn't able to return to the cottage 'til dawn so she spent all that time not knowing what was happening and imagining the worst. She's very relieved that Cormac and Cathy are safe but she passes on her sympathies to you regarding your mother.'

'That is very kind of her,' said Bridget automatically.

172

'She said she'll come up here as soon as she can get someone from the village to mind the boys. She doesn't want to have that rowdy pair running around in the middle of all the commotion.'

Bridget nodded. She hoped Ellen would come before too long. She felt suddenly desperate for her companionship and counsel.

'I hear you decided on a sentence of transportation,' said Liam, his face grave.

She sighed. 'I did. Do you believe it was the right course of action?'

''Tisn't my place to say. But I do think your mother would've been less lenient.'

'I know. She would probably have had them hanged on the spot for the irreparable damage they have done to the manor.'

'Such a reckless thing to do,' he said, shaking his head. 'And wicked how they dragged Mick McKinty into it. I met Maisie on the road and she's fit to tear strips off them. Least they're off your hands now. You're far better off without tenants like them.'

Bridget became aware of Cormac's gaze upon her and turned to see him leaning up on one elbow. He glanced sharply from her to Liam.

'What are you two talking about?' he asked in his hoarse voice.

She shifted uncomfortably. Her gut told her that this was going to make matters even worse. 'Joseph Hayes and Bernie Cuddihy. They are going to be transported to Australia.'

'On whose orders?' said Cormac, but he looked like he already knew the answer.

'Mine,' she said unwillingly. Then she added in desperation, as though to justify the act, 'I hold the Courcey title. There was nobody else to give the command.'

His face darkened. He said nothing aloud but a current

173

of communication flowed from him to Bridget through his expression. She understood at once that the last thing he wanted was for her to assume the management of the Oakleigh Estate. That would tie them to a level of society from which he wished to escape. They would not be free to lead a simple life with such a burden of responsibility on her shoulders. In the short term, they might even be forced to separate if she chose to remain on her estate while he continued to look for his family. Her new status created a web of complications which would only exacerbate the strain that had mounted between them after the events of the previous night.

A fresh flood of guilt washed over her.

'I need to get some air,' she blurted and hurried out of the stall, brushing past Liam who, oblivious to the silent message Cormac had just conveyed, looked confused by her abrupt departure.

She hastened out of the stables and across the cobbled courtyard, avoiding the startled stares of Mrs Kavanagh and Kitty Brophy. Rounding the corner of the ruined manor, she made for the tree-lined gravelled avenue. The constables' horse-drawn wagon was gone; the two criminals had been whisked away in it after the altercation in the harness room. She pounded the loose stones beneath her feet, putting distance between herself and Cormac with every step.

What did he expect her to do? Should she abandon Oakleigh and leave it to decay the way her mother had done? It was her duty to take care of the tenants' concerns; they had been neglected for far too long. Whether Cormac liked it or not, undertaking that task was her birthright. Perhaps it was not a position she desired to hold but she could not shirk it for that reason alone.

Still, she abhorred the other consequences of that decision. If she stayed to manage the estate and he left to seek his family in Dublin, they might be parted for weeks, maybe longer. Who would keep Emily? Their little family would be broken up after it had only just been formed.

Then there was the question of whether the tenants would even welcome her. What was to stop them from rising up against her as they had her mother? It could likely be quite a dangerous course of action and that made her fearful.

Through the mire of her thoughts, she heard the braying of a donkey and looked up in surprise. The animal was labouring into view further down the avenue, pulling a cart. She recognised the driver at the front as Farmer Hogan and, to her relief, Ellen was perched next to him.

She kept walking to meet them. When they reached her, the farmer pulled on the reins and the donkey came to a halt, letting out another 'Hee-haw!' as it strained its head towards Bridget to greet her. Ellen climbed down to the ground with a protective hand over her pregnant bump and, in an atypical move for a former lady's maid whose old habits were hard to break, hugged Bridget tightly. She took a great deal of comfort from the embrace.

When they pulled apart, Ellen said, 'We brought someone with us.'

She led Bridget around to the back of the cart where a figure sat propped up in its bed. Stuffed sacks had been positioned on all sides to keep him upright and secure in spite of the jerky movements of the cart. He was fully clothed but he wore no spectacles or boots, and bandages bound his hands and feet.

'Mr Enright!' Bridget exclaimed. 'What are you doing here? Ought you not to be resting in bed?'

The land agent gave her a wan smile. 'Perhaps, but I insisted on coming.'

'Wouldn't take no for an answer,' said Farmer Hogan, twisting around in his seat. 'Said I had to figure out a way to get him here. This was the best I could come up with.'

'And then they passed me in the lane so I hopped on too,' said Ellen. 'A grand way to save my boots from the mud after the heavy rain.'

Bridget rested her hand on the side panel of the cart. 'Mr Enright, I'm pleased to say that Mr Abbott, my mother's physician, is still on the grounds. I had intended to ask him to call upon you at Hogan Farm, but now he can examine your wounds while you're here.'

He shrugged. The clothes Farmer Hogan had given him didn't fit well across his muscular shoulders and the action looked awkward. 'That can wait. Firstly, I would beg you for a word in private.'

Farmer Hogan and Ellen exchanged glances.

'Looks like a mighty fine spot for a quick stroll, don't you think?' the farmer said.

'It does,' she agreed. 'I spotted a fine clump of daffodils back along the avenue which I should like to go back and admire, if you'll accompany me?'

Before they departed, Farmer Hogan helped Bridget into the cart so she could sit opposite Mr Enright for their conversation. Then he and Ellen disappeared down the avenue, chattering blithely about spring flowers.

Mr Enright waited until they had vanished from view before saying, 'You'll forgive me but a significant degree of discretion is required for some of the things I'm about to say.'

Bridget shifted her weight to avoid one of the sacks digging into her knee. 'I shall exercise prudence in all that we discuss. You have my word.'

'Thank you, my lady.'

'Oh, you don't need to address me —'

'Yes, I do,' he interrupted. 'That is one of the first lessons you must learn. You held a title in London so you understand how it works but I suspect you might not regard it the same way here, where you once lived as a child. However, you are the Lady Courcey and others must accord you that respect.'

She viewed the issue somewhat differently but did not argue the point, given that he had already begun to grow paler with the effort of talking.

He continued, 'As well as my respect, I must offer you my thanks. You treated me with great compassion at the farm when I was struggling to come to terms with my ordeal. Thank you for your kindness and for encouraging others to act likewise.'

'It was the least I could do,' she murmured. 'I cannot describe how sorry I am for what you have suffered.'

'There are many on this estate who will believe I got my just reward.' His hands twitched, like he wanted to clench them but couldn't. 'I tell you plainly, I have hated the role I've been forced to play these past years. I could see the estate falling to ruin around me but could do nothing to stop it. Your mother sat in her privileged seclusion and would not entertain any of my pleas to show leniency to the tenants. It was truly devastating both to witness it and to be an unwilling participant.'

He paused and she waited, sensing he had more to say and was steeling himself to say it. By now, all colour had drained from his face.

'I...' he said slowly. 'I tried to reason with her. I said I would inform Lord Wyndham. I threatened to resign from my role as land agent. But she — she had incriminating information about me which she promised to use against me if I hindered her in any way.' He ground his teeth. 'By a foolish oversight on my part, I left a document of a...personal nature in among the accounts which I had brought to the manor for her perusal. She discovered it, read its contents and comprehended that she had the means to keep me under her thumb for the rest of my life.' He looked Bridget directly in the eye. 'My lady, would you consider yourself to be of a similar character to your mother?'

Barely a heartbeat passed before she said, 'No, not in the slightest. I have long believed that almost all of who I am was given to me by my father. I have my failings,' she added, once more recalling with regret the events of the previous night, 'but they are not the same as my mother's.'

177

'I suspected as much,' he said, 'having witnessed your spirited disposition as a child and your solicitous conduct at Hogan Farm. I hope and believe that I can trust you.' He lowered his gaze. 'I will not go so far as to describe the subject matter of the letter, but you may well guess its substance. I received it from a gentleman with whom I have been...acquainted for many years. Our connection is not known in upper class circles.'

Bridget kept her expression composed but she could fully see why her mother had identified the letter as an instrument of power.

'My acquaintance's rank in society is much higher than my own. For his sake, I could not risk our connection becoming exposed. So I did as your mother bade me. I ensured the forced collection of rents, liaised with the tithe proctors, carried out the evictions. I had no other choice. And I am reviled the length and breadth of the estate for it.'

Bridget pressed her fingertips to her lips, shocked at what the agent had been compelled to endure. 'I am appalled that she coerced you in this way. At least you are now free from her control.'

He glanced up. 'Yes, and I believe you can put her mistakes to rights.'

Bridget gulped. 'There are many aspects of the situation to consider, not to mention some complications which may prove challenging to overcome.'

'I can perceive some of them myself already,' he said, nodding. 'Chief among them is that the tenants have developed a thirst for independence. You may find it difficult at first for them to accept you in this role, given the damage your mother has done to it.'

'There may be other impediments that you have not foreseen,' she said weakly.

'I understand that your husband is the legal owner of the property,' he went on, 'but he has never expressed an interest in running it himself. Now that your mother's guardianship has ended, a new arrangement could be reached whereby you are contracted to be the overseer of the estate in your husband's name. Such a contract could easily be drawn up by Webb & Brereton in Dublin.'

'Mr Enright,' she said. 'I do appreciate your thoughts on this and I acknowledge that your contribution is highly valuable. However, there are particular circumstances of which I must make you aware before any decisions can be made.'

'I'm certain whatever they are they can be overcome,' he said with a confidence she did not share. 'My lady, you know you must do this. It is your obligation. You alone can restore Oakleigh to what it once was.'

Some colour had returned to his features. In his animation, he accidentally knocked one bandaged hand against the other and he let out a hiss of pain at the contact. As she offered him a sympathetic look, she noticed Ellen and Farmer Hogan strolling back up the avenue. Ellen clutched a small bunch of daffodils; they appeared to be past their best but she raised them towards Bridget with a smile.

'Perhaps we can continue this discussion at a later stage,' she said to Mr Enright. 'But please know that I will treat everything you have disclosed to me with absolute discretion.'

He dipped his head in gratitude.

The ambling pair reached the cart and Farmer Hogan called out a greeting. His donkey, upon hearing its master's voice, brayed enthusiastically in return. The farmer helped Bridget back down to the gravel and, after thanking him, she turned to Ellen.

'May we talk?' she asked. 'I am in need of your advice.' She peeked back hastily at Mr Enright. 'On a separate matter to what you and I have just discussed, needless to say.' Well, the two conversations were related but she would not be delving into the agent's private affairs.

He waved one bandaged hand in acknowledgement as

179

Ellen said, 'Yes, of course.'

'You go on ahead,' Bridget said to Farmer Hogan. 'Please take Mr Enright up to the stables to be examined by Mr Abbott. We shall follow on foot.'

Farmer Hogan climbed back into his seat and clicked his tongue at the waiting donkey. The animal trotted forwards and the cart moved on, carrying Mr Enright in the direction of the house. Bridget hoped the men there would keep their resentment towards him to a minimum; he had already suffered enough.

As they receded from sight, Ellen said, 'What happened last night was just dreadful. How is Cormac faring?'

Bridget looked away.

'What's the matter?' asked Ellen. 'He hasn't taken a turn for the worse, has he?'

Bridget shook her head and, in a brief summary, related the circumstances of the previous night and that morning which had led to her current dilemma, culminating in Mr Enright's insistence that she was now obligated to run the Oakleigh Estate and Cormac's unmistakable opposition to that role.

'I don't know what I should do,' she finished. 'I feel like my head and my heart are at war with each other.'

Ellen chewed her lip. 'And you'd like my opinion?'

'Very much so.'

'Well, I think it's quite plain what you must do.'

'It is?' said Bridget, startled.

'Of course. You must go with Cormac, no question about it.'

'But Oakleigh—'

'You shouldn't be concerned about Oakleigh. You've spent enough of your life doing your duty. Now you should satisfy your own heart.'

'But all the tenants—'

'Sell the estate. Or appoint a steward to manage it on your behalf if you wish to keep it in your family. But whatever you do, pass the responsibility on to someone

180

else. You don't want to be parted from Cormac again, not even for a short time, knowing how much it's cost you both to get to this point. You should follow him wherever he wants to go because where he is lies your happiness.'

Bridget stared at Ellen as the murkiness cleared from her brain. It was so glaring in its simplicity. Ellen was right. Bridget belonged with Cormac but there was still a way to ensure that the estate was managed as it ought to be. Her mind toiled feverishly as she pictured how it might come together. Yes, it could work.

'Oh, Ellen, bless you for such excellent enlightenment,' she said, giving her a fervent hug.

She slipped her arm through Ellen's and they walked back up the avenue towards the house. Ellen gasped when the blackened and crumbling building came into sight.

'What a crying shame,' she murmured.

They made their way around the corner of the manor house back to the cobbled courtyard. Farmer Hogan had stopped his cart in the middle of the courtyard and Mr Abbott was perched in the back of it next to Mr Enright, removing the bandages from one of his hands and examining the fingertips. Denis, Ben and a few of the other men milled around, some averting their eyes, others watching in morbid fascination and not a little antipathy. To Bridget's surprise, Cormac was standing at the front of the cart and speaking to the farmer. What was he doing up and about already? He glanced past the farmer's shoulder, saw Bridget and Ellen coming and hastened towards them. Bridget was taken aback to perceive that he had a slight limp.

'What is wrong with your leg?' she asked before he could say anything.

'It's fine. I think I just twisted my ankle when I fell out of the drawing room window.' His voice was still husky but his eyes did not seem quite so heavy. 'Why did you leave? I followed you outside but I could not find you anywhere.'

'I just needed some space to think,' she said. 'I did not go far.'

Looking troubled, he said, 'I'm sorry about the way I reacted before. It wasn't fair of me to be like that.'

'Never fear,' she said. 'I believe I have a solution to our quandary.'

He tilted his head, wary. 'You do?'

In response, she went up to the group of men gathered near the cart and asked, 'Could one of you please fetch John Corbett to me?'

They stared sullenly back at her until Denis dropped his gaze and disappeared into the stables. She returned to Cormac and Ellen.

'Why are they all looking so surly?' Cormac asked, his brow furrowed.

She focused on the cobbles, remorse flooding her insides once more. 'They bear a rather strong dislike towards me for what I did to you last night.'

His eyes narrowed. 'That is a matter between you and me and nobody else.'

He limped over to the men. One of them called out, 'Good to see you on your feet, lad.'

'Thank you for your concern,' he said shortly. 'Now it seems I have to remind you that, regardless of your opinions on the events of last night, that lady over there is a *lady*. You need to treat her with the proper courtesy. Please ensure you do so from now on.'

An array of burning cheeks received his rebuke. Then each man tipped his cap at Bridget and mumbled, 'M'lady.'

Astonished, she nodded back in acknowledgement. Cormac returned to her side and put a protective arm around her shoulders just as John and Denis emerged from the stables. John was beaming.

'Your little girl is a pure gem,' he said to Bridget and Cormac. 'Mrs Kavanagh's in there now learning all about the importance of washing paintbrushes right after use.'

They laughed. 'That sounds like our Emily,' said

182

Cormac.

Turning serious, Bridget extricated herself from his grasp. 'John, could I ask you to approach the cart with me, please?'

Curious, he followed her to the back of the cart where she looked up at the physician. 'Mr Abbott, might I beg you to pause your ministrations for just a few minutes? There are some matters I need to discuss with Mr Enright and Mr Corbett.'

The physician huffed but lowered himself down from the cart. 'As you wish.'

Bridget said to Mr Enright, 'Please do accept my apologies for the fact that you are not in a more dignified position for this. I hope you will forgive me but I would rather not delay.'

Baffled, he said, 'It's fine.'

She continued on, addressing both the agent and the stable master, but allowing her words to carry to Cormac, Ellen and the other surrounding men. 'As you are aware, the responsibility for Oakleigh passed to me at the moment of my mother's death in the early hours of this morning and I am expected to take on the management of the estate. However, this is a position that I do not wish to fill for I have family obligations to which I must adhere first and foremost.' Mr Enright's mouth opened to object but she raised her voice to forestall him. 'This means that I shall need someone else to run the estate on my behalf. I therefore propose that, in my absence, I appoint you as joint stewards of the Oakleigh Estate.'

A shocked silence greeted her speech. She glanced over at Cormac to see that he was as astounded as the others. She looked back at John and Mr Enright.

'What say you?' she said when they still did not speak.

'M'lady,' John spluttered. 'I can't speak for Mr Enright but I'm telling the truth when I say I'm in no way qualified for a role of such magnitude.'

'I am also not worthy of it, after the part I have played in

183

Oakleigh's downfall,' said Mr Enright, so flummoxed that he swung his arm out in a gesture of bemusement and hit one of the stuffed sacks. He grimaced.

Bridget lifted her chin, dismissing their arguments. 'On the contrary. Mr Enright, for many years you supervised the running of Oakleigh under my father's direction to the point where it was once one of the finest estates in the country. I am fully aware that its recent deterioration was not of your voluntary doing and I bear witness to the fact that you have always had the people's best interests at heart.' She turned to John. 'And you, Mr Corbett, used to run the most efficient stables I have ever seen. You have a thorough understanding of this land and, more importantly, you know the men, women and children who have lived and worked here for so long. You have been their leader in the uprising and only you can convince them to desist or carry on with their rebellion. But I am confident they will come back to Oakleigh in an instant if it is to be under your management.' She pushed her shoulders back, unshakable in her conviction. 'I believe both of you will be fair and you will restore the estate to its former splendour and dignity.'

Further silence. The jaws of all the surrounding men gaped open. Some of them didn't seem to grasp yet exactly what was happening, but Denis's face was shining and he was gazing at Bridget with something close to reverence as she threw away decades of tradition. Ellen, too, looked very pleased.

Bridget took a slow, steadying breath. Once again, she felt the intoxicating sense of power she had experienced upon meting out punishment to Joseph and Bernie – it surged beneath her skin like fire. Only this time she was no longer scared of it. Her mother had abused such power but Bridget would not let it consume her.

'I envision a very different future for Oakleigh,' she declared. 'It shall not be a dictatorship in the Courcey name. I shall leave it almost entirely in your hands and I encourage you to take your guidance from the people. But I have just three stipulations. Firstly, I desire you to release the constables imprisoned at Hogan Farm. Secondly, Oakleigh must undertake the payment of the tithes on behalf of the tenants again. And thirdly, I should like to see the manor rebuilt.' She registered their dumbfounded reactions. 'It will be years in the making, I appreciate that. But it will provide a significant source of employment for those who might otherwise have served within its walls or on its grounds.' She could have said more but she suspected any further revelations might cause them all to faint. She offered John and Mr Enright a gentle smile of encouragement. 'I can think of no two better men for the job. Will you accept this honourable task?'

After a pause, John said, 'Thank you, m'lady, I will.'

Mr Enright added, 'Good gracious, yes.'

'That is wonderful.' She clasped her hands together in delight. 'We shall need to go through a formal process with the solicitors in Dublin in order to make the appointment official, but at least it is agreed upon now. I am very glad.'

Her sentiment was not shared by all around her. Several of the watching men looked distrustful and some muttered under their breath to each other.

Cormac came to her side, looking dazed. 'Are you certain this is what you want to do?'

'Yes. I could not be more certain.' She dropped her voice to a murmur so only he could hear. 'The alternative would have been for us to part, at least for a time, and I could not abide that thought. I love you and I will go with you to the ends of the earth if that is where you need to go. We belong together, always and everywhere.'

His face filled with the utmost relief. He wrapped his arms around her and kissed her warmly on the lips.

They heard little footsteps pattering on the cobbles and then a scandalised voice rang out, 'Papa, you're kissing Mama in front of all these people!'

Bridget and Cormac smiled at each other and kissed again.

Chapter 15

'Get your fresh fish!' bellowed a woman as she pushed her laden wheelbarrow across the street.

'Get out of the road!' a coachman roared back at her.

She made an obscene gesture at him and continued to holler about the freshness of her produce. He flung a curse in her direction and drove on, avoiding a collision with her barrow by mere inches.

Ben Bracken manoeuvred his donkey and cart carefully around the fishwife and carried on along the Dublin street. Cormac, sitting in the back of the cart with Bridget and Emily, hoped his daughter hadn't caught the coachman's swear word.

He tugged at his cap, pulling it more securely over his head. Liam had given it to him for his own had been lost in the fire, but it was looser and didn't fit quite as well. He was also wearing a long coat that had belonged to Denis – of all the men, the footman was closest in height and stature to Cormac and the coat was actually a decent match in size. Despite their protestations, he had paid them both for their contributions.

He gazed around, absorbing their environs: the footpaths thronged with jostling men, the orphans begging on street corners, the cacophony of shouts and clattering wheels and hoof beats, the stench of the gutters. It was all so familiar and not one bit of it brought back a welcome memory.

In the midst of the smoky city, he longed for the green fields they had left behind. He felt the sting of regret deep inside him; their time at Oakleigh had been all too brief.

187

'We will be back,' he and Bridget had promised Ellen and Liam on their departure, but who knew how much time would pass before they could keep that promise?

Leaving his family's cottage yet again had been a difficult parting, made easier only by the fact that he knew good people lived there and would look after it. Without the threat of tithe proctors or eviction notices, the Kirwans could now keep a happier home and Liam would get employment in the rebuilding of the manor house, so the arrival of their third child could be an impending event of joy rather than concern.

Next to Cormac in the cart, Bridget directed Emily's attention to a cluster of four pigeons perched on the roof of a nearby building. They were eyeing the fishwife's wheelbarrow with avid interest. Emily waved enthusiastically at the birds and encouraged her mother to join in; Bridget did so, but her smile was forced.

The loss of her own mother weighed upon her, Cormac knew, because she could not grieve openly. She had no mourning clothes to wear but, more than that, she was alone in her sorrow; no other person of her acquaintance suffered any distress over Lady Courcey's death. Cormac could offer support but not sympathy, and Bridget's closest surviving family was her uncle, Lord Walcott, with whom Lady Courcey herself had said she had become estranged. Bridget had written to her uncle's estate at Lockhurst Park in England and informed him of his sister's death but they had not stayed at Oakleigh long enough to receive his reply.

Very few people had attended the burial of the lady's scant remains recovered from the rubble of the house. Ellen and Liam had come out of respect for Bridget, while Mr Enright, John Corbett and Mrs Kavanagh, who could recall a time when Lord Courcey had been alive and Lady Courcey had not been quite so tyrannical, had also made an appearance. Cormac and Bridget had told no one that the lady's death had been an intentional act instead of an accident, thus allowing her to be buried in consecrated ground. Cormac felt it was more than Lady Courcey deserved but he had not objected for Bridget's sake.

After Lady Courcey's burial in the graveyard at St Canice's, he had visited the graves of his father and brother at St Mary's and, beyond the graveyard's wall, his sister. He had knelt before the mossy earth concealing their bones and made an earnest vow that he would not rest until he had located the remainder of their family.

'Help me, Da,' he had implored. 'Help me find Ma and the others. Let you and Patrick and Mary guide me to them.'

They would be his spiritual guides, but his actual guide came in the form of Ben Bracken. He had very kindly arranged an unscheduled trip to visit his sister in Dublin in order to take Cormac, Bridget and Emily all the way to the street where he had brought Cormac's mother, sisters and nephew seven and a half years previously. Mrs Bracken, being too frail to make the journey, had remained behind in the hospitality of Farmer Hogan, a source of relief for all concerned, except perhaps the farmer.

Ben sat at the front of the cart, driving his donkey on through streets that grew more crowded the closer they got to the centre of the city. He turned his head from one side to the other and Cormac caught a sidelong glimpse of the man's frown. He experienced a ripple of worry; had Ben forgotten the route he had taken with Cormac's family? But then his weather-beaten countenance cleared and he directed the donkey onto another street lined with a variety of establishments, from pawnbrokers and grocers to wine and spirit merchants. The strong smell of hops from a local brewery drifted on the air, causing Emily to screw up her nose.

Ben called over his shoulder, 'This area's the Liberties and we're heading along Meath Street. I'm sure it was up here on the left...' A few seconds later, he let out an exclamation of satisfaction. 'I was right, there 'tis.'

He brought the cart to a stop in front of a narrow, three-storey building. Many of the premises along the street were in a ramshackle state and this one was no exception. Its windows were grimy, their frames were warped and peeling, and bird droppings plastered the sills. Two signs hung crookedly in the window on the ground floor: one read 'Tobacconist' and the other read 'Lodgings' and both included crude illustrations of those services. Flaking letters above the front door spelled 'O'Hara's'.

Ben turned around in his seat, looking pleased. 'I'm right glad I could remember the way.'

'You have my deepest gratitude,' said Cormac. His voice was still a little rough, though the hoarseness was not as pronounced as it had been in the immediate aftermath of the fire; he sounded mostly like himself again. 'I can never thank you enough for bringing us here or for the assistance you gave my family so long ago.'

Ben shrugged away the compliment. 'Happy to help. Only wish there was more I could do. You sure ye'll be able to manage from here?'

'Yes,' said Cormac firmly. They could trespass upon the man's generosity no further. 'We'll be fine. You must go visit your sister now.'

Ben nodded, his face serious. ''Tis been longer than I'd like since I've seen her. The last time I got to Dublin was before we lost our brother. And she's got an anxious nature, does Annie.' He brightened. 'Mayhap my good news will cheer her up. Jaysus, she might even come home with me to work behind the counter. Now wouldn't that be a tonic for my ma?'

When Ben returned to Oakleigh, he intended to take over the proprietorship of The Pikeman, left vacant by Bernie Cuddihy. Cormac thought it was a splendid idea; an upstanding fellow like Ben would transform the place from a seedy drinking hole to a more respectable establishment. Mrs Bracken, impossible to please, had not shown any approval of the notion but perhaps the return

190

of her long-absent daughter might soften her.

Cormac jumped out of the cart, helped Bridget and Emily down to the footpath, and retrieved their valises from the cart's bed next to a small parcel of clothes and food for Annie. Handing one of the valises to Bridget, he went to the front of the cart to bid farewell to Ben. His limp had all but disappeared but he still wore a light bandage over his burnt fingers. He offered his unhurt hand to grasp Ben's.

'Thank you very much again,' he said.

'I wish ye the best,' Ben replied. 'And I hope you find your family, lad.'

He took his leave; they watched him and his donkey and cart merge into the flow of other carts and wagons along the street until he had disappeared from sight. Then they turned and stared up at O'Hara's.

Cormac was filled with apprehension. This was the last known location of his family. Had they stayed here for long? Could they in fact still be here now? Perhaps that was the shadow of his mother beyond that upstairs window or the voice of his sister Margaret floating out through it. There was only one way to find out.

He led Bridget and Emily up to the building's entrance. The door, scratched and stained, was partly open, possibly to entice passersby to make a purchase or to stay the night – there was nothing else about the place to encourage them to stop. He pushed the door open further and they entered.

The front hall of the building was unwelcoming, cold and poorly lit. A couple of threadbare chairs stood against one wall and opposite them was a high counter behind which an old woman was half obscured. Above her head were a few dusty shelves piled with pipes, pipe cleaners and snuff boxes. When she saw that she had three potential customers, she hurried around the counter to greet them. She was short and stooped with wiry, grey hair and more than a few bristles sticking out of her chin.

She grinned, revealing several gaps among her teeth. Cormac felt Emily shrink closer to his side.

'Good day to yous,' she leered. 'Looking for a new snuff box, sir? Take a look at my fine range here where I guarantee you'll find something to suit your tastes. Or mayhap yous are in need of accommodation? I've got a cosy family room available on the first floor, very comfortable.'

Cormac shook his head. 'We are not looking for snuff boxes or lodgings.'

The woman's grin disappeared. 'What d'yous want then?'

'Are you Mrs O'Hara?' he enquired, ignoring her abrupt change in attitude.

'I am. Who's asking?'

'Mr McGovern,' he said with a slight bow. 'I am looking for some members of my family and I heard a rumour that they are staying here or at least stayed here once. Can you confirm whether that is the case?'

Mrs O'Hara eyed him. 'Would their name be McGovern too?'

'Yes.'

'I've no one by that name on the books right now.'

His heart sank. 'Are you sure? Perhaps you could check —'

'I'm sure.'

'Or did anyone by that name reside here in the past? They may have moved on since.'

'No one by that name's ever been a guest here,' she said stubbornly.

'Maybe they used a different name,' he said in desperation. 'If I could just describe them to you —'

'Stop wasting my time,' the old lady cut in and went back behind the counter. 'D'yous think I can remember the face of every person who's walked through that door?'

He persevered anyway. 'It would have been about seven and a half years ago, if you were the proprietor back then.

A woman, three girls and a baby boy, all with dark hair. They would not have had many belongings with them.'

Mrs O'Hara opened her mouth to make another angry retort but then she shut it again. She peered at Cormac more closely and squinted at Bridget and Emily too.

'I do remember them,' she admitted.

Hope leapt inside Cormac. 'Please tell me what you know. How long did they stay here for?'

'They didn't stay here,' she said with a scornful look.

'But you just said you remembered them,' said Bridget.

'Just 'cause they came in the door doesn't mean they got a room, lovie. They couldn't afford to stay.'

Cormac looked around the dingy hall, wondering what kind of extortionate prices the old woman was charging. 'How is it that you remember them then?'

Mrs O'Hara pursed her lips. 'They were so desperate to get a room. They'd only a few coins on them but they were willing for all five of them to share a room the size of a broom closet and they offered to do work for me to make up the difference.'

'And you didn't help them?' Cormac said in a terse voice.

'This here's a business, not a charity,' she said indifferently. 'No money, no room. I just wanted them to leave. The baby wouldn't stop bawling.' She scowled at the memory.

Anguished by the fact that their promising lead was turning into a dead end, Cormac entreated, 'Do you have any idea where they might have gone next?'

She shrugged. 'None whatsoever.'

Deflated, his shoulders slumped. 'Thank you for your time,' he said flatly and steered Bridget and Emily back towards the door. He could sense Mrs O'Hara's gaze upon him all the way. Outside, he walked a few paces and halted.

Bridget placed a consoling hand on his arm. 'What do you want to do now?'

193

He sighed. 'Let's go to the solicitors' office and get that out of the way. Then we can figure out where to continue our search next.'

Mr Enright had given them the address of Webb & Brereton Solicitors on Baggot Street. They asked for directions in one of the pawnbroker establishments further up the street from O'Hara's and set off towards the solicitors' office. It was in a more prosperous part of the city so, as they neared it, they began to see cleaner streets, smarter shop fronts, and pedestrians and carriages of a more affluent sort.

They found Webb & Brereton Solicitors nestled between an apothecary and a dressmaker's. Cormac took a breath and gently tugged Emily's bonnet to make her look up at him.

'Do you remember the game we played on the ship where we pretended to be different people, *a stór*?'

She nodded.

'I'm going to play that game again today, for a little fun. You don't need to be anyone else, just Emily. Let your mama and me do all the talking here.'

She nodded again, a slight crease between her fair eyebrows, and he hated himself for having to be a liar in front of her.

But this was his area of expertise.

Looking to Bridget for one final glance of reassurance, he stepped up to the building's front door and rapped the brass knocker twice. After a pause, they heard footsteps beyond the door and it opened. A neat young man peered out.

'Yes?'

'Viscount Wyndham,' Cormac announced, his voice cultivated and confident. 'I seek an immediate interview with Messrs Webb and Brereton. Extenuating circumstances, which I shall divulge presently, prevented me from writing in advance.'

The young man gaped. 'S-sir?' At Cormac's outraged

glare, he amended hastily, 'I mean, m-my lord. I—your presence is…unanticipated…'

His gaze travelled downwards, taking in the valises in Cormac and Bridget's hands and their very ordinary clothing.

Tone clipped, Cormac said, 'I reiterate, extenuating circumstances have brought me here today. For that same reason I do not have a calling card to show you. Do please let us continue this discourse on the doorstep.'

The man leapt back, pulled the door wide and admitted them inside. They entered a long hallway with a parquet floor.

'I'm Mr Croft,' said the man. 'Apprentice to Mr Brereton. P-please allow me to notify him of your arrival, Lord Wyndham.'

'Indeed, and shall I wait in the hallway until such time as he is ready to receive me?'

Blushing, Mr Croft ushered them into a chamber off the hall with plain furnishings and a single sofa. Bridget and Emily sat down but Cormac remained standing.

Looking around at them disconcertedly, Mr Croft said, 'You—you travel without a servant, my lord?'

'My valet has gone ahead to arrange our accommodation. I do admire your talent for procrastination, Mr Croft.'

Cowed, the apprentice disappeared for several minutes. When he returned, he was still red-faced.

'Please accept my deepest regrets for keeping you waiting, my lord. Mr Webb is poorly and not here today but Mr Brereton would be honoured to receive you.'

'My wife's attendance is also pertinent to the proceedings,' said Cormac, and Bridget stood to join them.

'May we prevail upon you to keep an eye on our daughter for a brief time?' she asked Mr Croft with a smile full of apology and charm. 'She will not give you any trouble.'

Speechless, the apprentice bobbed his head. Leaving

Emily and the valises behind with a murmured 'Be good' from Bridget and no acknowledgement at all from Cormac, they re-entered the hallway with Mr Croft and he directed them to another door further along it. He knocked, announced them, conducted them inside, and bowed out of the room again.

The furnishings in this office were more luxuriant than in the previous chamber, with wood panelling on the walls, comfortable chairs, and a broad desk. A large portrait hung above the desk portraying a man with a bulbous nose, a clean-shaven chin, and an impressive set of whiskers on both cheeks. Its subject sat beneath it, identical in every way, save that the artist had generously given the nose a more proportional shape to the rest of the face.

Mr Brereton stood when they entered and greeted them with a bow. 'It is an honour, Lord Wyndham, Lady Wyndham. We have communicated in writing but never had the personal pleasure.'

This was what Bridget had suspected but until this moment they had not been certain. The tension inside Cormac uncoiled the tiniest bit.

'Please sit.' The solicitor motioned them to two chairs opposite his desk and continued, 'I do lament the fact that you were kept waiting. Mr Croft still has much to learn. He was rendered quite confused by your appearance.'

All three of them sat and Mr Brereton said no more, evidently viewing this as an opportunity for the unexpected arrivals to explain themselves.

Cormac took time to settle himself in his seat before replying, 'We have been through quite an ordeal, so you will have to forgive our lack of forewarning. The first thing I must tell you, and it grieves me to say it, is that my mother-in-law, Lady Courcey, has passed away.'

He resolutely avoided eye contact with Bridget at his blatant lie.

Mr Brereton rocked back in his chair, shocked. 'Good

gracious. My sincere condolences. How did this happen?'

'Unfortunately, the Oakleigh Estate has fallen foul of tenant unrest. In a most barbaric act of rebellion, two disgruntled tenants set fire to Oakleigh Manor. I'm afraid the manor succumbed to the blaze and Lady Courcey perished inside it.'

Mr Brereton's eyes bulged. 'Mr Webb and I had heard vague reports of some dissatisfaction on the estate, but Lady Courcey had assured us in her correspondence that it was but a trifling matter. I am most sorry to hear that it grew to such a scale and that her life was the deplorable cost.'

Cormac lowered his gaze in a moment of respectful silence. When he looked up again, he said, 'My wife and child and I had reached Carlow only the day before to commence our sojourn with the lady. We too were caught in the conflagration—a most traumatic experience—but we managed to escape the house with our lives.' He raised his bandaged hand and then waved his other one to indicate the clothes he and Bridget wore. 'You must excuse our modest travelling attire. All of the possessions we had brought on our journey were lost in the fire. We have just arrived in the city but our next call will be to a tailor's and a dressmaker's. I trust this explanation will allay Mr Croft's concerns about our humble appearance.'

Mr Brereton's hands fluttered and his protuberant nose went crimson. 'Of course, of course, and I do beg your pardon if he caused you any offence—'

'It is fine,' said Cormac levelly.

For a few awkward seconds, no one spoke. Then Mr Brereton said cautiously, 'And you are here today...'

'To address the legal ramifications of Lady Courcey's death,' answered Cormac.

'I see. Yes, her guardianship has ended with her passing. Do you wish to appoint another guardian in her place?'

'I do. My wife.'

Mr Brereton blinked and looked at Bridget. 'Your wife?'

'That is correct,' said Cormac, affecting an inflection of impatience. 'She holds the Courcey title and bears an inexplicable concern for the fate of the estate and its tenants. I have no wish to be bothered by it so long as it becomes a profitable asset again. Therefore the arrangement will be thus: Lady Wyndham will be named the new guardian of the Oakleigh Estate in perpetuity, and she in turn has identified two individuals, Mr Laurence Enright and Mr John Corbett, to act as joint stewards on her behalf. There is a great deal to be done to revive the property. All monies earned from the collection of rents shall be funnelled directly back into its restoration and shall not be channelled towards any other purpose. I desire you to draw up a contract to reflect this arrangement.'

He made a show of taking out his pocket watch and checking the time in order to achieve two objectives: the first was to put pressure on Mr Brereton to hurry along with the proceedings, and the second was to place the watch on display for the solicitor's discreet observation. Lord Courcey's pocket watch would be noted in their records as being in Lord Wyndham's possession. It was irrefutable proof that the gentleman in question sat right now in this office.

Mr Brereton did indeed take notice of the watch and, without making any reference to it, said, 'Very good, my lord. It will be done as you have requested. We shall need some time to prepare the document. Can we make an appointment for you and Lady Wyndham to return to our office next Tuesday to provide your signatures? We shall require the signatures of the stewards as well.'

Cormac had expected this delay so he did not object. 'Tuesday is acceptable,' he said. 'However, the stewards must remain in Carlow to oversee the beginning of the reconstruction of Oakleigh Manor. You will have to send the document to the estate with instructions for it to be signed in the presence of witnesses and they will return it to you. In addition, any future correspondence may be sent directly to Oakleigh for the attention of Mr Enright and Mr Corbett. I do not wish to be troubled by it in London. I trust this will all be satisfactory?'

'Yes, my lord,' said Mr Brereton.

One potential impediment to this plan was that Cormac might not be able to forge Garrett's signature accurately when the time came to sign the document. But he had flaunted his injured hand; if he kept the bandage on next Tuesday, he could blame it for any defect in his penmanship.

The greater concern of course was that Garrett would get wind of their machinations and expose the fraud. He would be bound to hear about it sooner or later, especially if he made enquiries into the running of the estate once the news of Lady Courcey's death reached him. But overturning their decision would require him to take on the management of the estate himself, or else place it back in the hands of a steward, with Mr Enright being the most likely candidate. Perhaps he would see that Oakleigh would prosper and eventually bring him revenue with no effort at all needed on his part.

Mr Brereton and Cormac spoke back and forth about the particulars of the contract, seeking no input from Bridget. She sat by meekly and neither of them acknowledged her again until the end of the discussion when, as they all stood, Mr Brereton said to her, 'Have you informed Lord Walcott of Lady Courcey's death?'

'Yes,' she said, 'I wrote to Lockhurst Park before we left Oakleigh.'

He scratched his whiskers, looking surprised. 'Your uncle is not in England. He currently resides in Dublin, on Rutland Square.'

She too was startled. 'He does? How do you know this?'

'He has written to us on a number of occasions enquiring after his sister's affairs at Oakleigh. I gather they have not been on speaking terms for some time which

199

prevented him from corresponding with her directly. Naturally, we could not divulge anything to him due to the agreement of confidentiality that exists between us and our clients. But he does persist in asking.' Mr Brereton's lips pressed together in a prim line of displeasure.

Cormac exchanged a glance with Bridget. Why would Lord Walcott take that level of interest in Oakleigh?

Frowning, Bridget said, 'Could you direct us to Rutland Square, sir? As his niece and closest kin, it should be my duty to deliver the news of my mother's death to him in person, given that we are both in the same city.'

The solicitor described the route and then said, 'It would be quite a distance to walk. Allow me to arrange a conveyance for your service.'

'Thank you, no,' said Cormac. 'We shall be paying a visit to the adjacent dressmaker's next so we shall make our transport arrangements from there.'

They began to turn for the door but Mr Brereton asked, his brows knitted together, 'And where will you be staying while in Dublin?' He added hurriedly, 'If we need to alter the date of the appointment, that is?'

'Courcey House on Merrion Square,' Cormac said with cool composure, though he had no desire for anyone to be able to trace their whereabouts. 'And do kindly adhere to the Tuesday appointment. We wish to return to London as soon as possible.'

'Indeed, my lord.'

Mr Brereton darted around his desk to hold the door open for them and they took their leave. In the other chamber, they found Mr Croft staring nonplussed at Emily as she chattered about how she would soon be mistress of a fine hen coop. Cormac hastened to extract her from the conversation, ordering her to his side. Downcast, she scurried to obey. He bent and grasped the two valises, dismissing the pinch of pain in his burnt fingers.

'I hope you had a productive meeting, s — my lord?' said Mr Croft. Cormac didn't like the crease of doubt on the apprentice's forehead.

'It was satisfactory,' he replied curtly. 'We now have other places to be.'

Mr Croft scuttled to escort them to the front door. He bowed them out and they turned aside in the direction of the dressmaker's as he lingered, shutting the door. They eventually heard it close and, instead of entering that establishment, they continued to walk along Baggot Street.

Bridget exhaled. 'My nerves are overwrought. I can't imagine how you had the mettle to keep up such a performance for nearly five years.'

He didn't want to think about that time. Assuming the persona of Oliver Davenport and dwelling in England as the nephew of Lord and Lady Bewley had released him from the shackles of poverty and iniquity that had plagued him in Dublin, but it had been another kind of imprisonment. What was worse, the Bewleys had been truly honourable people which had made his deception all the more reprehensible. It was not a talent in which he was proud to claim proficiency.

Shutting out those thoughts, he said, 'Do you really want to visit your uncle?'

'I think so, yes,' she said. 'It would be the decent thing to do.'

'How will you explain my presence?'

Her eyes twinkled. 'I happen to have an idea for that.'

Chapter 16

They chose to walk to Rutland Square, following Mr Brereton's prescribed route which took them over the River Liffey via Carlisle Bridge. The bridge was busy with pedestrians and carriage traffic; Bridget kept a firm hold on Emily's hand and a wary eye on the strangers rushing by. A jumble of noise filled the air, along with the pervading stink of the river. Undeterred by the smell, Emily tugged on Bridget's iron grip.

'Can I look over the edge? Please?' She swivelled to Cormac on her other side. 'Please, Papa? I can see a boat coming!'

He smiled at her exuberance. 'Why not?'

Whooping, she dragged them over to the parapet and Cormac relinquished the two valises to Bridget so he could lift Emily up. They watched as the vessel neared the bridge, glided under the arch below them, and vanished out of sight. Though it was only a barge and much smaller than the ship that had brought them down the Thames in London, it reminded Bridget of their escape that day. To her, the expanse of flowing water signified a flight to freedom. If one held one's nose.

Cormac let a beaming Emily back down to the ground. He plucked at her chin. 'Now, don't forget, you're not to call me Papa at the next place we're going to visit.'

Her bright expression dimmed. 'I won't.' Then she asked the question Bridget had dreaded to hear. 'Why?'

This was not exactly the ideal place but Cormac straightened his shoulders and Bridget steeled herself for the truths their daughter needed to learn.

'I'm afraid we can't explain some of the reasons properly to you until you're older, *a stór*. But there are a lot of people in this world who think your mother and I should not be friends. She was born in a fancy house like you, while I was born in that cottage where we stayed with Auntie Ellen. Many people believe this means we are not equal and that we can never associate with each other. So sometimes we need to pretend we are not friends when we go to certain places.'

A man hurrying past brushed roughly against Bridget's shoulder and she heard him mutter that the bridge wasn't a place for idle chat. Disregarding him, she crouched in front of Emily and held her solemn blue gaze.

'What your papa said is true. People make judgements based on social status and not on whether we are kind to others. You must remember, Emily, the most important thing is not how much wealth or property you own but that you're a good person. And if you find love, seize it with both hands, no matter what way it comes to you.'

The little girl rocked forwards on her toes. 'I shall, Mama,' she promised.

Bridget pressed a kiss to Emily's forehead. 'Let's keep going, gooseberry. Your feet must be getting tired but we're nearly there.'

When she rose, Cormac gave her a look full of tenderness and she felt the conviction deep in her heart that they were wholly right to lead Emily down a different path to the one imposed upon them by the established social order. He took back the valises and they carried on across the bridge.

They reached Rutland Square just as a chilly rain began to spit down. Seeking out the number of the house where Lord Walcott was residing, they located it along the north side of the square; a broad flight of steps climbed to its front door. Cormac rapped the knocker, then stepped back to the footpath, leaving Bridget and Emily alone on the top step. A tall footman answered the door.

'Good afternoon,' said Bridget. 'Could you please inform Lord Walcott that his niece and grandniece are here to see him?'

The footman acknowledged the request with more aplomb than Mr Croft. 'Certainly, my lady. I shall have to check if his lordship is disposed to receive callers. Would you care to step in from the rain?' He sent a quizzical glance in the direction of Cormac who was hovering in the background.

Bridget waved a dismissive hand behind her. 'My manservant. He will escort us, if that is agreeable to you.'

The footman bowed and permitted the three of them to cross the threshold into the entrance hall of the house, which had a staircase of shallow steps leading up to the next level. For the second time that day, they were ushered into a room to wait and, after taking Bridget and Emily's cloaks and bonnets, the footman withdrew to announce their arrival to his master.

Cormac peered out the window at the increasing rainfall. 'Perhaps we should take a hackney back to Merrion Square afterwards.'

'I think that's a good idea,' said Bridget. Emily didn't look like she could walk much further; her head was sagging like a wilting flower.

When the footman returned, his expression was sombre. 'His lordship will receive you but he respectfully requests that your visit be kept short as he is not feeling very well at present.'

'Oh,' said Bridget. 'Yes, of course. In light of that, may my manservant accompany us? I should like Lord Walcott to meet his grandniece but she has a boisterous nature. If she grows unruly or fatigues him overmuch, this fellow can take charge of her.'

If the footman thought it strange that Bridget would have a man instead of a maid for such a task, or that Emily's weary demeanour appeared the exact opposite of boisterous, he did not comment upon it. Inviting Cormac to leave the valises behind, he led them out of the room and up the stairs.

They waited outside a door as he announced Bridget and Emily and then he directed them inside. They found themselves in the library: richly furnished and well stocked, it was a welcoming space with a roaring fire in the hearth. Lord Walcott reclined on a chaise longue to one side of the fireplace. Bridget could not believe her eyes – her portly uncle had grown even larger since the last time she had seen him. Any trace of his neck had become lost in folds of fat that started at his chin and disappeared beneath his loosely tied cravat. His belly spilled out before him, stretching his enormous waistcoat almost to the point of bursting, and each of his thighs had to be the size of her waist. One of his legs was propped up on the chaise longue and a cloth lay over that foot.

A small dog was curled up next to his outstretched leg. It raised its head at the new arrivals, let out a weak yap, and rested its snout back on its paws.

'The maid will bring refreshments shortly,' the footman said and departed.

Cormac assumed a discreet position in the corner of the room, while Bridget and Emily approached the chaise longue. Lord Walcott's breath came in short, shallow pants and his face was mottled and sweaty.

'Greetings to you, Uncle Stuart,' said Bridget. 'This is my daughter, Emily. I hope we find you in good health.' She felt absurd even saying it.

He emitted a wheezy chuckle. 'I regret you do not. Forgive me for not rising to welcome you.' He gestured towards his covered foot. 'Gout. I am recovering from a recent attack and am still in a great deal of discomfort.' He shifted a little and winced. 'Confounded affliction. I wouldn't wish it on my worst enemy.'

'I am very sorry to hear it.' Bridget eyed her uncle uneasily, recalling how her mother had said his heart was failing. He looked like he might expire in front of them at any moment.

'Thank you for saying so. You were always my favourite niece.' He laughed at his own joke – Bridget was his *only* niece – and gestured to the chaise longue on the other side of the hearth.

Bridget and Emily sat with their backs to Cormac. Lord Walcott twinkled at Emily.

'And this delightful lamb is your daughter? Can you give me a curtsey, little girl?'

She obediently got up and dropped into a neat curtsey. 'Greetings to you, Granduncle.'

As she took her seat again, he grinned. 'What a pretty young thing. If she keeps those looks, she'll be snapped up once she comes out. I wager she'll have ten proposals before the end of her first season.' He pointed a pudgy finger at Bridget. 'You and Wyndham better keep a close eye on her. Some of those libertines might not have the patience to wait for her answer.'

Bridget could practically hear Cormac grinding his teeth behind her.

'Thank you for your advice, Uncle,' she said, feeling an odd twinge of regret that Emily would never experience the thrill of her first season. 'I shall take it into due consideration.'

He fished a handkerchief out of his pocket with some difficulty and mopped his damp brow. 'So what brings you to Ireland, my girl, and to my own doorstep?'

'My original purpose was to sojourn in Carlow for a little while but, alas, I come bearing ill news. I must inform you that my mother has died.'

Given the rift that had existed between him and his sister, she had not expected a great outpouring of emotion, but neither had she anticipated the veritable gleam that came into his eyes. He leaned forwards, insofar as his great bulk allowed him to.

'Is that so?' he said, looking intrigued. He made a poor attempt to veil it by passing a hand over his face in an attitude of distress. 'What a very sad loss. Can you tell me how it happened?'

She nipped the tip of her tongue with her teeth. 'I believe you are aware that my mother made some rather drastic changes to the way Oakleigh was managed over the past few years?'

'It had...come to my attention.'

'As it turned out, she pushed the tenants too far. They rose in rebellion against her, a conflict that culminated in two of the tenants setting fire to the manor. My mother did not escape the conflagration.'

Lord Walcott's skin grew even more patchy as he absorbed this. 'Indeed?' he murmured. 'So the insurgence was a direct cause of her death.' He sat back. 'And what will happen to the estate now?'

'I have taken responsibility for it,' she said.

His eyes flashed with anger. 'You have?'

Perplexed by his reaction, she said, 'So to speak. My role will be nominal for the most part. I have established an arrangement whereby the management of the estate has been placed in the custody of the land agent, Mr Enright, and the stable master, Mr Corbett. Mr Enright provides experience while Mr Corbett holds a strong link to the tenants. Between them, they will work in the best interests of the people. I hope in time that the tenants will gain greater autonomy over the land.'

'Oho!' cried Lord Walcott. He smacked a fist on his meaty thigh. 'I am very pleased to hear it. Well done, my girl, I highly approve. You'll do a far better job than your mother ever did if you can already see that the power of Oakleigh should rest in the hands of the people. That's where it belongs for it exists on their land.'

She stared at him. She had the strong impression that she was missing a vital component of their conversation.

Behind her, she heard Cormac mutter, 'The money,' but his words went unnoticed by Lord Walcott as the library door opened and a maid came in carrying a tray. While she bustled about setting out the teapot, milk jug, sugar bowl and cups on a table next to Lord Walcott, Bridget's mind worked furiously. The money…the anonymous benefactor…could it be possible? She accepted a cup of tea with an absent-minded thanks. The maid also handed a cup of milk to Emily, who took it with a wide yawn.

After the maid had left the room, Bridget studied her uncle with a fresh perspective. He was contemplating his own tea with faint disdain while darting a glance of longing at a decanter of whiskey standing on the mantelpiece.

'Remember the physician's advice,' he grumbled to himself and took a small sip from his teacup.

'Uncle,' Bridget began slowly.

He swallowed the tea like it was a particularly nasty tonic. 'Hmm?'

'Has your interest in Oakleigh been…more than academic?'

His expression turned cagey. 'I don't know what you mean.'

She raised her eyebrows. 'I think perhaps you do.'

He set his cup down on the table beside him and clicked his tongue softly at his dog. The creature stirred itself, crept sluggishly up the chaise longue, and crawled onto its master's vast lap. Lord Walcott scratched the dog's ears as it settled and shut its eyes. He looked back at Bridget.

'What is it that you suspect?' he asked.

She clutched the delicate handle of her teacup so hard she thought she might crack it. 'It was you, wasn't it? You sent the money to the rebels.'

He shrugged one large shoulder. 'Yes.'

It took all her willpower not to turn around to Cormac. 'I am dumbfounded, Uncle. When did you become a revolutionary?'

He laughed. 'What, does it surprise you that I fell in love with the Irish land as much as you did?' He daubed his handkerchief once more across his forehead. 'Before I first

208

visited Oakleigh, I was merely curious. The rebellion in 1798, the Act of Union in 1801. Who was this savage race who spilled so much blood for the sake of their homeland and whose overbearing neighbour felt the need to crush their independence in every conceivable way?' Stroking the dog's back, he focused his gaze on the blazing fire. 'But once I came to Ireland to assume the guardianship of Oakleigh and I beheld the beauty of this country, I understood why they fought so hard. And I came to sympathise with their cause.'

At a loss for words, Bridget took a gulp of her tea. Next to her, Emily had finished her milk and now slouched forwards, looking listlessly at her toes.

'The Irish are justified in coveting sovereign control over their own land. I did what I could to assist one small faction of them in that aspiration.' He grunted. 'Though I suppose, given the consequences of their uprising, I now have my sister's blood on my hands.'

Bridget flinched. Even if her uncle felt remorse for his actions, he could not change what he had done. That chapter in the life of their family was now closed.

But another chapter was only just beginning.

'Uncle Stuart,' she said, hoping she was taking the right gamble, 'if you are sympathetic to the Irish people, does that mean you believe they are not inferior?'

His answer was interrupted by the reappearance of the footman. 'My lord, you desired me to intervene if the visit became prolonged—'

'Go away, Simon, go away,' said Lord Walcott, flapping his hands. 'We are having a far more interesting conversation than I had anticipated. Leave us be.'

Rebuffed, the footman exited again, red all the way to the tips of his ears.

Lord Walcott regarded Bridget with squinting eyes. 'That is quite the fascinating question, my girl. If our countrymen are to be believed, the Irish are an uncouth, dim-witted race ruled by Rome. But I conjecture you and I are cut from a different cloth to our compatriots and view them with greater perception.'

She didn't consider the English her compatriots but that was beside the point. 'Without a doubt, Uncle.' She turned around deliberately to Cormac. 'Shall we tell him?'

He rubbed his chin with the knuckles of his bandaged hand. 'If you think so.'

She nodded and, guarded, he came forwards to stand at the end of the chaise longue she and Emily sat upon. Lord Walcott peered at them, puzzled.

'I must reveal something to you, Uncle,' said Bridget, enunciating her words so he could not pretend he had misheard. 'When it comes to the Irish, I am more broad-minded than you might ever have believed. This is Cormac McGovern, once a stable hand on the Oakleigh Estate. In the past month, I have deserted my husband and run away from London to be with him.'

'What the devil—' Lord Walcott spluttered.

She barrelled on. 'I fell in love with him that summer my mother and I returned to Oakleigh. Well, I do believe I always loved him but that was when I first realised it.'

She reached out to grasp Cormac's hand. His gaze was warm when he looked down at her but his jaw tightened as he glanced back at Lord Walcott. Her uncle's eyes were bulging out of their sockets.

'Are you being serious?' he said, his complexion almost purple.

'Quite,' she responded. 'Come sit with us,' she added to Cormac and, after a slight hesitation, he joined them on the chaise longue.

Emily slithered into his lap. As he wrapped his arms around her, she said sleepily, 'I thought you weren't supposed to be my papa in this house.'

A second exclamation of 'What the devil!' erupted from the other chaise longue.

Calmly, Bridget said, 'Take a closer look, Uncle. And recall what I said about that summer at Oakleigh...and how long ago that was.'

She watched her uncle compare the two fair heads, the two pairs of clear blue eyes, the way Emily nestled into Cormac's paternal embrace. His mouth opened and closed like a fish.

At last, he said, 'Does Wyndham know?'

'He has known since her birth. And he has punished me time and again for it. Ours was not a happy marriage.'

He twisted his lips. 'And you view that as justification for taking leave of your senses? Good Lord, the mind boggles!'

She tried to quell the disappointment welling inside her. 'I thought you believed the Irish were not inferior to us.'

'Race is a different matter to class. He's still a stable hand.'

'And proud of it, my lord,' said Cormac, his voice controlled. 'I feel no shame at my humble beginnings. I know what it is to be a man who possesses nothing but his name and that has proved a far more valuable education than that which any gentleman's tutor can provide.'

Lord Walcott gaped. His fingers convulsed in the hair on his dog's back and the animal gave a faint bark of disgruntlement. He patted it distractedly while he contemplated the improbable family in front of him.

At length, he said gruffly, 'While I don't pretend to approve, I am too old and ill to concern myself with it. Do what you will, if it makes you happy. Though in truth I ought not to be surprised, given that your mother's blood runs in your veins.'

Startled, Bridget said, 'What on earth can you mean by that? My mother opposed any hint of a connection between us, even an innocent childhood friendship.'

The corner of her uncle's mouth turned up. 'Ah, the hypocrisy of it. How amusing.' At Bridget's obvious confusion, he went on, 'Must I remind you that Lockhurst Park is the seat of an earldom? Your mother was an earl's daughter. Lady Constance married down when she wed a

211

mere baron.'

'But my father was a member of the peerage,' she protested.

'And two ranks below your mother. Our parents had it in mind to match her with a marquess so to see her sink to the lowest possible level of the aristocracy was deeply displeasing to them. Nevertheless, she was intractable and would have no one else. Their love match was the talk of London.'

It was Bridget's turn to gape. No one had ever told her that her parents' union had been viewed in a negative light. But her astonishment quickly transformed into indignation. Hypocrisy indeed – how dared her mother censure her for favouring Cormac over Garrett when she herself had flouted the expectations of society? But then, perhaps her objection had risen from the bitterness of experience.

Faltering, she said, 'Did my mother regret it?'

'Not when Angus was alive,' he said. 'But I'm sure acutely so once he was deceased.'

For a single second, Bridget allowed herself to envision a future where Cormac was dead and she and Emily were left utterly alone. The horror from the night of the fire swept over her and she shied away from the frightening picture she had conjured up. She pressed a surreptitious hand to his thigh to reassure herself of his solid presence. He offered her a comforting wink; he could not otherwise move to respond to her touch for Emily had fallen asleep in his arms.

Bridget scrutinised her uncle. 'Were *you* against my mother's choice?'

He fidgeted with a button on his waistcoat. 'At first, yes. Not only was he at the lower end of the peerage, but he was also Anglo-Irish and that made me mistrustful. Of course, once we became acquainted, I comprehended that he was the best of gentlemen.' He picked up his cup of tea, regarded it dubiously and placed it back down. 'He was the one who stirred my curiosity about Ireland. He encouraged me many times to visit Oakleigh but, alas, I did not make it there until after his death. I do believe he and I would have seen eye to eye on the plight of the Irish people.'

Cormac cleared his throat. 'On that matter, my lord, I would ask you a question. You have involved yourself in the rebel cause, but what of the lawful route? Would you speak for the Irish in Parliament?'

'I'm afraid it's too late for that,' said Lord Walcott, sweeping one thick arm out to indicate his giant frame. 'I shall never sit in Parliament again. In fact, it is likely I shall never leave this house again, save for in a wooden box.'

'Oh, Uncle,' said Bridget, 'is your health truly that precarious?'

'It is,' he said without dramatics as he touched his chest. 'The pain has become my frequent companion. It is only a matter of time before my heart gives out entirely.' He smiled sadly at the dog in his lap. 'My other companions have left me one by one. Brutus is the last fellow still by my side and not for long, I fear. This is a house of creatures waiting to die.'

'I don't wish to be indelicate,' said Bridget, 'but what will happen to Lockhurst Park? You are a bachelor.'

'Yes indeed, and I suppose it is not too late to marry, is it? Some women might still consider me a tempting catch—those of the money-grabbing sort, at least—but it wouldn't be worth the effort. At any rate, I doubt my ability to produce an heir at this stage.' He grimaced. 'There is a second cousin gleefully anticipating the day I go to meet my maker. He will inherit the title and Lockhurst Park, and I believe he has had the audacity to spawn two sons already so his own line is secure. I'm confident that when I encounter my father in the afterlife he will box me soundly for allowing the estate to slip away down a different branch of the family tree, but there you have it. I'll hold out as long as I can anyway, just to spite my cousin.'

By the end of this speech, he was taking a short breath after every three or four words. Alarmed, Bridget said, 'We should leave you to rest. This has been quite enough agitation for one afternoon. Might we call on you again while we are in Dublin?'

'Eh?' he said. 'You'll stay here, of course.'

'That is very kind of you but we intend to stay at Courcey House.'

'Do they know you are coming?'

'Not yet but—'

He lifted his hand in a feeble motion; he might have been aiming for a dismissive wave but it flopped back into his lap after rising only an inch or two. 'The house won't be ready. It'll be cold and they won't have a good joint of beef in. Stay here. I can assure you, a fine roast beef will be served this evening.'

Bridget glanced at Cormac and then down at the slumbering Emily. From the little girl's perspective, staying in Rutland Square was the more appealing option. Moreover, it would mean not having to go back out into the rain, and there might even be enough time before dinner to bathe properly, a true indulgence in their current way of life.

'Perhaps just the one night then,' said Bridget. 'If you're certain we shall not be a nuisance to your staff.'

'They'll have the rooms ready in no time,' said Lord Walcott. He arched one eyebrow. 'How many rooms?'

She tried not to blush. 'Two. Cormac and I shall share.'

'Hmm,' muttered Lord Walcott, but he said nothing more.

Chapter 17

Waking up in a large bed was a luxury to which they were not accustomed. Eyes still closed, Cormac stretched out, relishing the feel of the comfortable mattress under his back. Turning on his side, he reached out blindly for Bridget and found her drowsily reaching out for him too. His forehead bumped against hers and, with a soft laugh, he opened his eyes.

She looked up at him from beneath her eyelashes. 'Good morning,' she murmured, her voice husky with sleep.

He answered her with a kiss. He meant it to be chaste, a simple morning greeting between two lovers, but their love was still so new – and the bed was such a novelty – that the purity of the kiss degenerated into something altogether more hot-blooded.

They took full advantage of the rare occasion of privacy and, amid the rumpled sheets, made a more intimate acquaintance with the secret parts of each other's bodies. He inhaled the aroma of her skin and his senses ignited. She had abandoned her lilac perfume back in London and without it her own innate scent had come to the fore – it was even more arousing than the lilac fragrance and he could not get enough of it.

As he slid her nightdress up, he discovered a trio of freckles clustered on her right hip in the pattern of a triangle; he pressed his lips to them before removing her nightdress entirely. When it was her turn to disrobe him, she stripped him from behind and, with a hushed exclamation of surprise and delight, informed him that a faint blemish sat at the base of his spine, which he himself had not even been aware of.

'It looks rather like the shape of a leaf,' she said. 'How unusual. Let me examine it in more detail.' But, strangely, her attention became fixed on the area just below it instead.

Their tumble was swift and joyful and satisfying. They kept their sounds of pleasure as quiet as possible, conscious that the other inhabitants in the house would be waking too, and afterwards, when she still held him inside her, she whispered 'I love you' and he thought he might melt with devotion.

It would have been so easy to fall back into slumber, but the day ahead beckoned. They rose and dressed and Bridget went to waken Emily in another bedchamber down the corridor, while Cormac sought out Lord Walcott. He found him in the library, where they had dined the previous evening at a table the servants had carried in. Had they not later heard the footman assisting his master to bed, Cormac would have believed the man had not moved from this very spot. He supposed that with a bulk so great climbing the stairs had to be a daunting prospect and one to be entertained only in necessity.

Lord Walcott was reading a newspaper on his chaise longue, his leg propped up as it had been the day before. As Cormac entered, he gave a snort and folded the paper over in disgust.

'Good morning, my lord,' said Cormac. 'How does your foot fare today?'

'Hurts like blazes,' Lord Walcott replied, but at least his shortness of breath seemed to have abated. 'Where is my niece?'

'Rousing our daughter. They will be down shortly.' Cormac took a seat on the other chaise longue, avoiding Brutus who lay asleep at one end, legs extended.

Lord Walcott gave him a menacing look. 'You will do right by them?'

'I guarantee you I will. Nothing matters to me more than

their safety and happiness.'

Lord Walcott cocked his head. 'Does my niece truly comprehend all that she's forsaken? Her behaviour has been so very reckless, and there will be consequences for the girl too.'

Cormac kept his voice level. 'She understands.'

'And what do you plan to do next? Where will you build your life together? In what capacity can you provide for them? Have you given a single thought to those considerations or are you still too drunk on love to recognise the uncertainty of your situation?'

Gritting his teeth at being lectured like a schoolboy, Cormac said, 'Thank you, my lord, for your concern. I assure you, I am fully conscious of the nature of our situation and have deliberated at length over the many precarious aspects of it. I have a happy and secure future in mind for us, but there is another pressing matter which I must address first.'

He went on to describe the particulars relating to their ongoing search for the missing members of his family, beginning with the eviction that took place seven and a half years ago and concluding with their unsuccessful visit to O'Hara's yesterday.

When he had finished, Lord Walcott scowled. 'Good Lord, my sister must have been made of ice to do such a thing and not feel any compunction about it.'

Cormac could have added a litany of other colourful adjectives to describe Lady Courcey but decided there was nothing to be gained from it. 'We intend to continue our search, even though we are currently without any promising leads. But I wonder, my lord, would you be in a position to also make enquiries about my family? Could you use your connections to gain access to certain records? I'm thinking we should seek out the names of mission society converts or' – he swallowed – 'death notices and the like. Would you be willing to assist us?'

'Hmm,' said Lord Walcott. 'You do realise, my boy, that

217

if their circumstances deteriorated to the worst degree and they strayed into the most destitute areas of this city, their activities or deaths might not have entered any records?'

'I do realise that,' said Cormac, willing his voice not to crack. 'But I at least have to try. Will you help?'

Lord Walcott did not reply at first. He smoothed out the creases on the folded newspaper in his lap, fastidiously lining up the edges. At last, he said, 'You strike me as quite the singular man. You were born to nothing and yet you speak as well as any gentleman. You defy the conventions of society and yet your moral compass is evidently strong. Your fervour does you credit. I can see why my niece is so drawn to you.' He sighed. 'Yes, I shall help.'

Bridget and Emily entered the library just then and the business of breakfast commenced, the servants bustling in to accommodate the meal in the most convenient manner for their corpulent master. While they ate, Lord Walcott interrogated them on their next steps.

'I would like to begin today by going back to Meath Street,' said Cormac. 'It was the last known whereabouts of my family. Perhaps we can trace their movements to somewhere else in that locality.'

'And you will return here this evening?' Lord Walcott urged.

'Thank you for your generosity, Uncle,' said Bridget, 'but we shall stay in Merrion Square tonight. We gave that address to the solicitor so we must at least make an appearance, lest he try to contact us there.'

Her uncle looked disappointed. 'Very well. But you will come visit me again soon?'

Bridget gave him a fond smile. 'We shall.'

They took their valises with them when they departed from Rutland Square. The day was dull but dry. As they crossed the picturesque Wellington Bridge over the River Liffey, having paid a ha'penny each for the service, Cormac pondered the Grace of God Mission Society.

Could his family have happened across it, or another like it? He hoped they would not have been as bull-headed as himself and that they would have taken the soup. If seeking them in the vicinity of Meath Street proved fruitless, he decided they would try the mission society next.

They had no difficulty relocating the Liberties district – the smell of hops guided their way. Standing at the top of Meath Street, they gazed down its length.

Refusing to be daunted, Cormac said to Bridget, 'We'll commence our search here and then explore the surrounding streets. My family's chief priority would have been finding somewhere to stay so we must be on the alert for any lodgings or shelters.'

They started down the street, peering at names painted above doorways and signs placed in windows. Emily trotted between them, holding Bridget's hand. As they passed the dilapidated front of O'Hara's, Cormac gave it and its surly proprietor within a surreptitious glower. They were nearly gone past the building when the door opened wide and a figure appeared in the doorway. Looking back in alarm, he wondered if the old lady had caught his dirty look and come out to upbraid him. But it wasn't Mrs O'Hara.

The main difference to how he remembered her was her clothing. Stepping out onto the footpath, she wore full petticoats and had wrapped a shawl over her bodice, which covered a great deal more of her than she had customarily displayed. But her long curtain of black hair was the same, as were her round lips – and the provocative smile that curved them upwards.

His stomach turned over.

'Good day, Mr McGovern,' Thomasina called.

At the mention of his surname, Bridget stopped and looked back too.

'Let's keep going,' he muttered to her, but Thomasina was approaching them with quick steps and it was too late to ignore her.

She grinned. 'Oh, I was so hoping you'd return to Meath Street. What a happy reunion this is.'

Stiffly, he said, 'I'm afraid we have an urgent matter to attend to and really can't delay.' He tried to encourage Bridget and Emily on down the street but Bridget stood her ground.

'Won't you introduce us?' she said with a frown.

He cringed. How could he introduce Thomasina when he did not even know her last name?

Her grin practically split her face as she comprehended his predicament. Altering her expression to one of pure innocence, she parroted, 'Yes, won't you introduce us?'

His face burned with mortification and anger. 'What are you doing here?' he said through clenched teeth.

She gestured behind her. 'Biddy O'Hara is my auntie. Sometimes she lets me take clients here if she's got a room free.'

Bridget shot a sharp glance at Cormac. He sensed the situation slipping out of his control, the pieces of it crumbling through his fingers. Unable to look at her, he asked Thomasina, 'Why in God's name were you hoping I'd return to Meath Street? How did you find out I'd even been here?'

'Auntie sent a message to me. She recognised your name and knew you and I had been...on familiar terms.' She adopted a look of angelic sorrow. 'I had told her how important you were to me and how much I missed you.'

Next to him, Bridget went rigid. 'Cormac,' she said. 'What is going on?'

Thomasina beamed. 'Cormac,' she said with an air of satisfaction. 'I never knew your name.'

Seething, he said to Bridget, 'Nothing's going on. This conversation is over.'

Before he could turn away, Thomasina grabbed his arm, the smile wiped from her features.

'Just you wait a second,' she hissed. 'Aren't you

forgetting something?'

He shrugged her off. 'Leave me be, Thomasina. We haven't got anything to say to each other.'

'Fine,' she said, putting her hands on her hips. 'But don't you remember where I work? I can go back to the lodgings right now and tell them I've seen McGovern here in the city. How d'you reckon Cunningham will react to that?'

His blood went cold. He scanned the busy street, half expecting the money lender or his chief lackey, Munroe, to sidle out from the crowd with murder in their eyes. That kind of danger hanging over them was the last thing they needed.

He levelled her with an icy gaze. 'What do you want?'

'Money,' she replied promptly. 'Enough to get out of Dublin and away from those brutes.'

She tucked her black hair behind one ear and he saw it: the faint trace of a healing bruise on her cheek.

He exhaled slowly. 'Very well. I'll get you some money.' Bridget twitched but he continued to avoid her eye.

'You better,' Thomasina said. 'It'll go badly for your daughter if you don't.'

He took a protective step in front of Emily. 'Don't you *dare* threaten my daughter,' he growled.

'Oh, is she your daughter too?' Thomasina bared her teeth. 'No, I mean your *other* daughter.'

He was certain he had misheard. Two wagons were passing each other on the street just then and the drivers were shouting greetings and good-natured obscenities to one another. They were so loud that he could convince himself he had not heard Thomasina properly.

But one glance at Bridget's frozen countenance told him he had.

He shook his head. 'You're lying,' he said to Thomasina.

She looked genuinely hurt. 'Why, because all whores lie?'

'No, because it's not possible,' Bridget bit out, addressing Thomasina for the first time. Her voice shook on the last word.

Thomasina winked at Cormac. 'Been keeping me a secret, have you?' She crossed her arms and jutted out her chin. 'Sorry to disappoint, lovie. The brat's yours. Born on Valentine's Day after the summer you ran off without a trace.'

He closed his eyes briefly. He had bedded Thomasina a month before he boarded the ship to England. A birth the following February added up and meant the child was four years old now. His insides churned. Could it really be true? When he opened his eyes, both Bridget and Thomasina were staring at him expectantly.

Despising himself, he mumbled to Bridget, 'It's possible.'

A tiny gasp escaped her, while Thomasina looked smug.

Wanting to quash that infuriating satisfaction, he retorted, 'But it's not beyond all doubt. How many other men did you service around that time? What proof is there that the child is definitely mine?'

Her face fell and he was dismayed to see tears welling in her eyes. 'There's no need to be so vulgar, 'specially with little ears listening.' She motioned to Emily, who had tucked herself under Bridget's arm. 'As a matter of fact, I was…less active 'round that time. I took ill, but you never noticed 'cause you were acting like I didn't exist after what had happened between us. And then by the time I knew for sure, you were already gone.'

He felt rotten, for the way he had treated her then and the way he was treating her now. Holy God, what was he supposed to do?

Bridget looked like she was biting the tip of her tongue hard enough to draw blood. But when she spoke, her tone was surprisingly gentle. 'Do you want him to acknowledge her? To give your daughter his name? Tell us what you seek from him.'

Thomasina appeared taken aback at her unexpected ally. 'Just the money. I want to take Henny away and live in the

222

country, far from the misery and violence and dirty dealings that go on in that place. That's all I want.'

'Henny?' said Cormac. 'That's her name?'

'Henrietta.' Thomasina's lip twisted wryly. 'I called her that so both of us would be reminded that our mas wanted boys instead.'

They were all silent after that, a cluster of mute figures in the midst of the street's hectic activity.

Thomasina gnawed on her full bottom lip. Hesitantly, like the thought had never occurred to her, she said to Cormac, 'D'you...d'you want to meet her?'

Bridget answered for him. 'Yes,' she said. 'Could you bring her here tomorrow? We can give you the money then as well.'

Thomasina squinted at her. Cormac couldn't blame her if she was doubting Bridget's motives, because he was wondering about them too. 'You mean it?' she said.

Bridget nodded, her face an impassive mask.

Thomasina tugged her shawl a little tighter around herself. 'We'll be here tomorrow afternoon so. Come at five. If yous don't show up, I'll go straight to Cunningham.'

She spun on her heel and went back to O'Hara's, slipping through the door with one final backward glance.

Cormac dredged up the courage to look at Bridget and was unsurprised to see her mask fracturing, shafts of fury glinting in the cracks.

'Feel free to slap me,' he said. 'It might make us both feel better.'

'I certainly don't want to do anything to make *you* feel better,' she said, her voice brittle. 'Nor do I wish to strike you in front of Emily. Perhaps I'll save it for later.'

He fiddled with the handle on his valise. 'I won't try to stop it when it comes. You must consider me an awful cad.'

'I don't think you grasp why I'm so furious,' she snapped. 'It's not because you lay with another woman.'

She jabbed her finger in the centre of his chest. 'It's the fact that you *lied* to me about it.'

He rubbed the back of his clammy neck. 'I do see now that it was a colossal mistake to do that. But my encounter with Thomasina was not something I was proud of. I preferred to forget it had ever happened.'

'Well, you can't forget about it anymore,' she said with a short, grim laugh. 'There were consequences to what you did.' She added, almost plaintively, 'Do you think she's telling the truth?'

He blew out his cheeks. 'God, I don't know. I'd rather not believe her, but I'm so afraid it's true.'

'We may have a clearer idea tomorrow. That's why I agreed that we should meet Henrietta. If she takes after her mother, we shall be no better informed. But if she has Emily's colouring...'

They both looked down at Emily who peeked up at them with interest. 'Colouring? Can I take out my watercolour box?'

'Not right now, *a stór*,' said Cormac. 'Let's keep walking for the time being.'

He urged Bridget and Emily onwards and they moved down the street until O'Hara's was no longer in view.

It felt like a nest of snakes had taken up residence in the pit of his stomach, writhing and trying to slither up his throat. He was disgusted with himself. How could he have let this happen – twice?

The revelation about Emily had been a wonderful discovery, an unforeseen marvel that had taken his breath away with joy. Henrietta was a shock of quite a different kind. If she was truly his, she had been conceived in an act between virtual strangers that had been without love or even tenderness, only lust and a dull rage.

He heard Bridget gulp in a lungful of air. Pale-faced, she said, 'If she is your child, you cannot forgo your responsibilities to her.'

'I know,' he said at once. Now that he was aware of the

situation, he could not shy away from it. But he didn't have a notion how Thomasina or Henrietta might fit into the future he planned to share with Bridget and Emily, and the rest of his family if they were ever found.

'For now, let's return to our original purpose, shall we?' he said and was relieved to receive a nod of acquiescence in response. He supposed he wouldn't see the full extent of her anger until they were alone.

They continued along Meath Street, on the lookout for signs displaying any type of accommodation. Cormac got his hopes up when they found two more sets of lodgings, both in better condition than O'Hara's, but neither of the proprietors recognised the description of his family at all.

They came to a corner where another narrower street met Meath Street. At first glance, the buildings appeared to be more residential than mercantile. On impulse, Cormac led Bridget and Emily down it. This was not an area he had ever wandered into during his period of poverty in Dublin. As he gazed around, he realised that, despite the fact that the inhabitants could boast of a roof over their heads, they were not much better off than he had ever been. The dwellings squatted in a long, sullen line on either side of the street and made O'Hara's look like a palace. Many of them had no doors, and most of their windows were cracked, broken or altogether missing. Rubbish littered the ground and the smell of hops could not quite conceal the odour of human waste. There were some people walking along the footpaths here too but they lacked the purpose of those hurrying up and down Meath Street and were far more bedraggled.

Cormac sensed Bridget's unease as two men across the way gave them a hard stare.

'We won't linger here long,' he assured her.

He halted at the next open doorway and decided to make an enquiry within. The way these rundown houses practically sat on top of each other, it was reasonable to assume that the occupants would be familiar with their neighbours and, judging from the attitude of the two men who were still watching them closely, suspicious of strangers. If a family of five had roamed into their midst, someone would have noticed.

Taking the glares of mistrust into account, he debated whether it was wise to bring Bridget and Emily inside.

'I'll just take a brief look myself,' he said. 'If it seems unsafe, we won't go any further.'

As he stepped across the threshold straight into the front room, he glimpsed six or seven scrawny figures crouched in the shadows. Low voices told him there were more people in another room beyond, and sporadic footsteps tapped on the ceiling above. He put out his hand to make sure Bridget and Emily did not follow him in. It was a tenement building, with numerous inhabitants occupying a space designed for far fewer. These poor souls were only a hair's breadth away from destitution and he knew from past experience that such people were dangerous when their territory was threatened.

Proving his point, one of the figures in the front room leapt up, a youth with a scarred face and a hostile expression.

'There's no more space,' he said roughly.

'I'm not looking to stay,' Cormac said in a clear, calm voice. 'I'm just searching for some people.'

'You won't find any of *your* people here.' The youth narrowed his eyes at Cormac's clothes which, while plain and unassuming, were still finer than anything worn by the ragged occupants of this tenement.

'If I could just—'

'Get out!' the fellow yelled, raising two clenched fists.

Bridget and Emily both jumped in fright behind Cormac. It was time to retreat – he did not want to risk putting them in danger and there was no telling what the youth might do to force him out.

Then he heard another voice say, 'What's going on?' and the frail form of an old man emerged from the back room.

He looked weak with hunger and clung to the door frame for support.

'Intruders,' growled the youth.

Cormac lifted his free hand in a non-threatening gesture. 'I only wish to ask about some family relatives and then I'll be on my way.'

'You can be on your way right—'

'Shut up, Marty,' the old man said wearily. He offered Cormac an apologetic shrug. 'He don't like strangers. You're best off leaving.'

'I understand,' said Cormac. 'But could I just take one moment of your time to ask if you know of a family named McGovern? Or if you remember a woman, three girls and a baby who might have been in this vicinity seven or eight years ago?'

The old man shrugged again. 'I wasn't here then.'

Cormac started to turn away.

'But Tess was,' the old man added. 'You could ask her. She knows everyone 'round these parts.'

'Tess?' Cormac repeated. 'Where is she?'

A third shrug. 'She's not here right now. Can't say when she'll be back.'

'Might she be here tomorrow?' Cormac pressed.

'She might. She might not. Tess makes her own rules.'

Cormac nodded. 'Very well. I'll call again and hope our paths will cross. Thank you for the information.'

The old man said nothing. Marty was still simmering with hostility, so Cormac backed out and rejoined Bridget and Emily beyond the doorstep.

'You heard all that?' he asked.

'Yes,' said Bridget. 'It's better than another dead end. Perhaps this Tess will know something.'

'I hope so.' He shot her a guilty look. 'And I suppose this means we have two reasons to return to this area tomorrow.'

She pursed her lips. 'I suppose it does.'

Chapter 18

They took a hackney to Merrion Square that evening and Bridget was glad of it, not caring one jot about its shabby appearance and grubby interior. It felt positively regal after their long day walking the Dublin streets. Her fingers ached from carrying the valise and she suspected she had a blister on her left foot. Emily, the little angel, had lasted as well as she could but she had grown more and more fractious as time wore on until Cormac had agreed it was best to call a halt to their search for the day. They had left the Liberties with no better lead than the absent Tess and a great deal of unpleasantness to process.

Bridget avoided Cormac's gaze as they were jolted about inside the hackney. She was still trying to come to terms with what she had learned today. He had lied to her, and so successfully that she had not had an inkling of the deceit. She knew he had been a practised liar in his guise of Oliver Davenport, but she had made the arrogant and erroneous assumption that she was immune to his abilities. Now her trust in him had taken a blow and she wondered what else he might still be keeping concealed. If she asked him outright, would she recognise the truth?

But then, she had lied to him too. She had said her wrath wasn't attributable to the fact that he had lain with another woman...except that it was. His admission of it had stung bitterly. He had led her to believe that she was and would forever be the only woman to know him in that intimate way. But now there was Thomasina with her sultry smiles and full lips and Bridget could not stop herself from picturing the two of them together, their bodies entangled

228

and those luscious lips pressed to places they had no business being.

Her heart ached. He had given something so precious to someone he clearly held no regard for – a physical transaction, nothing more. She herself had been obliged to carry out such emotionless transactions in her marriage bed but she couldn't conceive of the idea of doing so voluntarily. A sense of dismal disillusionment filled her.

Emily tugged on her arm. 'I'm hungry,' she whined.

They had eaten a swift meal at a tavern earlier – in a snug away from the disgruntled men who frowned upon the presence of a woman and a child in their domain – but that had been hours ago.

'We'll have supper very soon,' Bridget promised. She did not know what kind of supper the cook at Courcey House might be able to prepare for them at such short notice but it would do fine, despite her uncle's opinions on the matter.

Part of her wished they were returning to Rutland Square for the night. Her affection for her uncle had grown immensely in consequence of his revelations the previous day and, besides, she would have liked to check that he had not keeled over since they had departed after breakfast.

But another part of her acknowledged the sense in making the staff at Courcey House aware of their presence in Dublin. They needed to ensure no suspicion would be aroused should Mr Brereton find the need to send a message there.

Cormac cleared his throat and she glanced at him; he looked uncomfortable and she got the impression that more unwelcome news was on its way.

'I think we should only stay in Merrion Square for one night,' he said.

'Why?' They had been on the move for so long now that it was an attractive prospect to reside in one place for a few days and not have to carry those accursed valises everywhere.

'I believe it would be wise not to settle for long in any single location while we're in the city.'

'Why?' she said again, sounding like Emily when she was in a particularly inquisitive mood.

He took off his cap and fidgeted with it in his lap. 'I would harbour some concern that we may soon be at risk of being followed.'

Alarmed, she said, 'What do you mean?'

He cringed. 'Thomasina,' he said, muttering her name like it was an expletive. 'After she disappears from Cunningham's lodgings, they will likely come looking for her. Not out of any worry for her personal welfare, but because they would consider her a piece of their property with no right to walk out of there whenever she pleased. If they trace her steps to Meath Street, they'll question Mrs O'Hara and she will be able to inform them that she's seen me.' He rubbed at the peak of his cap and then abruptly fixed his eyes on Bridget's. 'There's no doubt that they will attempt to hunt me down. We shall need to be vigilant. The best way to elude detection is to cover our tracks and never stay in any place for more than one night.'

Her resentment at hearing Thomasina's name on his tongue (which triggered an unpalatable image of their tongues converging in a heated kiss) was supplanted by fear. His apprehension was palpable: Cunningham and his men were to be avoided at all costs.

'Very well,' she mumbled as the hackney lurched to a halt.

'Merrion Square,' the driver called out.

They stepped down onto the footpath with their valises. Dusk was falling and the street lamps were being lit. As Cormac paid the driver, Bridget took Emily's hand and scanned the square, trying to get her bearings to identify Courcey House. In the next pool of light on the footpath, a well-dressed lady was approaching, accompanied by her maid.

'Good gracious,' Bridget heard her say. 'Who would have the indecency to show up to this square in a tatty contraption such as that?'

Startled, she thought she recognised the voice – and when the lady drew nearer and her auburn ringlets became discernible, she was left in no uncertainty. She turned towards the hackney, hoping to go unnoticed, but the lady came to a sudden standstill a few feet away.

'Bridget?' she exclaimed.

As Cormac froze next to her, Bridget turned back reluctantly, plastering a smile onto her face. 'Oh, my goodness, Madeleine!'

Her old friend stared at her, stunned. 'Good grief, what on earth brings you here?' She let out a happy laugh. 'I haven't seen you in so many years. I am speechless with delight!'

She stepped forwards as though to embrace Bridget but faltered. Her gaze focused upon the hackney she had derided so vocally, and then roved over Bridget's plain clothing and the minimal baggage she carried. It came to rest upon Cormac, who had finished paying the driver and had adopted a subservient attitude behind Bridget with his head lowered. As the hackney rolled away from them, Madeleine's bewildered expression returned to Bridget.

'What is going on here?' she asked, her brow furrowed.

Bridget kept her smile fixed in place. 'I made arrangements to sojourn in Dublin for a time. I have long been overdue a visit home to Ireland and I yearned to show my daughter the place where I spent my formative years.'

Madeleine looked down at Emily but, instead of gushing over her as most women were wont to do, she squinted back at Bridget.

'But where is Lord Wyndham? And why do you dress like that, and travel in such a conveyance? And this man –' She gestured towards Cormac. 'Why is *he* with you?'

231

'He is my manservant and escorted us on our journey.'

Madeleine shook her head, her ringlets bounding emphatically. 'That cannot be correct.' She peered at him. 'I recognise him by his hair. The shade of it is so distinctive.'

It was only then that Bridget realised Cormac had forgotten to replace his cap; it was clutched in his hand along with the valise he carried.

'Yes, you would have encountered him at Oakleigh when you came to visit that summer –'

'That is true,' Madeleine cut across her, 'but I have seen him more recently than that.' She glared. 'Although his hair and clothes were much dirtier at the time, I am certain it was him. I came upon him here, in this very square. *Begging.*'

Bridget cast a quick glance at Cormac and he gave her an infinitesimal nod. She scrabbled to amend her story.

'I admit he has had to cope with many struggles in the past. He travelled to London a few years ago to make a new life for himself. My husband and I agreed to offer him a position and he has given us no cause to regret it. He is very hard-working.'

'Forgive my impertinence,' said Madeleine, her voice hard, 'but I do believe you are lying to me.' All of a sudden, her jaw dropped and she said in a horrified whisper, 'Has he *abducted* you?'

Bridget clicked her tongue. 'Come now, you are letting your imagination run away with you.'

'Well then, tell me the truth and I won't have to imagine!'

Behind Madeleine, her maid was standing agog. There was no one else walking along the footpath on this side of the square but Bridget saw a curtain twitch in the window of the nearest house.

'I confess all is not what it seems,' she said, 'but we cannot discuss it out here in the open. Let us go inside and I can explain everything.'

Peeking about furtively, Madeleine scowled and said, 'Very well. Do you intend to stay at Courcey House?'

'We have yet to make our presence known,' said Bridget. 'And I expect the commotion that will ensue upon our arrival would not be conducive to a serious discussion between ourselves.'

Looking as though it pained her, Madeleine said, 'We shall go to my own residence then. I live here on the square now,' she added proudly.

She led the way along the footpath, chin in the air and her maid scuttling close behind her. Bridget, Cormac and Emily followed at a discreet distance.

'Miss Wallace, is that her name?' Cormac muttered.

'Mrs Matthew Parnell since her marriage,' Bridget replied in a low voice. 'She wed an acquaintance of Garrett's. They first met during his birthday celebrations at Oakleigh.'

'Are you going to tell her the truth?'

'I think I may have no choice.'

They trailed Madeleine down the next side of the square where she paused halfway along it. When they caught up to her, she said frankly, 'I cannot receive you in the drawing room. It would be inconceivable.'

Bridget concealed her sigh. 'Then receive us in whichever room you deem the most appropriate. The kitchens, perhaps?'

She meant it half in jest but Madeleine gave a grave nod. 'Yes, that ought to do.'

However, once inside the grand townhouse, Madeleine absurdly had to ask the surprised footman where to locate the kitchens and, once they got there, they found it in an uproar preparing for dinner because the master had sent a message to say that he would be late.

The housekeeper goggled to see her mistress below stairs but offered her own room for them to speak in private and even procured some biscuits for Emily. They shut the door on the noise from the kitchens and

Madeleine took the most comfortable chair, while Bridget and Emily sat at the housekeeper's small table. Cormac remained standing by the door, his posture tense.

'This is most unseemly,' said Madeleine with a sniff. 'Matthew may not have inherited his title yet but I shall be a viscountess one day and this subterfuge is really quite beneath me.'

'We can leave whenever you wish,' said Bridget tightly.

'Not until I hear it all.' Madeleine's eyes gleamed and it struck Bridget that she could very well be the topic of discussion in every drawing room in Dublin before the week was out.

'I suspect you have already guessed what is afoot,' she said. 'Do you need me to say it out loud?'

Madeleine's gaze flitted to Cormac and back to Bridget. 'Yes.'

Wondering if their past friendship would count for nothing after this, Bridget said, 'I shall not meander around the issue then. I am guilty of infidelity. Cormac is my lover and we have run away to be together.' She decided not to mention anything about Emily's parentage. Madeleine could draw her own conclusions if she was perceptive enough to see it.

Madeleine let out an abrupt breath. 'That is an even more fantastic tale than an abduction.'

Bridget splayed her hands out on the table. 'It's the truth.'

Incredulous, Madeleine said, 'What could have possessed you to do such a thing? Have you lost your mind?'

'I have not.'

'Pray, be rational,' Madeleine implored. 'You were a well-respected lady of London society. You had wealth, position, servants, a life of leisure. What would prompt you to discard all that for a miserable existence with a beggar? He can offer you nothing that Lord Wyndham does not already give you.'

'He offers me love.'

'You ought to know your place and keep to it rather than reaching for the ridiculous notion of love. It does not exist.'

'It does, and it transcends all else. I am far happier with Cormac than I ever was with Garrett. Our marriage was a failure.'

Madeleine's gaze darkened. 'That does not give you the right to abandon your vows whenever you choose. What woman is truly happy with her lot? The rest of us have learned to tolerate our circumstances. Why not you?'

Bridget read the jealousy in her old friend's eyes. She thought back to the letters she had received over the years in London, pages filled with reports of married bliss and family blessings. Had Madeleine been lying through her teeth every time she put pen to paper? That would have been Bridget's fate too, had she stayed with Garrett – decades of pretence for the sake of appearances.

'I know I have made the right decision,' she said quietly. Even the reality of Cormac's indiscretion with Thomasina could not change that.

Madeleine appeared not to hear her. Countenance brightening, she said, 'Perhaps there is still time for you to rectify your mistake and save your reputation. You could go back to London and beg Lord Wyndham's forgiveness. His anger might be great but I'm certain his gratitude would be greater.'

'There is no inducement in this whole world that would compel me to return to Garrett.'

'But your standing in society will be forever ruined,' Madeleine lamented. 'And your daughter! Good gracious, have you considered for one moment the damage you are inflicting upon her? She will be a social pariah for the rest of her life.'

They all looked at Emily who was munching contentedly on her biscuits. Cormac winced at the accusation but Bridget remained composed.

'We do not rank social status as a measure of happiness,' she said.

Madeleine threw her hands up in the air. 'What a luxury for you. And what a pity we cannot all afford to adopt such ideals. Might I point out, your misdeeds will be a detriment to those who must claim to have associated with you. I cannot fathom your selfishness.' She crossed her arms, sulky and reproachful.

Bridget set her jaw. 'Please accept my apologies for any inconvenience this may cause you.'

She wished they had never come here. She had been hopeful that Madeleine would relent as Lord Walcott had done, but there was no hint of understanding in the other woman's attitude.

Rising from the table, she said, 'I think we should leave now.'

'You are not going to Courcey House, are you?' Madeleine asked. At Bridget's nod, she touched her fingers to her lips, her expression shocked. 'How can you have the audacity? You will bring shame to the square.'

Before Bridget could reply, Cormac interjected, 'I believe we have had quite enough of your censure, Mrs Parnell. Our activities need be of no concern to you or the other inhabitants of this square.'

Madeleine displayed the usual surprise that came from those who did not expect any level of eloquence in Cormac's speech, but then her eyes blazed with anger. 'This cannot be permitted to happen. As soon as Matthew comes home, I shall tell him what has transpired here and he will do all that is within his power to run you out of the square.' She raised her voice as Cormac opened the door and the sound of bedlam from the kitchens came rushing into the housekeeper's room. 'Furthermore, I shall press him to write at once to Lord Wyndham to inform him where you are. It will only be a matter of time before you are traced and this farce is brought to an end.'

Appalled, Bridget urged Emily to her feet. 'Come,

gooseberry, we must go.' As Emily snatched up the last biscuit, Bridget said to Madeleine, 'I beg you to recall the friendship we once shared. Please do not act against us. We have no intention to cause harm to anyone else.'

'I am acting in your own best interests,' said Madeleine primly. 'You will comprehend that in due course.'

She tailed them back to the entrance of the house, clucking her disapproval. Just as they reached the front door, the footman opened it and Matthew Parnell came striding through. He checked at the sight of strangers in his home but Cormac, leading the way, did not stop. He brushed past Mr Parnell, beckoning Bridget and Emily to do the same.

As they hurried down the steps, they heard Madeleine say shrilly, 'Oh, Matthew, there is such a scandal. I beseech you to write to Lord Wyndham directly…'

Fleeing down the street, Bridget knew she would never see Madeleine again.

***

There was no question of them staying at Courcey House now, not even for one night; the necessity of disappearing into the city without a trace had become a more immediate consideration. Instead, Cormac posed once again as Bridget's manservant and left a message with the butler at Courcey House that his mistress and her husband were in Dublin but that they were residing with her uncle for a few days. Any letters addressed to her or Lord Wyndham could be forwarded to Rutland Square. They could trust Lord Walcott, he felt sure of that.

He didn't think it would be wise to avail of the gentleman's hospitality for a second night in a row, however, and neither he nor Bridget felt inclined to traipse all the way back across the Liffey again anyway, so they sought out a room in a nearby inn instead. Thanks to the anonymous letters he had been sending his mother for years, and even though he had given a portion to Liam and Ellen, money was not a significant problem for them at present – although their funds would take a blow after their meeting with Thomasina tomorrow.

As he closed the curtains across the narrow window of their room, he shot a guilt-ridden glance towards Bridget. She had finished tucking Emily into the low truckle bed – the little girl was already fast asleep – and was opening her valise to extract her nightdress.

'Do you want me to sleep on the floor?' he asked.

Her shoulders tightened and she did not look at him as she shook out the garment.

He shrugged out of his coat and draped it over the back of the single chair in the room. 'I'm ready for that slap too, if now is convenient for you.'

The corner of her mouth twitched but she covered it up by pursing her lips, tugging at a loose thread on one of the nightdress's cuffs.

He crossed over to her and turned his head, presenting his cheek. Her hand came up, but only to pat it lightly.

'I'm too tired to put the effort in,' she said.

'But you are still angry?' he said cautiously.

She returned her attention to the loose thread, plucking at it until it came free. 'I don't have any right to be. After all, neither of us believed we would ever meet again. You were entitled to engage in a relationship with whomever you chose.' She looked up at him. 'Though between Maisie McKinty and Thomasina, I am feeling like quite the jealous woman.'

'Don't be,' he said. '*Táim i ngrá leatsa amháin.*'

'You love only me,' she repeated in a murmur. 'I am very glad to hear it.'

He touched a gentle kiss to her forehead, but that was all.

She did not make him sleep on the floor.

Chapter 19

Cormac kept looking over his shoulder after they left the inn the next morning, valises in hand. It was too soon for Cunningham and his men to harbour suspicions about Thomasina's whereabouts for she would not flee the lodgings until that afternoon, and of course Matthew Parnell's letter would have to travel across the sea before Garrett would receive the information he needed to pursue them, but that did not prevent Cormac's nerves from jangling at every shout or striding step behind them. The Dublin streets seemed ominous, with unseen threats lying in wait around each corner.

The first place they visited was the premises of the Grace of God Mission Society. His mouth soured when he saw the bronze plaque and recalled the fleeting hope he had felt when he had lurched through those open double doors. The cruelty of this institution was unfathomable – how could they be in such an influential position to help the needy and yet only offer aid to those of their own Protestant religion?

Next to him, Bridget said, 'I received a letter from here once, in response to my futile attempts to locate you. The deacon said you refused to take their soup.'

He stared up at the deceptively welcoming facade. 'I couldn't conceive of renouncing the faith in which my parents had raised me. I could no more stop being a Catholic than I could stop being an Irishman. It's in my blood.' He sighed. 'And I suspect my mother would have been too devout to capitulate either.'

Nonetheless, they made their enquiries within. It was

not Deacon Haybury but a different deacon who greeted them. He was very pleasant and checked their register of converts but, as expected, he came across no one by the name of McGovern. He advised them where they could find other mission societies situated nearby and, with no better leads, they decided to visit them one by one.

Later in the morning, emerging from yet another of these institutions without success, Cormac spotted an establishment further along the street selling a variety of goods, including children's toys. On impulse, he went inside and purchased a doll to give to Henrietta. Bridget didn't comment but he wondered if she was thinking the same as him – would the gift be tantamount to an acknowledgement of fatherhood? Still, it would be unkind to meet the child empty-handed.

He could not neglect Emily so he bought a doll for her too and she gasped with delight upon receiving it.

'Oh, Papa,' she breathed, hugging it to her chest. 'She is just beautiful.'

As he gazed down at her happy face, so easy to please, he speculated on what Henrietta's reaction might be. Did she have any playthings of her own? What had her four years of life been like so far, growing up in that cesspit that was barely one step away from a brothel?

The day progressed with one negative response after another to all enquiries about his family. By the time they reached O'Hara's at ten minutes to five, Cormac's spirits were very low. After this, they would go back to the tenement, where he hoped the mysterious Tess would be present and able to impart some scrap of helpful information. But first, he had to brace himself for a meeting with Thomasina and her daughter.

When they entered the dingy front hall, Mrs O'Hara peered at them from behind her high counter with a gap-toothed sneer.

'Oh, it's yourself, is it? Come to take responsibility for your recklessness?'

He ground his teeth. 'Is Thomasina here?'

She jerked her head towards a door at the rear of the hall. 'They're in the back room. Thought yous would want a bit of privacy. Straight down to the end.'

He strode past her with a clipped word of thanks and pushed open the door she had indicated. Bridget and Emily followed him into a narrow, shadowy corridor. There was one door off to the side and another down at the end, both closed. He proceeded down the corridor, his stomach in knots at the coming encounter.

At the last possible second, it occurred to him that this might be a trap. What if Thomasina's plan was actually to hand him over to Cunningham via this ruse? Could Munroe and the other men be lurking behind the door?

'I've suddenly got a bad feeling,' he muttered to Bridget. 'If this turns out to be some sort of ambush, grab Emily and run out of here as fast as you can. I'll be right behind you.'

Eyes wide with alarm, she gave a shaky nod.

Taking a deep breath, he nudged open the door with his elbow, ready to forestall a blow if it came his way. Nothing happened. He stepped across the threshold and scanned the room swiftly. There were only two people in it and he loosened his held breath in relief – only for it to hitch again in his throat.

Thomasina was perched on a chair against the opposite wall, and next to her on a low stool sat her daughter. The girl was her offspring without a doubt for she was the image of her mother, with an identical head of black hair and the same shaped mouth in miniature form. Her simple frock, threadbare and stained, fell to her shins and beneath its hem she was barefoot. Cormac wished he had bought her shoes instead of a doll. He set his valise down on the floor as Bridget and Emily came in behind him. Bridget shut the door and stood awkwardly in front of it, looking like she didn't know whether she should partake in the conversation or not. Emily stared curiously, her new doll cradled in her arm.

Thomasina prodded Henrietta's shoulder. 'Go on, get up. Here he is.'

The girl got to her feet. She was small for her four years, a mere slip of a thing. She stuck a finger in her mouth and started biting the skin around the nail.

Thomasina stood too. 'Let me get this right,' she said. 'May I present Miss Henrietta Brennan?' She dipped into a mocking curtsey, wobbled and caught her balance with a laugh.

Cormac knelt in front of the little girl. 'Good afternoon, Henrietta,' he said.

She said nothing back, only kept gnawing on her finger. Her nails were caked with dirt. Flinching, he took a gentle hold of her wrist and coaxed the finger out of her mouth.

'It is nice to meet you,' he tried but she still did not speak.

He looked into her eyes, which were not his shade of vivid blue but a warm light brown. He had never taken much notice of Thomasina's eyes before but now he stole a glimpse to compare them to the girl's. They were also light brown – the only difference appeared to be some lighter golden flecks in Henrietta's irises. She took after her mother in practically every respect.

Her lack of fair hair and blue eyes alleviated some of his fears, though only marginally so. There was no solid evidence to say that she was his daughter, but equally there was nothing conclusive to say that she wasn't.

'Come on, Henny,' said Thomasina. 'Say "It's nice to meet you too after all these years". Tell him your favourite colour and the songs you like to sing. Y'know, things he'd already know if he'd been around.' She gave Cormac a wicked grin.

He did not credit her with a response. Instead, he reached behind him and pulled over his valise.

'I have a present for you,' he said and, withdrawing the doll from the valise, held it out to Henrietta.

242

She gazed at it and then peeked up at her mother. Thomasina's brow was puckered in surprise but she said, 'Go ahead, you can take it.'

Hesitant, Henrietta accepted the doll, clutching one arm gingerly.

'Do you know what to say when someone gives you a present?' Cormac asked her.

Thomasina glowered. 'She never gets presents, so no.' She prodded Henrietta's shoulder again. 'Say "Thank you", Henny.'

So quiet that she was scarcely audible, the girl whispered, 'Thank you.'

'You're very welcome.' Cormac rose and motioned to the stool. 'Do you want to sit again?'

She did as he suggested and he took the chair Thomasina had vacated.

'You'll have to come up with a name for her,' he said. 'What do you think you will call her?'

She didn't answer. Her grimy fingers were tracing the painted hair on the doll's head (black like her own), the closed mouth with its sombre expression, the wooden limbs, and the pretty cream dress with lace cuffs. She was wholly captivated by this new creature that now belonged to her.

Then she touched the doll's head to her cheek and, with a subtle splintering of his heart, it became clear to Cormac: all little girls just want someone to hug them.

Without thinking, he lifted her onto his knee and put his arm around her. She did not resist and leaned back against his chest, although her attention remained fixated on the doll.

He glanced at Bridget but her expression was unreadable. Thomasina was staring with open-mouthed astonishment. Emily walked past them both and came right up to Henrietta.

'I have one too,' she said, holding out her own doll. 'Do you want to play?'

243

Henrietta considered for a moment before sliding down off Cormac's knee. Emily led her over to the corner of the room and they hunkered there, Emily doing most of the chattering while the two dolls and the two girls – could they be half sisters? – met for the first time.

Cormac got up again, his legs somewhat unsteady. Thomasina threw him a baffled look.

'You must have a way with children,' she said. 'The brat usually runs and hides when she sees a man coming.'

He didn't like to think what kind of mistreatment Henrietta might have been subjected to by the men in the lodgings – they were liable to kick a child out of the way as easily as a dog.

'She's very small for her age,' he said reprovingly.

Thomasina arched an eyebrow. 'She's underfed. What did you expect?' She put her hands on her hips. 'We need to be going soon. Where's my money?'

He withdrew a pouch from the pocket of his coat; it jangled as he held it out to her. She snatched it from him and opened it to examine its contents.

'Make sure you use a portion of it to buy her some shoes and better clothes.'

She closed the bag, satisfied. 'I will.'

'Ow!' The cry came from the corner of the room. Emily swivelled to them with an injured expression, holding up her hand. 'She pinched me!'

Henrietta looked innocent, stroking her doll's head and balancing its feet on her bare toes.

Thomasina tutted at Emily. 'Or are you telling a fib, little miss tattler?'

Cormac frowned. 'You don't get to talk to her that way.'

'Well, we know who'll always be the favourite, won't we?' Thomasina said with a huff. Tucking the pouch of money inside her bodice, she snapped, 'Get up, Henny. We're leaving.'

Cormac felt a shard of unhappiness lodge inside his gut. Was that all the time they would have? It seemed far too short.

He caught Thomasina's elbow. 'Where are you going next?' he asked.

'Smithfield Market,' she said. 'I've made arrangements to meet a fellow there. He's going to take us north out of the city.'

He didn't ask who the fellow was and she didn't offer any further information, but he hoped he was a decent man who would treat her and Henrietta well. There had been a distinct shortage of decent men in their lives up to now, that was for sure.

As she shrugged out of his grip, he asked, 'Do you need anything else? Is there any other way I can help you both?'

She shook her head. 'I promise you'll never see us again.'

Bridget stepped aside as Thomasina stalked to the door. She hurried into the corridor beyond and Henrietta followed on her heels. The little girl didn't look back but she still grasped the doll tightly.

Cormac released a slow exhalation, while Bridget checked the red pinch mark on the back of Emily's hand and kissed it better. His mind was in a whirl. Surely he hadn't done enough. He ought to go after them and offer to do more – but then what exactly could he offer? He had no fixed abode right now and any sort of settled existence was impossible until he had found his family. Perhaps they were far better off without him.

Dispirited, he stooped over Emily and gave her a kiss too. She snuffled but shed no tears. Then, lacking the energy to discuss what had just happened, he said, 'Shall we go?'

Bridget nodded wordlessly. They picked up their valises and returned to the front hall. Mrs O'Hara flung a few more choice accusations at him but he didn't register what she said. Emerging onto the street, he swept his gaze in both directions but Thomasina and Henrietta had already vanished. With a sigh, he led Bridget and Emily along

245

Meath Street until they came to the corner where it crossed with the street of tenement buildings. They turned onto it and walked along until they found the one they had entered the previous day.

Marty was once again ready to disabuse them of any notion that their presence might be welcome. The scars on his face stood out vividly as he hollered, 'Get out of here!'

Cormac raised his voice to be heard over him. 'Don't you remember us from yesterday? We're looking for Tess, that's all. Is she here?'

'Go away!'

Exasperated, Cormac tried to see past Marty into the back room, wondering where the frail old man was. The silhouette of a figure appeared in the doorway – a womanly shape, shorter and curvier than the old man. She stepped through into the front room and Cormac got such a shock that he nearly fell over.

She was several years older and she had a harsher countenance but he would have recognised that distinctive shade of red hair anywhere. Although the only time he had ever met this girl was nearly five years ago, it was not an encounter easily forgotten: it had been his last night in Dublin before he had got on a ship out of the country and it had been her first night attempting to sell herself for money.

Her hair was still the same but her demeanour was quite different. In that warehouse on the docks she had seemed self-conscious, timid, hunched over with the shame of what she had tried and failed to do. Now she stood with her shoulders back and her chin thrust out, her manner self-assured and her gaze unsympathetic. Her rouged cheeks and painted lips, together with her low-cut bodice and the raised hem of her skirt which exposed an unseemly amount of ankle and stocking, led Cormac to the regrettable conclusion that he had not succeeded in turning her away from that objectionable profession.

She regarded them with suspicion. 'What d'yous want?'

He did not know what to say. 'Do you—do you remember me?'

Her eyes narrowed and then opened wide. She took a step back in amazement. It had been a long time ago but he supposed she would not easily forget the face of a stranger who had handed her a lot of money without expecting something in return.

'You!' she blurted. 'What're you doing here?'

'I'm looking for my family. I had no inkling that I might come across you.'

She started to say something else but Marty interrupted her. 'They've got to leave. There's no space for them.'

'I have already told you that we don't want to stay,' Cormac said stridently.

Marty's eyes flashed and he took several menacing paces forwards. Cormac felt Bridget tugging at the back of his coat to pull him out of harm's way, but Tess put a firm hand on the youth's shoulder.

'Marty, we've talked about this. If your behaviour gets too out of hand, we'll throw you out. Calm down. These people aren't going to harm you.'

He still looked mutinous, growling low in his throat. She shook her head and turned to Cormac.

'Maybe we should speak outside. I was getting ready to leave anyway.'

Her day's work was only about to start, he inferred, but he just nodded.

'I've got to fetch my shawl. I'll meet yous out there in a moment.' She disappeared into the back room.

He felt the heat of Marty's glare and ushered Bridget and Emily back out to the footpath where they waited for Tess to emerge. The same two men from yesterday were once again scrutinising them from across the street.

'Who is she?' Bridget demanded, and it was plain she was beginning to fear he had bedded all the scarlet women in Dublin.

'I was never a customer of hers,' he hastened to assure

her. 'She was barely more than a child when we met. Do you recall, when I told you about my past, I mentioned saving a girl from a thug and giving her some money? She's that girl.' He blinked. 'That incident was actually what prompted me to board the same ship as Oliver Davenport. I suppose we have a great deal to thank her for, when you think about it.'

The distrust faded from Bridget's expression and she looked relieved. 'Perhaps we do.'

He felt sad for Tess. She had seemed so young back then but now she appeared old beyond her years. Life on the streets had toughened her, and she had been compelled to assume the most unspeakable occupation for a woman. Of course, he could not condemn her when he recollected the path he had been forced to take himself, but he was sorry that the money had not helped her enough to avoid it.

She materialised in the doorway a minute later with a frayed shawl wrapped around her shoulders, concealing her low-cut attire. She joined them on the footpath and the two men opposite turned away, satisfied.

Cormac offered her a smile. 'So your name is Tess?'

'Teresa,' she said. 'Tess to my friends,' she added, one corner of her mouth upturned. 'Sorry about Marty. He gets awful fretful 'round strangers.' She stared at him in wonderment. 'I never thought I'd see you again.'

'Nor I you. This is quite the chance encounter, just like that night was.'

She gave a wistful smile. 'I used to think of you as my guardian angel. I longed so much for you to reappear so's I could thank you right.'

Bridget cleared her throat; from Tess's ardent gaze, it was not hard to guess in what manner she would have liked to thank him. He hastily introduced Bridget and Emily so that the relationship boundaries could be made quite clear. Tess looked Bridget up and down, disappointment registering on her face. This was palpably not how she had imagined the scene playing out.

Discomfited, Cormac said, 'I hope the money was a help to you?'

'Oh,' she said, focusing on him again. 'Yes, it helped us a lot.'

'Us?'

'I shared it with my friends.'

'That was generous of you,' he said, surprised. 'Alone, that money could have lasted you for months.'

She shrugged. 'Their ma was sick. She needed it more than I did.'

'I take it that it was not long then before you had to...' He trailed off.

Her eyes hardened. 'That's none of your business. I did what I had to do. Now, if you'll 'scuse me.'

She swung her red hair over her shoulder and brushed past them.

'Wait,' he called after her. 'I did not mean to offend you. But I just have one question to ask you before you go. Please.'

He was not sure why she stopped and turned around, but maybe she felt she owed him for the good deed he had done for her so long ago.

'What is it?' she said irritably.

He set down his valise, holding out his hands in a conciliatory way. 'We are looking for some members of my family who have been missing for many years. Their last known whereabouts is only around the corner from here so there is a high possibility that they may have wandered into this area. We were led to believe that you know the local inhabitants better than anyone. All I am asking is if you can tell me whether they ever came to this street or even whether they might still be here now.'

She folded her arms. 'Not likely. Most of the people 'round here are new enough. We'd a disease that wiped out a lot of us a couple of winters ago.'

He flinched.

'Sorry,' she said, softening a little. 'Maybe your family

249

was lucky. What do they look like?'

He repeated the familiar description. 'A woman, three girls — two in their adolescence and the third a good deal younger — and a newborn baby boy, although he must be nearly eight years old by this stage. They all have dark hair and their surname is McGovern.'

She stumbled backwards, total disbelief written all over her features. She seemed too stunned to speak.

Hope rose in Cormac. He took an urgent step towards her. 'Do you know them?'

She stared open-mouthed at him. At last, she whispered, 'Are you Maggie's boy?'

He felt a burst of emotion inside him. 'I am!' Was she about to tell him that his mother was inside that very tenement building? Was he on the verge of being reunited with his sisters? 'Are they here? How do you know my family?'

She hesitated for the longest time before answering. 'They were my friends.'

He heard her use of the past tense but he did not want to acknowledge it.

'Where are they?' he demanded. 'Where is my mother?'

She was unwilling to meet his gaze. 'Your mother's dead,' she said softly.

Something seemed to have happened to Cormac's senses. Tess continued to speak but her voice had grown distorted and distant, and everything around him had gone foggy. The boulder in the pit of his stomach, his constant companion throughout his search for his missing family, felt like a ton weight. He became vaguely conscious of a pair of arms encircling him but he could not move, either to lean into the embrace or shake it off. It was only when he felt a pressure on his right knee that he regained a proper sense of awareness and glanced down. Emily was hugging his leg and staring up at him with huge eyes.

She should not have to hear any of this.

'Let's go somewhere,' he muttered. 'I need to hear it all from the start.'

Tess shook her head. 'I can't. Time's passing. I've got places to be.'

'Forget about that tonight.'

'That's easy for you to say,' she said, her tone rising. 'You won't be the one with no money for food in the morning.'

'I will give you money,' he said, digging his hand into his pocket and pulling out some coins.

She eyed the money but did not take it. 'I'm not going to be in your debt again.'

'There will be no debt.' His voice was laced with desperation. 'You know what happened to my family and I am offering payment for that information. It will be a fair exchange. Please, I am begging you.'

She twisted her lips as she weighed up his proposal. Then she relented. 'Fine so.'

He looked at Bridget, whose arms were still around him. 'We should put Emily to bed. This is not for her ears.'

She nodded in agreement, pain and compassion in her eyes.

Chapter 20

They had to walk the length of several streets before they located an inn in the vicinity that seemed reputable enough. They paid for two rooms beside each other and, after cajoling Emily into eating a bowl of watery stew from the inn's available fare, put her to bed in one of the rooms. It was early in the evening but she was so exhausted from their day's walking that she did not gripe. Bridget hummed a lullaby to her and Cormac silently stroked her hair, while Tess observed without comment, her brows drawn together with something like envy.

Once Emily had fallen asleep, they went into the other room so that they could talk freely. The only furniture in the room was a bed and two worn chairs with arms by the window. Cormac offered Tess a chair but she sat on the edge of the bed so he and Bridget claimed the chairs. The light outside was still bright, although the timbre of it implied that twilight was not far away.

'Would you care for something to eat too?' Bridget said to Tess. 'We can ask the innkeeper to bring it up.' She did not suggest food for herself or Cormac and he was glad; he didn't think he would be able to stomach it.

'No, thanks,' said Tess. 'Best be getting on with it.' She dropped her shawl onto the bedcover and pulled her mane of red hair over one shoulder; it was long enough to reach the top of her bodice and covered the swell of one breast, though the other remained exposed. 'So what d'yous want to know?'

'Everything,' said Cormac, both dreading and aching to hear the truth. 'Don't omit a single detail. Where did you

252

first encounter my family?'

'Right in that shelter where yous met me this evening. It was their first winter in the city. They always said afterwards if I hadn't found them they'd all have been dead by New Year's. And they were right—that winter was cruel. But I'd been on the streets for three years at that stage and I knew how to survive.' She crossed one leg over the other, showing even more of her stockings. 'I had different hideouts but I often went to that place because there was a black boy who would trade blankets and things. I stumbled upon your family in one of the rooms upstairs. They were starving. It was a miracle the poor baby was still alive. At first, I was just going to ignore them—I wasn't too keen on trying to help others when I could hardly feed myself—but I took pity on them. The mother, Maggie, reminded me of my own ma before she died. She had kind eyes.'

Cormac twitched but said nothing.

'The building was in better shape then than it is now. If you were lucky enough to have a blanket, it was possible to warm up a little. Maggie used to stay there with Orlaith and the baby while I took Margaret and Bronagh out and showed them the best places to find food.'

At the sound of his sisters' names, Cormac gripped the arms of his chair. Bridget reached out and placed her hand over his.

'We survived that winter, every single one of us. Another girl in the shelter had recently lost her own newborn baby so she wet-nursed Patrick. I was sure he wouldn't make it but he was a strong boy. Then we'd a fine summer and it was much easier to find food. We all became very close and Maggie said I was like another daughter to her.' Tess bowed her head and fingered the unravelling hem of her shawl, hiding whatever emotion her face might have revealed. 'The next winter was mild but the following winter was much worse. Your ma took ill and she didn't get better when the spring came. We

253

didn't know what sickness it was but she had fever and chills and coughed all the time. I tried to steal some medicine from an apothecary but I was caught and whipped before I could get away. We wondered if we should take her to the workhouse but she wouldn't hear of being parted from her girls. Our last resort was to pay for the medicine and we knew there was only one way to get the money. The night I met you' – Tess nodded at Cormac – 'was the first time Margaret and I went walking the streets.'

'But you were just girls,' said Bridget in a hushed tone. 'You were just two young girls.'

Tess's mouth contorted into a hard smile. 'For some men, it's the younger the better. But I didn't have to go through with it 'cause my guardian angel appeared with more money than I'd ever seen in my life. Poor Margaret wasn't so lucky though. She had to see it through and her customer was quite brutal with her. She was in pain for days afterwards.'

Cormac shut his eyes. That was his sweet sister she was talking about. Gentle, kind Margaret, reduced to a whore. If only it had been her and not Tess whom he had come across that night in the warehouse, he could have put an end to all this.

He heard Tess continue: 'Between the two of us, we'd gathered enough money to buy some decent food and the medicine for Maggie. The apothecary said it would work if she took it for long enough. But it got used up quick so we went out again. I hoped my guardian angel would appear to me a second time but no such luck. It came to be a regular thing for us. Maggie didn't know what we were doing. Margaret told her we were making money by selling flowers on the street and Maggie believed her.'

Tess paused. When she spoke again, her voice was fainter. 'What happened next was unexpected. Maggie was the one who was sick and we concentrated all our efforts on trying to make her better. But what I didn't

254

know, and what your other sisters didn't know, was that Margaret had also fallen ill. It wasn't the same disease your ma had. I reckon it was something she picked up on the streets. She hid it as long as she could but it got so bad she couldn't keep it from us anymore. She'd a fever too so we tried to give her some of Maggie's medicine but she wouldn't take it. By the end she couldn't breathe proper and she got awful confused. It was unbearable to watch. She faded very fast and died one night in July. I'd known her less than three years.'

Cormac felt angry tears pricking his closed eyelids. While Margaret had been dying, he had been studying mathematics and philosophy at Bewley Hall. While his mother and sisters had been struggling to keep their family together, he had adopted a new aunt and uncle for himself. It was appalling.

Sighing, Tess said, 'After that, your ma gave up. There's no other way to describe it. She'd suffered too much and it was agony for her to try to bear the loss of yet another child. Even though she'd two daughters and a grandson yet alive, she just let go. I did all I could to convince a medical man to come see her but it was too late. She died only four days after Margaret.'

Cormac's hands whipped up to his head. He grabbed fistfuls of his hair and pulled as hard as he could. He needed to feel pain, he needed to punish himself, he needed to suffer. His mother had endured so much beyond what any person should have to tolerate in one life. He was consumed by immeasurable guilt; the night of sweet innocence he and Bridget had shared in the hay barn had set off the chain of events that had led to this unutterable horror. If he could turn back the clock and find his mother and transfer all of her pain onto himself, he would do it in an instant and he would be full of gladness that her torment was now his – it was no more than he deserved.

'Cormac, stop,' he heard Bridget whisper and felt her

tugging at his hands.

Dispirited, he let them drop to the arms of his chair again. Opening his eyes, he saw the tears on Tess's cheeks. She must have been very devoted to his family to go to such extreme lengths to try to save his mother.

'What about the others?' he said lifelessly. 'Bronagh, Orlaith and Patrick. How did they die?'

'They're not dead,' said Tess. 'Or at least, I don't think so anyway.'

He leapt from his chair, shock blazing through his veins.

'What?' he cried. 'I thought they were all dead! Why did you not take me to them at once when you found out who I was?'

''Cause I don't know where they are!' she responded with equal heat. 'It's been years since I've seen them.'

He tried to calm himself but remained on his feet. 'When was your last contact with them?' he asked, keeping his voice as steady as he could.

Still looking insulted, she said, 'A couple of months after Margaret and Maggie died. Bronagh was the first to disappear. We woke up one morning and she was gone. I think she ran away and my guess is she went to America. She used to talk about it a lot, even when her ma and sister were still alive. She wanted us all to go, thought we'd have a better chance of survival there. But by that stage Maggie was already too weak to walk, let alone travel on a ship, and where would we've gotten the money for six tickets anyway? After Maggie's death, Bronagh became so withdrawn. I figured it was her own way of dealing with her grief but now I think she was distancing herself to make it easier to leave. Selfish maybe, but it would've been the right thing for her own sake.'

That sounded like Bronagh, fierce and fearless. Only she would contemplate crossing the ocean to a new continent all by herself.

'So she might still be alive,' Cormac said with a measure of relief.

'She might,' Tess acknowledged.

'And Orlaith and Patrick? Do you know what happened to them?'

Tess's shoulders drooped. 'Poor little Orlaith. She'd to grow up so fast. She was laden with adult concerns at the age of only eight. I was willing to look after her and Patrick but she said I'd done enough for her family and she didn't want to burden me any longer. She began leaving the shelter every morning with Patrick and coming back very late at night. She'd never tell me where they'd been. This went on for weeks. Then one day they returned and she said it was the last time I'd see them. They came back just to say goodbye. I begged her to tell me where they were going but she refused. She claimed she was too ashamed of what she'd done.'

Cormac blanched. 'Not Orlaith too…'

'No. She swore to me she hadn't resorted to that. But it was still something so disgraceful she wouldn't speak of it. We hugged and they left. I haven't laid eyes on them from that day to this.'

He sank back into his chair. 'So they may still be alive but we have no idea where. They could be gone to America too, for all we know.'

Tess hesitated. 'I don't think so. I've a feeling they're still in Dublin.'

He looked up sharply. 'Why do you say that?'

'That black boy in our shelter, Eli. He came and went as he pleased and he'd an awful temper but he always had a soft spot for little Orlaith. Used to give her spare bits of food and the like. He buggered off to some other hideout a while back but I bumped into him about a year ago in an alley behind a grocer's shop and he told me he thought he'd seen Orlaith the previous week.'

Cormac's breath snagged in his throat. 'Where?'

'On a square of fine houses in the centre of the city. He goes scavenging there every now and then 'cause rich people throw out so much good food. I've always stayed

257

away. There are more constables on watch and I don't want to risk getting caught. But I went there after what Eli told me. He said the girl had looked like Orlaith from a distance and she'd been wearing maid's clothes so I wondered if she'd managed to get employment in one of the houses. I searched 'round for her but I never saw her walking on the street and I couldn't exactly go knocking on doors. So I left and I didn't go back again. It's possible Eli was mistaken.'

'It is also possible that he was correct,' said Cormac, getting fired up again. It was the slimmest of leads but he was going to cling to it with all he had. 'In the morning, I want you to come with us to this square. We will keep looking for Orlaith and Patrick until we find them.'

Bridget bobbed her head fervently beside him. Tess nodded too and wiped her eyes on the corner of her shawl.

A sudden thought occurred to Cormac. 'This Eli. He had black skin? Did he have a milky eye too, by any chance?'

Tess gaped. 'He did. How did you know?'

Cormac rubbed his hand over his mouth. 'I believe we bumped into each other once. He tried to steal from me.'

Tess gave a cracked chuckle. 'That sounds like Eli.'

Cormac remembered how the black youth had attempted to wrest his blanket from him – the only thing he had possessed at the time apart from the clothes on his back. Now he wondered whether Eli had been thieving the blanket for further trade or to give as a gift to Orlaith. Anguish welled in him. How could his path have been so close to his family's and yet never actually crossed? If only he had known...could he have saved them?

He swallowed. 'Ma and Margaret. What happened to their bodies?'

Tess winced. 'I was hoping you wouldn't ask that.' Embarrassment coloured her cheeks and her gaze flicked away from him. 'Dublin's known for its medical men but they need to practise their skills to improve their knowledge. Their lackeys are on the lookout everywhere. If they're not grave robbing, they're hunting for corpses in the poorer parts of the city and they'll usually give a few coins. Two fellows came looking that July and I—I let them t-take—' She stuttered to a stop. Then, very formally, she said, 'Please forgive me. It was a hideous thing to do.'

'There is nothing to forgive,' said Cormac, even though it distressed him to imagine what had happened next. 'On the contrary, I am so very grateful to you. Thank you for everything you did for my family. They were lucky to have you as their friend.'

'I don't think luck was something they had much of.' She sniffed. 'I was happy to do anything I could to help them. They were such kind people and they never harmed anyone but this city just kept battering them 'til they couldn't get back up.' Her chin trembled. 'They meant a great deal to me. They were the closest thing I had to a real family after my own ma was gone.'

It had grown darker in the room as the daylight faded outside but no one moved to light a lamp.

Tess fingered a lock of her red hair. 'They used to talk about you all the time.'

Cormac felt deeply sad at this. 'Did they?'

'Maggie said you were an exact copy of your da in both looks and talents. There was nothing you couldn't do with a piece of wood. And Margaret always talked about how good you were with animals, 'specially horses. They never knew what happened to you but they hoped and prayed you were alive and well, wherever you were. Except—' All of a sudden, she fell silent.

'Except what?' he said, startled.

She pressed her lips together and her forehead creased. 'They were troubled,' she said in a low voice. 'We heard rumours of a vicious thug on the streets. He worked for that bastard money lender, Cunningham, and he went by the name of McGovern. He was ruthless. He terrorised the people who owed Cunningham money and even threatened their small children to make them pay up. Your family feared this man might be you 'cause of the name, but they hoped it was just a coincidence. Maggie couldn't believe her son would be capable of doing such things.'

The atmosphere in the room became tense. Cormac felt an icy chill run down his back. His family had heard about the despicable things he had done. They had not been certain it was him but they had harboured some suspicions. Wretched shame coursed through him. His throat tightened and he could not speak.

Tess stared at him with dawning horror as the silence lengthened between them. She swallowed audibly. Then, grabbing her shawl, she bounded to her feet and ran for the door.

Cormac got there just as she wrenched the door open with her two hands. He slammed it shut and stood in her way so she could not get past. She backed into a corner of the room, a mixture of terror and revulsion on her face. Her gaze flipped from Cormac to Bridget, who had also jumped up from her chair, and back to Cormac.

'Please understand—' he started but she cut him off.

'I don't want to hear what you've got to say,' she hissed. 'For the first time, I'm glad your family's no longer here. At least they never had to learn the horrible truth. They would've been heartbroken.'

'I know that.' The thought of it made his gut twist. 'I hate myself for what I did. It is a period of my life that I utterly regret. But I was desperate. I was as poverty-stricken as the rest of you when I came to Dublin and it was the only way I could stay alive. You know what that feels like. You have been forced to resort to an abject level of conduct as well.'

'My actions have harmed no one but myself,' she countered. 'We heard such terrible stories of cruelty. You laughed in the faces of mothers who begged for their children's lives. You took more than what borrowers owed just to line your own pockets. You tortured people for fun.'

He listened to these accusations with deep shock. 'The rumours you heard were grossly exaggerated. I never did any of those things.'

'You're a liar.' Her expression was full of loathing. 'I should've realised who you were. Back in the warehouse when you pulled a knife on that first disgusting customer of mine, you said you worked for Cunningham. But he'd a lot of toughs working for him. You could've been any one of them. And then I found out your name today but I still didn't make the connection. I'm such a fool.'

'Listen to me,' he said in exasperation. 'Yes, I worked for Cunningham but that was a long time ago and I am not that person anymore. You have spent this evening in my company. You can see that I have a child with me. Have I given any reason, by my behaviour or my language, for you to be afraid? I am not a threat to you or to anyone else.'

'You're a piece of slime. And slime just gets slimier over the years.'

He was astounded by the vitriol coming from the girl's mouth. She despised the person she believed him to be. But her opinion was based on hearsay which was wildly inaccurate – he could never have stooped so low as to torture someone for enjoyment. He was unable to fathom how such lies had spread.

'I gave you all that money,' he pointed out. 'That was an unselfish act which does not correspond very well with your image of the fiend known as McGovern.'

In the waning light, he could make out the obstinate expression on her face. She said nothing.

He exhaled. 'I am no danger to you but plainly you are not willing to accept that. Are you going to flee as soon as I step away from this door?'

'Yes,' she said without hesitation.

'Will you not come with us in the morning to find Orlaith and Patrick?'

'I'm not going anywhere with you tomorrow. I won't lead you within a mile of them if I can help it. They're far better off without you.'

Cormac looked at Bridget helplessly. She had been watching the heated exchange between him and Tess with increasing apprehension. Now, at his unspoken plea, she stepped forwards to intervene.

'Are you certain about that?' she said.

'What?' Tess snapped, glancing at her before returning her angry gaze to Cormac.

'Are you certain that Orlaith is better off without her brother? That Patrick is better off without his uncle? Would they not be grateful to piece some of their family back together?'

'Not when they realise who he is and what he's done,' Tess said through clenched teeth.

'You have a fallacious view of Cormac McGovern,' Bridget told her. 'You have heard these untrue reports about him and credited them as fact without verifying their validity. Yes, he did work for that money lender. He made a mistake. Who in this room has not? But I have known Cormac for most of his life and I know that he is a good man and that he loves his family. You told us how fondly they used to speak of him. Do you not think that the remnants of this family deserve to be reunited?'

Tess finally looked straight at Bridget. She appeared less sure of herself in the face of this unswerving loyalty from such a well-spoken lady. But she was stubborn.

'You know one version of McGovern,' she said, 'and I know another. Orlaith and Patrick shouldn't run the risk of encountering the worse of the two.'

'Is that not a decision they ought to make for themselves?'

Bridget's words hung in the air. Tess huddled in the corner, chewing on her lip.

'But they're still so young,' she said at last. 'Orlaith must be barely thirteen and Patrick can't yet be eight.'

'All the more reason for them to have an older family member to take care of them. Their own flesh and blood. That has to be better than whatever lives they are leading now. They could be children again.'

Cormac watched Tess anxiously. She vacillated for a few moments longer and then she gave a grudging nod.

'I suppose I don't have the right to decide for them,' she muttered. 'Maybe it's only fair they're allowed to make up their own minds. But I won't go out of my way to help yous. I'll tell yous where to go and then I want to leave. Understood?'

'Very well,' said Cormac. 'We cannot ask for more than that.'

Looking as though it was against her better judgement, she said, 'Stephen's Green. That's where Eli thought he saw Orlaith. But of course there's no certainty that it was her.'

Cormac pressed his nails into his palms with relief. He was very glad she had not said Merrion Square for he didn't know how they would have been able to show their faces there again. 'We will maintain hope that it was, and trust that we will find her there tomorrow.'

They stared at each other, a wary truce between them. Then she glanced at the door and he stepped away from it.

'Thank you again,' he said. 'I appreciate all of your help and hope you might come to realise in time that I am not the evil beast you deem me to be. Will you accept the money I offered you earlier?'

'No,' she said. She bolted for the door and they watched her red hair whisk out of sight.

With a shaky breath, he sank down onto the edge of the bed. Bridget sat next to him.

'It is difficult to come to terms with the fact that someone can hate me with such intensity,' he said weakly, looking down into his lap. 'I'm thankful you were able to convince her to help us.'

'Do you think she told us the truth?' Bridget cast a

263

worried look at the still-open door.

'We have no way of knowing for certain, but I think she did. She would not want to be the person who got in the way of the McGoverns finding a degree of happiness at last. Her affection for them all was genuine. It was apparent how much it cost her to speak of their deaths.'

His voice fractured on the last word. He turned to Bridget and saw the tears glistening in her eyes.

'Poor Maggie and Margaret,' she whispered.

The truth of it crashed over him, and some part of him deep in his very core compressed under the weight of it and shattered. A mangled sound, laced with agony and loss and remorse, slipped from his throat. He fumbled for Bridget's embrace, needing her to anchor him before it crushed him entirely. She held him in the darkness and together they mourned the passing of two gentle souls.

Chapter 21

There was no sleep to be had. Cormac felt as though someone were sticking pins into him throughout the night, jerking him back to wakefulness whenever he was about to drop off. Nightmarish images of his mother and sister's final excruciating days swam before his eyelids and guilt gouged out his insides, leaving him in shreds by the dawn.

He rose with sluggish limbs and his mind in a stupor. Bridget's bleary gaze told him she had spent the night in a similar fashion. While he made a weary effort to shave, she folded her nightdress and eyed their valises sitting side by side at the end of the bed.

'Perhaps we could leave them in the charge of the innkeeper?' she said hopefully. 'It would be a relief not to lug them about all day and we could return in the evening to retrieve them and seek out alternative accommodation.'

Exhausted, he made no objection. They arranged it with the innkeeper and also procured a parcel of black pudding and hard-boiled eggs to eat during the day, although he himself still didn't feel remotely hungry. It wasn't until they got outside, when the fresh air, damp with an early morning mist, struck his face, that some semblance of energy returned to his body. As Emily skipped ahead of them clutching her new doll, which she refused to leave behind, he reminded himself of their purpose and discovered that a tiny scrap of optimism still remained.

They made their way through the Dublin streets to the square of St Stephen's Green. Bridget knew it from her youth for it was one of the most respectable addresses in the city. Terraces of elegant, red-bricked townhouses lined the square on all sides, and in the centre was the green itself, a park enclosed by railings and accessible only to the square's inhabitants. The houses exuded affluence and had wide steps leading up to entrances topped with semicircular fanlights. Iron railings surrounded open wells at the fronts of the houses, with flights of steps allowing direct access down to the cellars.

The enormity of their task was quite plain to them. There had to be more than sixty residences on the square and Orlaith and Patrick could be in any one of them or none at all.

With a grimace at Bridget, Cormac said, 'I regret to say it but I think the best way to approach the matter is to be methodical and visit every house in turn.'

It would be immensely time-consuming but, if nothing else, they would be able to rule out each one with absolute certainty. It would also be more thorough than Tess's aimless wandering, but then she had been correct – there could have been no possibility of her going to knock on doors. Cormac and Bridget looked respectable enough that they would not be turned away at first glance and ought to at least get the opportunity to state their case.

The mist persisted and threatened to develop into rain as they approached the first house. Cormac opened the gate in the front railings and led Bridget and Emily down the steps to the cellar as that was where they were most likely to find luck, if there was any to be found. Perhaps Orlaith would be working in the kitchens or the scullery; maybe Patrick would be cleaning knives or shoes. He could also very well be shovelling manure in the mews at the rear of the houses, so that was another avenue they could pursue later if their enquiries via the front access proved to be in vain.

Cormac rapped on the cellar door. A cook answered it, her face and apron covered in flour. Her manner was civil as it was clear that Cormac was no mere milkman.

'Can I help yous?'

'I hope that you can,' said Cormac. 'I am looking for my sister. It is possible that she is a maid in one of these houses. She is thirteen with dark hair and there should be a little boy with her around the age of seven. Does this description sound familiar to you?'

The cook scowled when she realised that the callers were not there to serve any purpose for her master or mistress.

'They're not at this address,' she said and closed the door with a snap.

The day wore on in much the same manner. They visited house after house and met with varying levels of curiosity, suspicion and downright rudeness. They spoke mainly to cooks and maids and, once or twice, a housekeeper. From each one the answer was almost always the same: nobody on the staff fitted the description of either the girl or the boy. A number of times there was a dark-haired housemaid but it was never Orlaith.

They stopped to eat the black pudding and eggs in the early afternoon before embarking along the third side of the square. The rain had held off for the most part but now scattered drops were starting to fall in earnest. At the first house on this side, a maid stood at the top of the cellar steps, watching a coalman shovel a delivery down the coal hole in the footpath. She had dark hair but she looked like she was in her early twenties, too old to be Orlaith.

'Who're yous?' she said as they approached her.

'This is Mabel,' Emily said, holding up her doll, and the maid gave her an indulgent smile.

For what seemed like the thousandth time in his life, Cormac explained why they were there and who they were looking for. 'Are they here or have you ever seen them on the square?'

He was braced for the usual negative response but the girl did not answer right away. Her brow furrowed in contemplation.

'I'm not sure,' she said slowly. 'Maybe…'

He felt his spirits lift. 'Do you know them?'

She shook her head. 'Not the boy, anyway. There are no young lads employed in any of the houses 'round here. But the girl... There's a dark-haired girl working for a household two doors down from here. She's been there for a few years. I remember when she started 'cause I noticed how young she was, no more than eight or so, and I wondered how poor her family must've been to let her go out working at such an age. I don't know if maybe she could be your sister?'

There was a yell from the open cellar door below. 'Stop your dawdling, for pity's sake, can't you see it's raining!'

Alarmed, the girl thanked the coalman and scurried down the steps.

'My sincerest gratitude for your help,' Cormac called after her.

'You're welcome!' she exclaimed over her shoulder and was gone.

He looked at Bridget and Emily, feeling nervous. 'Well, let's follow her suggestion,' he said and led them past the next house on the street and on to the one after it.

He tugged his cap down against the raindrops as they descended the steps to the cellar door. A housekeeper answered his knock, a set of keys jangling at her waist. Beyond her was a storage room with a flagstone floor.

'Yes?' she said, her manner just shy of impatient.

He told her their purpose. She frowned in puzzlement as she listened but at the mention of Patrick her face changed. Shock and then fear filled her expression.

'Don't waste my time,' she said brusquely and tried to slam the door on them.

He put out a firm arm to hold it open. 'Do you know something? Tell me! Are they in this house?'

At that moment, an inner door into the storage room opened and a girl appeared, carrying a coal bucket. She was young and her dark hair was pinned back beneath her maid's cap. It had been seven and a half years since Cormac had last seen her but he recognised her at once;

she was almost identical to their sister Margaret except that her grey eyes were larger and rounder. Her eyes had always been her most prominent feature.

'Orlaith!'

She dropped the bucket and it toppled over; fragments of coal spilled across the floor and a cloud of black dust flew up into the air.

The housekeeper clicked her tongue. 'Stupid girl! Clean that up this instant!'

With a startled glance at Cormac, Orlaith fell to her knees on the flagstones and began picking up the pieces of coal.

'Can't that wait a minute?' he said indignantly to the housekeeper. 'I'm her brother. We haven't seen each other in years.'

'She was stupid enough to drop it so it's her responsibility to clear away the mess.'

'Stop calling her that,' he said, his temper rising with every word out of the woman's mouth. 'Orlaith, come here.'

She peeped up, frightened, as she tipped the coal lumps back into the bucket.

'You have no authority in this household,' the housekeeper barked and tried to force the door shut again.

To her outrage, he pushed it open and darted into the storage room. He seized Orlaith's wrist and pulled her to her feet.

'You're not staying here any longer. Where's Patrick? Let's find him and leave.'

At the mention of their nephew's name, her eyes grew even bigger and she shook her head.

'Is he not here?'

'No,' she said in a tremulous voice. 'Patrick's not here.'

'Then let's go.' He towed her towards the outer door, leaving sooty footprints on the flagstone floor.

'Where do you think you're going?' The angry housekeeper barred their way, one hand on her keys as

269

though she intended to lock them in. 'The girl works here. She can't just up and leave whenever she fancies. That coal dust needs to be cleaned up. It's everywhere.'

'Do it yourself then,' Cormac said curtly, sidestepping the woman and hastening outside with Orlaith. Bridget and Emily both gaped at the sudden development in events. The four of them hurried up the steps while the housekeeper stood in the doorway and shouted at Orlaith to come back at once. They emerged onto the street just as the rain became heavier.

'We need to find shelter,' Cormac said to the others.

'There's a church over on Whitefriar Street,' said Orlaith. ''Tis this way.'

She led them off the square and along one street and then another, circumnavigating other pedestrians who were dashing to escape the worsening weather. She said nothing, shoulders hunched as she pounded the footpath ahead of them. They reached the church just as the shower became a deluge and ran for cover inside its doors.

The vestibule was vacant of people but a few congregants knelt in pews further up the nave. Even though the rain drummed a loud and rhythmic beat on the doors, a hushed silence reigned within. Cormac felt a lump come to his throat. It had been so long since he had attended a Catholic Mass. In England he had been obliged to go to Protestant services with Lord and Lady Bewley, and since returning to Ireland there had barely been time for a quick, mumbled prayer at St Mary's in Ballydarry. He dipped his fingers in the holy water font and blessed himself. He thought of showing Emily how to bless herself too but she was bemoaning Mabel's wet face. While Bridget dug out a handkerchief to dry the doll, he turned to look at his sister.

She was filthy. There was coal dust all over her and the rain had mixed with it to leave streaky black stains across the front of her apron and on her arms and hands. But she was Orlaith. Those eyes were unmistakable. And yet they were different...they seemed empty somehow.

She stared at him. 'Are you really Cormac?' She had a thick Dublin accent and no wonder; she had spent more of her life in the city than she had in Carlow.

'I am. Do you remember me, chicken?'

She twitched at the endearment. 'I don't remember much of our old life,' she said. 'But your face is familiar. What're you doing here?'

'I came back to seek out all of our family but it seems that you are the only one left. I am sorry that I could not find you sooner. You have had an appalling ordeal here in Dublin.'

Instead of replying, she looked back outside to the pouring rain. He did not understand. There was no joy, no relief – just blankness. In fact, the only emotion he had seen her express since her appearance in the storage room was fear. It was almost as if she had not wanted to be found.

He took a tentative step towards her. She backed away from him. Then it struck him – she had said that Patrick was not there at the house. Had something bad happened to him for which she felt responsible? Perhaps that was why she was putting distance between herself and those who had known him.

'Orlaith, is Patrick dead?' he murmured, at pains to keep any trace of reproach from his tone.

She swallowed. 'No, he's not. Our nephew's alive and well.'

'Then where is he?'

'He's in the house you've just taken me from.'

Cormac was mystified. 'But you said –'

'I said *Patrick* wasn't there. And that was the truth. He goes by the name of Edward now.'

Cormac didn't know what to say. He glanced at Bridget; her brows were drawn together in confusion.

'Can you please tell us what happened?' she asked.

Orlaith clenched her jaw and turned her back to them.

271

She was tall for thirteen but her posture was stooped. When she spoke again, Cormac had to strain to hear her over the hammering rain.

'I hoped I'd never have to explain this to anyone.'

Without looking at them, she plodded into the nave, genuflected and took a seat in the last pew. After a hesitant moment, Cormac removed his cap and joined her. Bridget and Emily followed and slid into the pew in front of them.

'We must be very quiet in here, gooseberry,' said Bridget.

Emily nodded and whispered the same to Mabel. While she rocked the doll like a baby, Bridget half pivoted towards the back pew. Cormac faced forwards, not wanting Orlaith to feel like she was under interrogation, but he tilted his head slightly in her direction. She sat staring at her knees as the rain pelted the church's windows.

'Y'know, I wasn't even nine years old when I knew what it was like to be desperate,' she said, her voice pitched low. 'By then, most of my family were either dead or gone. Only myself and my nephew were left—two homeless, penniless children. What chance did we have? The easiest thing would've been to lie down and wait for death to take us too.'

Cormac listened with a horrible heaviness in his bones. There was such dejection in her words. That depth of hopelessness led one to commit the kinds of unspeakable acts to which Mary and Oliver had both resorted.

'But I wasn't like Mary,' said Orlaith, echoing what he was thinking. 'I didn't give up. I tried to find a way out. There was a girl, Tess, who said she'd look after us but she was living rough too which meant she couldn't do anything to help us really. We'd stay stuck where we were for the rest of our lives. And I didn't want that, not for me and not for Patrick who was only three years old and had lived practically his whole life in poverty. So I went out walking with him every day, not in places we knew, but in areas where rich people lived. I knocked on cellar doors and offered my services as a housemaid, a scullery girl, anything at all. But I'd no luck. Nobody was willing to take me on when I'd a little boy in tow. Still, I kept trying.'

She wiped her fingers on her apron, only succeeding in making the sooty smears worse.

'Then I knocked on yet another cellar door and came face to face with the nasty housekeeper yous just met. Mrs Twomey's her name. For the first time, I wasn't turned away as soon as I said I'd my nephew with me. She stared at Patrick in a very cold, calculating way. I remember it gave me the shivers. She told me to wait, disappeared inside and returned with the mistress of the house herself, Lady Anner. The lady said she wanted to help me and the best way she could do that was to take Patrick from me 'cause I was far too young to be looking after him but she and her husband could give him a happy home at Anner House. At first, I didn't understand what she was saying but then I realised she was offering to take Patrick in as her own son. I found out afterwards Lord and Lady Anner's five-year-old boy had died only two or three months before that and Lady Anner was unable to have any more children. Their one and only child was gone forever and Patrick was an unexpected chance to replace him, probably the only chance they'd ever have.'

Cormac resisted the urge to interrupt, though his tongue tingled with questions.

Orlaith's features were expressionless as she continued to speak. 'I suppose I should've said no. But it was an opportunity for me to shift the burden to someone else and for Patrick to grow up in a proper home. So I agreed on two conditions: that we could go back to say goodbye to Tess and that I could stay in the household too and still be allowed to see Patrick. Lady Anner said she was already doing me a great kindness and I shouldn't expect anything more, but she considered herself a generous woman so she offered me a position as a scullery maid. I was to work for free 'til my debt to her had been repaid. I took her at her word. After we came back from the shelter, Patrick was brought above stairs and I was set to work in the kitchens.'

For a few moments, Orlaith was quiet. An elderly man trudged from the vestibule up the nave, his hat and coat soaking and tiny puddles pooling on the floor in his wake. Her gaze followed him as he entered a pew halfway up towards the altar and knelt down. She shrugged.

'It took me several days to realise I'd been lied to. Lady Anner renamed Patrick as Edward and gave him his own bedchamber, a governess, rich food and fine clothes. I was never allowed to see him. She went out of her way to make sure we were always kept apart. It was more than a year later when I laid eyes on him again and by that stage he'd forgotten me. He recognised me only as a maid and had no memory of his first family. Lady Anner had succeeded in creating a new son and heir for herself. But it seems my debt hasn't yet been repaid 'cause I still work without pay, four and a half years later.' She bowed her head. 'So now you know the wicked thing I did. I as good as sold my nephew in exchange for regular meals and a proper roof over my head. I doubt if God or Ma will ever forgive me.'

'Don't be so hard on yourself,' Cormac murmured, his heart full of pity. 'Mrs Twomey and Lady Anner were the ones at fault for exploiting you. You were just a child and you only did what you believed was best in order to improve the quality of life for yourself and Patrick.'

Shaking her head, she rooted in her pocket, drew out a string of rosary beads, and pressed her lips to the cross that hung from them. At the sight of them, the air drained from Cormac's lungs.

'Are those—' he croaked. 'Are those Ma's?'

He reached out but she slid a few inches down the bench away from him, tucking the beads inside her closed fist.

'You don't get to touch them,' she snapped, loudly enough that the elderly man further up the pews half turned his head in disapproval. Bridget gave him a small wave of apology while Orlaith lowered her voice to a hiss. 'What right have you to lay your hands on anything that belonged to Ma? Where were *you* when the last members of your family were struggling to stay alive?'

Cormac sagged. 'You are quite right to accuse me. It is my fault your circumstances were so grim that you were driven to such wretched measures. I am to blame for all the troubles that have befallen our family.'

'We both are,' said Bridget, her knuckles white as she gripped the back of the pew.

'What d'yous mean?' Orlaith looked astonished that they were prepared to assume responsibility for every awful thing that had happened to the McGoverns.

Given that she was too young to remember much of their former lives in Carlow, Cormac went back to the start and provided her with a brief account of the most pertinent details of the past eight years, from his liaison with Bridget that last summer at Oakleigh right through to their encounter with Tess the previous evening. Orlaith reacted to nothing, not when he confessed that he had indeed been that McGovern of whom they had heard such shocking rumours, nor even when, hoping to redeem himself somewhat, he told her he had also been the mysterious stranger who had given Tess all the money that had been used to pay for their mother's medicine. He wondered if his questionable interactions with Oliver Davenport and Lord and Lady Bewley might elicit a response but, arms folded, she remained taciturn throughout.

'And, thanks to Tess, you are the one member of our family whom I have managed to locate,' he finished. 'Although it is possible that Bronagh is alive somewhere in America.'

When he stopped talking, he noticed the silence in the

church had deepened even further and realised the torrent outside had finally eased.

Orlaith's gaze narrowed. 'And what d'you plan to do with me now you've found me?'

He sensed her resistance and chose his language with care. 'What I hope is that you, and possibly Patrick, will come with me, Bridget and Emily to begin a new life as a family somewhere else, far away from this miserable city. But that is only if you wish it. I shall not force you into something you do not want to do.'

While it pained him to give her the option of rejecting them, he knew it was the correct thing to say. She was young but she was mature beyond her years, and she had both the entitlement and the capacity to make this decision for herself.

She mulled over his words. 'I thought what I'd done was wicked, but what you've done is worse. We heard dreadful stories about Cunningham's man McGovern. Were those things really carried out by my brother's hand?'

'Some of them, yes,' he admitted, 'but most of the nastier stories are untrue. Lies were spread which bolstered my reputation far beyond its due. However, for the terrible acts I did commit I have no excuse other than that I was in a hideously dark place and I thought I had no way out. I had believed I was alone in that regard, but now I am aware that my whole family shared the same nightmare.'

'And yet,' she said, glaring at Bridget, 'none of us would've had to experience that hell at all if your mother had been less vengeful.'

Bridget raised her chin against the girl's incriminating tone. 'I am conscious of my mother's failings and I make no attempt to absolve her. But she has since paid the price with her death and can no longer hurt anybody.'

'The damage has already been done,' Orlaith muttered. She looked back at Cormac. 'If I was to leave with yous, where would we go?'

He hesitated. He had been contemplating that question ever since they had met Tess and she had told them of his family's fate, but he had not yet discussed it with Bridget.

Taking the plunge, he said, 'I think perhaps America. I propose that we follow Bronagh across the ocean and search for her over there. If we find her, we can then settle down and make a new home for ourselves, either there or back here in Ireland.'

He glanced at Bridget. They would need to consider many aspects of his proposition before they could act upon it, and of course her responsibility to Oakleigh would be at the forefront of her mind. But a slow smile spread across her face and she laid a gentle palm on Emily's head, as though communicating a blessing from both of them.

Orlaith's countenance, on the other hand, was far more guarded. She stared down at Maggie's rosary beads, rolling one of the spheres between her thumb and forefinger. Cormac ached to hold them, the only physical thing he could remember his mother by – her nimble fingers had counted those beads hundreds of times.

Orlaith touched the cross, tracing her fingertip down the length of it. At last, she nodded. 'Yes. I'll go with yous.'

'Good,' he said, and the boulder inside him disintegrated into tiny pieces and melted away. 'I am glad.'

He hoped their mother and father were looking down on them. Although he could never repair his whole family, at least he and Orlaith had been reunited. He recalled with fondness the little girl who had taken such attentive care of her hens, but she was not the young woman before him. Thirteen-year-old Orlaith was cold and tough and, from her doubtful expression, she still harboured misgivings towards him. She was willing to come with them but it might take months or years for him to earn her trust again and even longer for any kind of sibling love to grow between them.

Bridget cleared her throat. 'What about Patrick? Are we going to attempt to make contact with him?'

'Yes,' said Cormac. 'We shall go back to Anner House and explain how this unusual situation arose. Patrick ought to be with his true family now.'

The corners of Orlaith's mouth tightened. 'Yous can try, but I don't think yous'll succeed.'

On this pessimistic note, they left the church pews and Cormac led his lover, his child and his sister back along the wet streets the way they had come. It was time to retrieve the last remaining member of his family in this city which had treated them all so cruelly.

Chapter 22

The rain had ceased but the trees in the park in the centre of St Stephen's Green still dripped with moisture. When they reached Anner House, Orlaith opened the gate in the railings to go down the cellar stairs but Cormac stopped her with a shake of his head.

'None of us are servants anymore,' he said. 'We shall announce our presence at the front entrance.'

She raised her eyebrows and followed him, Bridget and Emily up the steps to the broad space before the front door. He used the gleaming brass knocker to give two sharp taps. A footman in livery answered almost at once.

'We are here to see Lady Anner,' Cormac declared.

The footman gave him an appraising look. 'Who may I say is calling?'

'Mr Cormac McGovern. I wish to speak with the lady on a family matter of some importance.'

His tone was so sincere and urgent that the footman began to open the door wider to admit them. Then his gaze fell upon Orlaith at the back of the group.

'What are you doing?' he shot at her. 'You shouldn't be here. Get back to the scullery.'

Cormac stepped sideways to block her from the footman's line of sight and reproachful words. 'She is meant to be here. She is my sister and a vital part of the family matter I need to discuss with Lady Anner.'

The footman's countenance grew perplexed; it was plain he was ignorant of the arrangement that had brought Orlaith into this house. Cormac supposed very few of the servants were privy to the information – it was not a secret that the Anners would wish to be widely known.

Without warning, the door was jerked out of the footman's grasp and Mrs Twomey appeared in the entry, livid.

'It's time for you to leave,' she said.

'We are not going anywhere until we have spoken to Lady Anner,' said Cormac. 'She can receive us in her drawing room or she can meet us here on her front steps, but either way she *shall* see us. I know you are aware of the situation involving my sister and nephew and I am certain you are wise enough to concede that it would be best for every party concerned to resolve it as soon as possible.'

She ground her teeth, glowering at him like he was a nasty insect she wanted to squash beneath her heel. Then she pulled on the footman's elbow and they both vanished inside the house, shutting the door firmly behind them. Cormac glanced at the others – Bridget was biting the tip of her tongue, Orlaith was scowling, and Emily was fastidiously straightening Mabel's dress. He looked back at the brass knocker and waited.

It was several minutes before he heard muted speech on the other side of the door. It swung open and a lady materialised in the gap. She was tall with flaxen curls twisted up into an elaborate hairstyle. Her face was beautiful but not youthful.

'What is this about?' she said in a surprisingly soft voice.

'Lady Anner, my name is Cormac McGovern and I am here to discuss two issues of great consequence relating to my family. One is with regard to my youngest sister, Orlaith, and the other pertains to our nephew, Patrick.'

Lady Anner looked beyond him to where Orlaith stood. 'Your sister is shirking her duties and ought to return below stairs at once. As for your nephew, there is no one by the name of Patrick living under this roof.'

'As I understand it, our nephew goes by the name of Edward now.'

'There is a boy called Edward, but he is not your nephew.'

'We are all cognisant of the true state of affairs,' said Cormac levelly. 'There is no need to tell falsehoods.'

The lady's nostrils flared but when she spoke her voice was still silky smooth. 'What is it you wish to say to me, Mr McGovern?'

He sensed her anger beneath her calm exterior and it sparked his own; how could she stand there without any compunction for what she had done?

Unclenching his jaw with effort, he said, 'Four and a half years ago, my sister and nephew showed up at your cellar door and you seized the opportunity to acquire a son and a slave. You separated them until the boy no longer recognised his aunt and you worked her to the bone under the pretence that she was paying you back an enormous debt. Such cruelty and abuse is unpardonable. I was not there to stop it then but I am here to stop it now. I intend to take Orlaith and Patrick away with me today.'

Lady Anner's expression was derisive. 'And what makes you think that I shall give them up to you?'

'You have no right to keep them. Patrick is not your blood relation and Orlaith is not employed here by legitimate means. You took advantage of two small children who had no protector, but that power is no longer yours.'

Her lip curled. 'On the contrary, that power is still very much mine. Any number of servants and neighbours will attest to the fact that my husband and I took a small boy into our home four and a half years ago and that, in an unrelated circumstance, a young girl has worked in our kitchens for a similar length of time. If you take them away you will be branded an abductor and incarcerated.'

Baffled, Cormac said, 'But what lies have you fed those servants and neighbours? You hardly made it known that you had plucked a homeless boy off the streets.'

'Indeed I did not, for that is not what happened. It is

281

common knowledge that Edward is my husband's nephew.'

Cormac stared at her. 'I beg your pardon?'

With angelic serenity, she said, 'My husband's brother, Mr George Whitmore, was always a sickly fellow so he resided in the countryside for the sake of his health. When we lost our own dear son, George became heir presumptive to the Anner title. If he produced no issue, the title would go to a more distant, and shall I say less suitable, relative.' She smiled. 'Imagine our delight, therefore, when we heard that George had fallen in love and married a young lady of irreproachable birth. Sadly, their happy time together was all too brief. His wife did not survive childbirth and George's health worsened over the ensuing years so my husband and I agreed to take their young child into our own loving home. It was the least we could do to ease George's burden.'

Cormac blinked rapidly, unable to believe what he was hearing.

Lady Anner carried on, 'Edward knows we are his aunt and uncle but he has come to look upon us as his parents and he even calls us Mother and Father now. We are all he has left since poor George passed away not two years ago. Naturally, we shall continue to take care of him like a son. He is now next in line to inherit the barony of Anner.'

Cormac could barely speak. 'This is outrageous!' he spluttered. 'You have fabricated this story to serve your own ends.'

'That is a despicable accusation,' she said, unruffled. 'And one that nobody will believe.'

He was at a loss for words. Next to him, Bridget looked stunned but she found her tongue and said to Lady Anner, 'Do you genuinely claim this as fact to your acquaintances? Patrick is not your flesh and blood. And Orlaith is nothing more than a skivvy to you. Cormac is all that remains of their true family.'

'But you have no proof. You cannot even argue that they

282

look much alike.'

'Have you no *conscience*?' Cormac demanded. 'You know that you are at fault, that you have lied and used these children. Do you not have any scruples about what you have done?'

'How dare you speak to me in such a way?' she said, as soft-spoken as ever. 'Get off my property at once.'

'I want to see Patrick,' he insisted.

'That is preposterous. You will not set one foot across this threshold. My staff will make sure of that. And you, girl,' she added to Orlaith, 'you have been idle for long enough. Go back to the scullery right away. You will work as late tonight as is necessary to catch up on all your tasks.'

Orlaith folded her arms. 'I'm leaving with my brother. I don't work for yous anymore.'

For the first time, Lady Anner looked properly furious. Then her face changed. She twisted to look at someone out of Cormac's sight.

'Take him back upstairs,' she ordered. 'He is not allowed to go outside.'

'But I want to go splashing in the puddles!' a boy's voice whined.

'I said go back upstairs at once.' Her voice was now tinged with apprehension. 'Do you hear me? No, Edward!'

She stretched out her arms as a young boy came pelting through the doorway. He dodged her grasp and ran out onto the broad top step where he stopped short in his bid for freedom at the sight of all the strangers. Cormac seized this sudden chance.

'Greetings, Patrick,' he said, stooping to shake the boy's hand. 'My name is Cormac and I am your uncle.'

Lady Anner tried to drag the boy back into the house but he danced out of her reach again. He stared up at Cormac. He was a handsome child with thick, black hair, hazel eyes and a proud stance. He looked very much like Garrett but Cormac could detect a little of Mary around his nose and mouth.

'But I don't have any uncles apart from Father,' he said. 'And why did you call me Patrick? My name is Edward.'

'Come inside this instant,' Lady Anner commanded but he ignored her.

'Who are you really?' he asked Cormac.

Despite the wet steps, Cormac knelt on one knee to look the boy in the eye. 'I told you the truth. I am your uncle and you are my nephew. When you were born, you were named Patrick by your mother who is now dead. You spent the first three years of your life with your grandmother and aunties until this lady took you into her home. She told you your name was Edward but that was a lie. While we are grateful that she looked after you, we have come to take you away with us for we are your true family.'

The boy's features were alight with excitement; this was an adventure far beyond what he had expected when he had run outside. 'And who are the rest of these people?'

'This is my wife, Bridget,' said Cormac. 'And this is our daughter, Emily. She is your cousin.'

Emily beamed and waved Mabel's arm.

'And this is Orlaith.' Cormac indicated his sister at the back. 'She is your aunt.'

The boy frowned at her. 'But she is a servant.'

'She used to be,' Cormac acknowledged.

'Then it cannot be real.' The boy's face fell in disappointment. 'I thought it would be a lark to run away for a little while but you are not telling me the truth. I know I am not related to any servants.'

'In fact, you are. I was once a servant too, a stable hand. But it doesn't make a difference. We are still your family.'

'No, you are not,' the boy said rudely. 'Look at her. She's dirty. She is not part of my family and neither are you. I am only related to people of noble blood.'

'Patrick—'

'You will address me as Master Whitmore, I'll thank you

to remember that,' the boy said, drawing himself up to his full small height.

Cormac stared at him incredulously and then looked up at Lady Anner's smug expression. He got to his feet, incensed.

'You have indoctrinated him with notions of nobility,' he said, the disgust of it making his blood boil. 'Notions which will only breed arrogance and conceit. You have ruined him.'

'Edward merely takes pride in his class and his heritage,' she said with satisfaction.

He shook his head in disbelief. She knew as well as he did that this boy had lived on the streets for three years. Just because he couldn't remember it did not mean it hadn't happened. She and her husband were fooling him and fooling themselves.

He glanced over his shoulder. Orlaith's face was easy to read; she was unsurprised, for the scene had played out just as she had predicted it would. She did not look sad – he supposed she had given up on their nephew a long time ago.

Was there any prospect of convincing him of the truth? Discouraged, Cormac surveyed the boy's contemptuous countenance. His nephew was entrenched in his new persona. On the one hand, he appeared to be content, and they could be guaranteed that his physical and financial needs would be met. But what about his character? It had already taken a great deal of damage – if Lady Anner continued to rear him on such supercilious principles, the boy would end up even vainer than his father. Patrick was his sister's son; Cormac did not want to fail Mary by abandoning her child to this contemptible woman.

With one last effort, he bent again to the boy's level and said, 'We are planning to travel to America. How would you like to come with us and visit a whole new continent? We can tell you all about your real parents. We are your true flesh and blood and we promise to look after you.'

The boy took a step backwards to Lady Anner's side. 'Please leave our home now.'

The lady placed her hand on his shoulder and smiled sweetly.

Cormac shrugged and rose. 'Very well. I am sorry to leave you behind, but I hope that you have a happy life.'

He turned to head down the steps. Bridget, Emily and Orlaith made to follow.

'Where are you going, girl?' Lady Anner said, raising her voice the tiniest bit. 'You are still our scullery maid.'

Orlaith looked back at her with open disdain. 'You might be able to control the boy but you've no more power over me. I'm no longer your slave. Good riddance to you and Mrs Twomey.'

Lady Anner and her 'son' watched in shock as Orlaith marched down the steps and away from the house. Cormac, Bridget and Emily hurried to catch up with her.

'Did you leave anything behind that you wanted?' Bridget asked. 'Any possessions or keepsakes?'

'No,' said Orlaith, pressing her hand to her pocket where Maggie's rosary beads were stowed. 'Everything I want is in America. Let's go there.'

Chapter 23

As they walked back in the direction of the Liberties to fetch their valises from the inn, Cormac and Bridget apprised Orlaith of some more things that had occurred during their years of separation, including the uprising and the burning of Oakleigh Manor, and – though it pained Cormac to admit it – their contact with Thomasina and Henrietta. He felt ashamed to reveal such an appalling indiscretion, but it was best to be honest about everything family-related; if Thomasina had been telling the truth, then Henrietta was Orlaith's niece.

Orlaith showed no signs of condemnation. While they waited for a fine carriage to pass by so they could cross the street, she said thoughtfully, 'We used to have a hen called Henrietta, didn't we?'

'We did,' he said with a smile. It made him glad to see her remembering their old life.

The carriage rattled past and they crossed over to the other side; the inn was located just a little further down the street. It was growing late in the evening, but the sun had emerged before dusk and a slanting shaft of light struck the inn's windows. The streets were still wet from the earlier rainfall and they too glimmered in the rays of the setting sun.

As they approached the inn, they passed an alleyway where three men loitered at its mouth sharing a smoking pipe between them. Cormac and the others had almost gone by when one of the men spoke.

'Oliver Davenport?'

Cormac's head whipped around in recognition of the

name – too late he realised his mistake. Two of the men leapt forwards and seized his arms. Bridget screamed and Emily cried 'Papa!' as the men dragged him into the alley and shoved him up against the wall, nearly wrenching his shoulder out of its socket.

'Shut your traps afore I shut them for you,' the third man in the group snarled and he herded Bridget, Emily and Orlaith into the alleyway too.

There was no direct sunlight in the narrow passage and it took a few moments for Cormac's vision to adjust to the gloom. He did not recognise the faces of any of the men. The two pinning him to the wall were both clean-shaven and one of them had pockmarked cheeks. The third had a rust-coloured beard and had taken up a menacing stance in front of Bridget, Emily and Orlaith, who cowered against the opposite wall. He still held the pipe and brandished it at them, forcing them into a tighter huddle. From the little the men had said, Cormac could tell by their accents that they were English.

'What do you want from us?' he demanded. The mention of Oliver Davenport's name was ominous; this was no ordinary robbery.

'There's someone who fancies a word with you,' growled the man with the pockmarks.

Pinioned in place, Cormac could only twist his head towards the entrance of the alleyway. The fine carriage they had glimpsed hardly a minute earlier had returned, coming to a stop out on the street. It occurred to him belatedly that a conveyance of that elegance was incongruous in such a working class part of the city; the sight of it ought to have rung a warning bell straight away. A footman came around and opened the door to allow its passenger to alight.

An older gentleman emerged, white-haired beneath his hat and carrying a beechwood cane. He stepped down to the footpath without any sign of frailty and strode forwards, stopping just inside the mouth of the alley.

There was silence until Emily burst out with joy, 'Uncle Bewley, are you here to save us?'

Lord Bewley had spent more than one entertaining afternoon kneeling on the hearth rug at Raynesworth House in London attending tea parties with Emily's imaginary friends, but he did not even respond to the little girl now. He leaned on his cane and his gaze swept over them all, leaving Cormac until last.

'Good evening, Oliver,' he said. It was a mocking greeting; every single person in the alleyway knew that Cormac was not Oliver Davenport.

Cormac did not know what to say so he just replied, 'Good evening, Lord Bewley.'

The earl's mouth curved wryly – he was 'Uncle' no more. He gestured to the two men who held Cormac in their grip. 'Release him.'

They let go and stood back from him, but remained poised for action. Massaging his shoulder, he cast a fleeting look towards Bridget. She was trembling with panic and held Emily's small hand tightly. The little girl clutched Mabel just as hard. Next to them, Orlaith surveyed the scene with her fists furled.

Lord Bewley regarded him coolly. 'Your true name is Cormac McGovern?'

Cormac nodded, recalling the letter he had left for the Bewleys before fleeing from London. Little had he known then that he would be facing the consequences of its contents in person.

'We have had some difficulty in tracking you down,' said Lord Bewley. 'It took us several days after you absconded to realise that you were not still in London and that you must have escaped on that ship after all. It was a cunning feat, but then all the evidence suggests you are quite the sly creature.'

Cormac did not protest. Lord Bewley deserved the opportunity to castigate him.

'How did you find us?' he asked.

'The law enforcement informed me that you were gone beyond their interest but if I was able to return you to England they would exact the proper punishment upon you. I therefore began my own investigation and approached this young lady's husband for information.' Lord Bewley waved his cane in Bridget's direction. 'He was happy to oblige and told us that the most likely place you would go would be Oakleigh Manor. A series of inopportune delays meant that by the time we landed in Ireland and reached the estate you had already departed from it. However, we learned you were not gone long and that you were bound for Dublin so we followed you here. My men asked for you in both savoury and unsavoury circles and struck lucky today when they met a girl who could say with absolute certainty that you had stayed at this inn last night.'

Tess. No doubt she had been all too pleased to assist.

'We did not think we would be so fortunate that you would return for a second night, until the innkeeper informed us that he was holding your luggage for you. So we placed ourselves in the vicinity and here you are.'

Cormac cursed himself for not insisting upon taking their valises with them that morning. They could have stayed at any other inn in the city tonight and Lord Bewley would have been none the wiser.

'I am afraid this is the end for you, Mr McGovern,' said Lord Bewley.

Heart sinking, Cormac believed him. The earl was a powerful man. 'What do you plan to do with me?'

'I will have you sent to prison for the rest of your life, though even that is too lenient. I can only hope there is a magistrate willing to bestow a greater punishment.'

'No!' gasped Bridget. 'Please, no!'

Lord Bewley turned to her, distaste written on his face. 'Lady Wyndham, my esteem for you has fallen to less than nothing. You may be considered party to Mr McGovern's crimes for you were aware of his duplicity and informed no one. In my opinion, you are just as guilty and ought to stand before a magistrate as well. However, your husband has bargained for your freedom. So you and your daughter shall both come with me. As for this other girl, I do not know who she is but she is of no concern to me. She may leave whenever she pleases.'

'I'll stay, thanks,' Orlaith said tartly at the same time as Bridget said, 'Emily and I are not going back to Garrett!'

'You misunderstand,' said Lord Bewley. 'He has not requested that I return you to him, only that I make arrangements to ensure your safety. He directed me to deliver you and the child into the protection of your uncle in England, your closest relative apart from your estranged mother. I confess that Lord Wyndham's resentment was palpable but his underlying regard for your wellbeing was unmistakable.'

It seemed that Garrett, too, had been unaware that Lord Walcott was residing in Dublin and not in England, but now was not the time to correct the mistake. Bridget was looking perplexed. 'Regard for our wellbeing? Well, even so, we shall still refuse to go with you.'

Lord Bewley stared at her. 'Why would you stay? There is nothing left for you here. This man's life is over, I will make sure of that.'

Bridget's eyes met Cormac's across the narrow space. Their future was disappearing like a wisp of smoke dispersing into the sky.

'Please,' she begged, reaching out imploring hands towards Lord Bewley. 'Have mercy.'

'*Mercy*? There can be no mercy for the wrongs that have been perpetrated. My wife and I have been robbed of our nephew, the only family we had left. Mr McGovern claims in his despicable letter that Oliver left this world by his own hand but we shall never have any proof of that. His passing may very well have been expedited by the imposter himself.'

'I didn't kill him!' Cormac exclaimed. He took a step

forwards and the pockmarked man immediately shoved him backwards. He lost his balance and fell back against the wall. 'I did not kill Oliver. Everything I wrote in my letter to you was the truth.'

'Then you cannot deny your other transgressions,' said Lord Bewley, his eyes bulging. 'That you stole Oliver's clothing and possessions, that you presented yourself to us as our nephew, that you made us believe for nearly five years that you were of Bewley flesh and blood. We gave you an education. We intended for you to inherit the family estate. But you were a stranger and a thief in our home. It was all a pretence. You betrayed us.'

There was a shake in his voice that told Cormac just how immense that betrayal was. The Bewleys had felt genuine affection for their 'nephew', had even begun to view him as a son, and to find out that those feelings of attachment had been based on a lie must have been a very painful discovery. Lord and Lady Bewley were grieving.

Cormac's words were quiet but heartfelt as he said, 'I am deeply sorry for the distress I have caused you both. It was never my intention to hurt either of you.'

Lord Bewley gave a sceptical grunt. 'Well, you did. My wife wept for two solid days after you ran off. She is distraught over what has happened. She had become exceedingly fond of you.'

'And I of her,' said Cormac, saddened to think of Lady Bewley crying over the sins he had committed. 'She had become like a second mother to me.' He pressed his palms to the wall behind him, his skin scraping the rough surface. 'Please understand, my actions were not driven by malice when I entered your lives. And equally there was no evil intended when I left. My departure was compelled by a profound love for that exceptional woman standing there and by a fear for the uncertain welfare of my first mother. My whole family was in crisis and I had to try my best to save them.'

Lord Bewley's grip tightened so much on his cane that

his knuckles looked ready to pop. 'I don't see how you can profess to uphold values of any sort,' he muttered. 'And particularly not when it comes to the sacred bond of family.'

'I do value the bond of family, I swear it,' said Cormac. 'I have travelled miles in search of my lost family members. To my despair, I was too late to save my mother and one of my sisters. But I have located another sister' – he gestured towards Orlaith – 'and am determined to find the third, even if it means crossing an ocean to do it. And I stood on a doorstep in St Stephen's Green this afternoon and did all I could to reclaim a nephew who has been taken in by a family there, despite the futility of it.'

Lord Bewley had appeared to be wavering but at this he drew himself up in indignation. 'Are you serious? You have a lowborn nephew living in the care of an upper class family?'

Cormac admitted, 'I do.'

The earl seethed. 'It seems being an impostor is an abominable family trait.'

Cormac lowered his gaze. 'I can only say again how remorseful I am for the way I deceived you. I was desperate and I made an irresponsible decision.'

'And you will pay for that decision now,' Lord Bewley said grimly, signalling with his cane for his men to take Cormac away.

'You'll pay for more than that,' came a voice from behind Lord Bewley before the men could even move.

All heads turned towards the mouth of the alley. Cormac's limbs went weak. The last rays of the dying sun framed none other than the money lender, Cunningham, flanked by four of his men, the thickset build of Munroe discernible among them.

An overwhelming sense of hopelessness invaded Cormac. Lord Bewley was a decent man and might have been persuaded to show leniency; Cunningham could never be swayed to be anything less than ruthless.

293

'Take them,' Cormac said urgently to Lord Bewley, motioning towards Bridget, Emily and Orlaith. 'Take them with you and leave right now.'

The earl did not heed him. 'Who are you?' he asked as Cunningham strolled forwards, his men following in his wake. Cormac spotted a thin-lipped sneer on one man's face and recognised him as Lawlor, the fellow who had thrown a stick of firewood at him the day he had first encountered this gang. How he wished he'd never retaliated and just walked away.

'The name's Cunningham,' said the money lender. 'I'd like a word with our man McGovern here.'

He casually let his coat fall open to reveal a pistol nestled at his side.

Lord Bewley looked at Cormac in horror. 'What sort of shady dealings have you been involved in?'

'The shadiest,' Cunningham said with a grin. 'Now, sir, you look like a gentleman of honour and I have no bone to pick with you. So why don't you and your men just walk away and we'll take over from here.'

Lord Bewley shook his head. 'Mr McGovern has committed acts of an unlawful nature. I came here to apprehend him and ensure that justice is served.'

'Mr McGovern will not be making it out of this alley alive,' said Cunningham, his tone mocking at the formal address. 'Is that justice enough for you?'

Aghast, Lord Bewley said, 'You are going to murder him? What has he done to merit such a violent end?'

'Acts of an unlawful nature. Against *me*, and in that case there's only one method of redress.'

'I cannot...' Lord Bewley swallowed. 'I do not think I can permit this to happen.'

Cunningham raised his eyebrows. 'It's going to happen whether you permit it or not. And the longer you stay here, the likelier it is you'll join him. I recommend that you and your men go back to your fancy carriage and head home in the happy knowledge that your goal has been achieved.'

A shadow of fear crossed Lord Bewley's face. Cunningham was not giving him an empty threat. He glanced at Cormac – was that regret in his eyes? Perhaps some vestige of affection yet remained. But Cunningham was serious and Lord Bewley's own life mattered more to him than the life of a lawbreaker whom he still wanted to see imprisoned. He nodded at his three men and they came to his side.

'We shall leave now,' said Lord Bewley. 'We do not wish to interfere. May we take the females with us too?'

'No, you may not,' said Cunningham. 'They will not be making it out of this alley alive either.'

Abject terror made Cormac's insides turn to ice. 'For the love of God, no!' he cried.

'Now, wait just a moment,' objected Lord Bewley.

Bridget scooped Emily up into her arms to shield her from harm. Both of them had tears on their cheeks. Orlaith was not crying but she looked like she very much wished Cormac had never knocked on Mrs Twomey's door that day.

'What is the matter?' said Cunningham with a look of innocent enquiry.

'You are talking about slaughtering a woman and two girls,' said Lord Bewley, white-faced. 'You have no reason to do so.'

'My reason is that they are connected to McGovern, and I want to obliterate him in every respect.'

Cormac started towards Cunningham and found himself in the vice-like grip of Munroe with a dagger at his throat.

'Where d'you think you're going?' Munroe snarled.

'Please,' Cormac said in a strangled voice. 'I am begging you. They have done nothing to hurt you. Just let them go.'

Cunningham laughed and clapped his hands together. 'Isn't this ironic? That is just what our borrowers always used to say to you. And how did you respond?'

'I never killed anyone! They always gave me what I wanted before it got that far. But you already have what you want. You've got me, you don't need them.'

Cunningham cocked his head to one side. 'True. But perhaps I would like to kill them for my own amusement.'

'For heaven's sake, man,' entreated Lord Bewley. 'The little one is only six years old. You do not want her on your conscience.'

'You'd be surprised what my conscience can tolerate.'

Lord Bewley went red with outrage. 'That is quite enough, sir. I imagine Mr McGovern's presence in this alley is non-negotiable, but I shall not leave the other three behind. You said your name is Cunningham. If you refuse to release them, I shall do everything within my power to find out who you are in this city and, make no mistake, I shall ruin you and whatever dastardly dealings you are involved in.'

Even as Cormac experienced the deepest gratitude towards Lord Bewley, he wondered if the earl could in fact exert that much influence in Dublin circles. Whether he was bluffing or not, he puffed out his chest like he could take over as Lord Lieutenant of Ireland if it suited him.

Cunningham looked bored. 'Very well, very well,' he said, flapping his hand. 'The females can go too. That just leaves us with McGovern which means we shall have to make him last an awfully long time.'

Cormac baulked as Munroe pressed the dagger harder into his neck.

'Rotten brutes!'

Orlaith's cry resounded off the alley walls. She ran at Munroe and pummelled his torso with her fists. He fell back in surprise, letting go of Cormac. He raised his hand to strike her but Lord Bewley's pockmarked lackey intervened, catching Munroe by the wrist. Lawlor darted forwards to assist his comrade and, in the chaos of the ensuing struggle, Bridget rushed to Cormac with Emily still in her arms. He embraced them both, burying his face in Bridget's hair, breathing in her familiar smell. He was terrified but he couldn't allow it to show.

'It will be fine,' he whispered. 'Go with Lord Bewley. I'll escape and meet you at Tess's shelter. I love you.'

She shook her head and began to sob. Emily grew hysterical and clutched the collar of his coat. In the crook of her elbow, Mabel's solemn eyes stared up at him.

He dropped a quick kiss on his daughter's wet cheek and choked out, 'Take good care of your mother, *a stór*.'

Over the noise of the skirmish, Lord Bewley barked, 'It's time to leave!'

The man with the rust-coloured beard tossed aside the pipe he still held and seized Bridget; she tried to cling to Cormac but the man pulled her and Emily away. His pockmarked associate ducked beneath Munroe's swinging arm and dragged Orlaith with him to the top of the alleyway where Lord Bewley's other man stood protectively in front of the earl. They all retreated to the carriage out on the street; Cormac heard Bridget scream his name before she, Emily and Orlaith were bundled inside it. Lord Bewley followed them and his men climbed up front with the coachman or onto the back with the footman. The coachman whipped the horses and the carriage rattled away out of sight.

Once it was gone, the alley became very quiet. Twilight had fallen and the gloom had thickened even further but Cormac could still make out the figures and hostile countenances surrounding him. Munroe spat blood on the ground and touched a knuckle to his split lip, his dagger hanging slackly from his other hand. Lawlor and the other two men looked to Cunningham for their next move. The money lender's expression was dispassionate.

'What possessed you to return?' he said to Cormac, tutting in mock disappointment. 'You should have known you were a dead man as soon as you set foot in this city again.'

Cormac attempted to quell his fear as he recalled the

promise he had just made to Bridget. Had it been wrong of him to give her what could very well be false hope? What prospect did he have of breaking free from this gang's clutches? He could try to run for it but he would have to get past five men first. He could fight them but they were armed and he had no weapons whatsoever. He couldn't conceive of any other route of escape.

God, he wished he could hold Bridget in his arms again. What would she do if he didn't come back? Would she still go to America with the girls? He and Orlaith had been reunited mere hours ago – now he might never get to know the young woman his sister had become. And Emily, his beloved baby girl. He could not bear the thought of never seeing her again.

He pushed down his burgeoning despair. He had to maintain hope.

Folding his arms across his chest, he said, 'How did you find me?'

'Thomasina Brennan,' said Cunningham with a grin. Cormac's stomach dropped. Had Thomasina taken the money and informed on him as well? But then Cunningham continued, 'Lawlor spotted her by chance at Smithfield Market, hopping onto a cart to flee the city. He brought her back to the lodgings and she eventually admitted that you had shown up at her auntie's place. We spoke to Mrs O'Hara and after that managed to trace you to the inn on this street. You know, with a reputation like yours, you shouldn't be throwing your name around so much.'

Cormac nodded. 'I've been hearing a lot about my reputation in the last day or two. It seems I was quite the animal in my heyday and yet I cannot recollect doing many of the things of which I have been accused. Can you explain that to me?'

Munroe gave a nasty chuckle. 'We might've embellished the stories a little. Fear's a powerful motivator when it comes to producing money.'

'And money is all I care about,' said Cunningham. He was not grinning anymore. 'What made you think you could steal from me and get away with it?'

'I didn't take it for myself,' Cormac said, recalling the wine merchant's profits he had bestowed upon Tess. 'I gave it to someone else who desperately needed it.'

'That doesn't make a blind bit of difference,' snarled Cunningham. 'It didn't end up in my coffers. But if you didn't use it yourself, then clearly you found some other way to make your fortune, given the generous sum we found in Thomasina's possession.'

'I suppose it's too much to hope that you'll let her leave with it,' Cormac said bleakly.

This time Lawlor laughed and the other two beside him joined in. 'She don't need it anymore.'

A chill ran down Cormac's back and his arms dropped to his sides. 'What do you mean?'

'Got what was coming to her, didn't she?' Lawlor gestured respectfully towards Munroe. 'All credit to himself.'

Cormac thought he was going to be sick. Swallowing bile, he struggled to speak. 'She's...dead?'

Munroe shrugged. 'Bitch couldn't take a beating.'

The wrath that rose up in Cormac threatened to strangle him. 'You goddamned monster,' he hurled at Munroe. 'Why couldn't you let her be? She just wanted to make a better life for herself and her child.'

'She knew you were back and didn't tell us. That kind of disloyalty doesn't go unpunished.'

A tremendous wave of anguish tore through Cormac. 'The little girl—Henrietta—is she—'

'She's still alive.'

'But you've left her without a mother!'

Unconcerned, Munroe said, 'The other wenches will make sure she remembers to eat. Probably.'

'I'm going to take her away from that place,' Cormac growled, even though he had no feasible plan for even getting out of the alleyway.

'She's not yours to take.' Munroe paused, then sniggered. 'Or is that what Thomasina told you? To get the money off you?'

Cormac hesitated as the others sneered. Even Cunningham's lips curved into a smirk.

Munroe flipped his dagger and caught it neatly by the hilt. 'The brat could belong to any one of a dozen men. But Thomasina picked me for the honour. Came to me on Christmas morning with the newborn, calling her a Christmas gift. As if any fellow would be pleased to see a girl instead of a boy.'

Christmas? But that was all wrong. If it had been the first Christmas after Cormac had fled Dublin, then the child would have been born at only seven months and surely wouldn't have survived. If it had been the second Christmas, then that would put Henrietta's age at not even three and a half years old and would mean he had left the country months before she had even been conceived.

'I chose not to believe it,' said Munroe, 'but Thomasina has stuck to the same tune all along. Even named the chit after me.' He made a mocking bow. 'First name's Henry.'

Cormac could only gape.

Cunningham clicked his tongue and said, 'You know, it strikes me as strange that you would be concerned about a whore and her spawn when you have far more pressing things to be worrying about, *Mr* McGovern.'

Munroe strode forwards and dug his fist into Cormac's stomach, making him double up in pain. Winded, he was unable to block the next punch to his face but he recovered enough to dodge the third shot and swing out at Munroe; his knuckles connected with the other man's chin. A stinging pain coursed through his fingers – he had used his burnt hand and, though the wound had nearly healed, the skin was still tender. Gritting his teeth, he drove his heel into Munroe's shin, causing him to stumble backwards. Munroe slipped on the dropped pipe and landed heavily on his backside.

Cormac might have seized that moment to make a dash for it, but the peak of the loose cap he had acquired from Liam fell into his eyes and he didn't see the blow coming from Lawlor. There was the fleshy sound of skin smacking skin and his head snapped sideways, the cap soaring off into the gloom. He bit the inside of his cheek and tasted the coppery tang of blood. Then the other two men stepped up to fight, leaving him with hardly an instant to breathe. One of them jabbed him in the shoulder he had twisted earlier and he let out a sharp hiss of pain. The other shoved him backwards and his skull slapped against the wall behind him. He slid down it, dazed, and they kicked at his legs and upper body until he managed to struggle to his feet again. He lashed out at them but his punches were becoming slower and fewer of them were making contact. Munroe and Lawlor joined back in too and he became progressively weaker under their concerted attack, while Cunningham observed with a look of deep satisfaction.

Cunningham was the key, he thought as the edges of his vision went momentarily blurry. These lackeys were nothing without their leader. If he could take Cunningham out, he might stand a chance. But it was impossible to get to him; four savage men stood in the way. And they were winning. He tried to duck as Munroe's fist came flying towards him once more but the blow landed on his ear and knocked him flat on his back on the dirty ground of the alley.

'Enough,' he heard Cunningham say as his head swam. 'Let us make the damage more precise.'

Cormac did not understand what he meant until Munroe knelt over him with the dagger, the smell of his sweat rippling off him.

'Where to begin?' he said, dangling the blade lazily over Cormac's face. 'Maybe your eyeballs. You're not going to need them for much longer.'

In such close proximity, Cormac had a detailed view of Munroe's own eyes. He saw the golden flecks in his irises, just like Henrietta's, and, with a surge of sadness for the little girl, recognised the truth in them.

'Or your tongue?' Munroe went on. 'You won't be in a position to kiss that strumpet of yours anymore.'

Cormac did not wait to hear more. In one swift movement, he reached out to grab the dagger and head-butted Munroe at the same time, ignoring the pain that rocked through him. Munroe fell backwards, clutching his nose, as Cormac rolled to his knees, secured his grip on the dagger and hurled it in Cunningham's direction. It sailed through the air and the point of it lodged in the centre of his stomach. Cormac had been aiming for the bastard's black heart but it had been a long time since he had wielded such a weapon. Though it was still a decent shot, he did not stop to admire it. In the short second when everyone stared in surprise at the unexpected turn of events, he was on his feet and bolting for the mouth of the alleyway.

He had just reached the street when a single shot rang out.

Chapter 24

Lord Bewley's carriage hurtled down the street away from the violent scene in the alleyway, its occupants tossed around like marbles in the coachman's haste to get away. Bridget clung to the arm strap for support and wrapped her other arm around Emily's shoulders. The little girl was still crying. Of course, she would not understand what had just happened, but she could sense her mother's anguish and tell that they had left her father behind with some very bad men. With an enormous effort, Bridget forced herself to stop weeping in order to put on a brave face for her daughter. Orlaith sat opposite them in a daze. Beside her, Lord Bewley was twisting his cane anxiously in his hands.

Nobody spoke for several minutes. Bridget's fingers were trembling, even though she, Emily and Orlaith were now out of harm's way. But Cormac was still in danger, the worst kind of danger imaginable. Those men had at least one dagger and a pistol while he was unarmed, and there were five of them and only one of him. What hope did he have?

No, she must not despair. She curled her left fist, feeling the coarseness of the thread ring in contrast with the smooth metal of the gold ring. Drawing courage from them, she dug her fingernails into her palm and clenched her jaw. She could not allow herself to contemplate the idea that he might die. In their last embrace, he had been confident of his escape and so must she be. To believe anything else would be unbearable.

'Where are we going?' she asked, breaking the tense

silence.

'To the docks,' said Lord Bewley. 'The sooner we get out of this infernal country, the better.'

'By no means shall we leave with you! We must go back.'

'Go back? Have you lost your wits?' He stopped twisting his cane to glare at her. 'It is best for everyone if we put this whole sordid affair behind us.'

'We need to turn around,' she insisted. 'He said he would meet us at the shelter.'

'My dear, he will not meet you. He is going to perish at the hands of those men. Forgive me for my brutal honesty, but it is a certainty.'

'I refuse to believe it,' she said desperately. 'You will take us to the shelter or we shall get out and walk there ourselves.'

He shook his head. 'Having seen the type of men who populate these streets, I think it would be unwise to let ladies walk them alone at night.'

'Then the gentlemanly thing to do would be to escort us where we wish to go.'

He shrugged helplessly. 'You are setting yourself up for a terrible disappointment.'

'No, I am not,' she said, digging her nails in even harder. 'I would appreciate your assistance in this regard, but we shall return on foot if we must.'

Disgruntled, he said, 'That won't be necessary. I have enough preying on my conscience tonight without adding the abandonment of three females to the list. Where do you want to go?'

'Thank you, I am grateful. The shelter is near Meath Street. If we return to the Liberties, I will recognise the correct street once I see it.'

Lord Bewley knocked on the coachman's partition with his cane and gave the instruction to turn back. It was clear from his frowning countenance that it was against his better judgement. As he settled again in his seat, he gave

Bridget a curious look. She arched her eyebrows in defiant enquiry.

He angled his head as though scrutinising a rare creature in a cage. 'I am trying to fathom what motivates you, Lady Wyndham. You had a fine life in London but you relinquished it to abscond with a liar and a thief. Now you are being presented with an opportunity to return to a privileged lifestyle, and yet you still choose the inferior option. What drives you to behave in such an unusual fashion?'

'It is all a matter of opinion,' she answered. 'To me, the inferior option would be to go back to the insipid existence of a lady of leisure with wealth but no love. Cormac has brought me happiness that I scarcely knew was possible. I would not forsake him for all the riches in the world. And I do not intend to forsake him tonight. If he says that he will meet us at the shelter, then he will.'

Lord Bewley absorbed this in astonishment and lapsed into pensive silence. Bridget wondered if her words would make any impact on his attitude. The walls of upper class society were high and thick but she would continue to whittle away at them brick by brick.

Next to her, Emily's tears had quietened to intermittent snuffles. Her eyelids were beginning to droop; the poor child was exhausted. Bridget kissed the top of her head.

'It won't be long until we see Papa again,' she murmured.

She glanced at Orlaith, caught the girl's dubious expression and raised her chin, challenging her to make a contradiction. Orlaith shrugged and looked out the window. Bridget could not tell what the girl planned to do but it appeared she was going to remain with them for the time being, at least until they knew her brother's fate.

Bridget peered out of the other window; night was falling quickly but she could still make out their surroundings. The carriage had retraced its route but the coachman had avoided the street with the inn and was travelling down a different street instead. This one was unfamiliar to her but then they turned onto the next one and she recognised the ugly face of O'Hara's.

'It is just around the corner from here,' she told Lord Bewley.

He nodded and passed the information on to the coachman.

'This is it,' she said a minute later. 'Please let us out now.'

The carriage came to a stop at Lord Bewley's order. The footman opened the door and first Orlaith and then Bridget and Emily stepped down. The little girl was whimpering from sheer fatigue; Mabel dangled limply from her hand.

'Lady Wyndham.'

Bridget turned back; Lord Bewley was leaning forwards in his seat. 'Yes?'

'Would you care for me to wait here until such time as you know for certain whether...?' He trailed off.

She pictured the mistrustful eyes of the local inhabitants. 'I regret to tell you that I do not think your prolonged presence in this vicinity would be appreciated.'

His gaze darted up the street. 'Then let me say this. I do not intend to linger in this country any longer than I have to. But I am going to delay my departure for another day. If your hopes are not realised, please know that you and your daughter, and the other girl if she wishes it, may have safe passage with me back to England.'

'That is very generous. However, we shall not be going with you. If we leave Ireland, we will travel west, not east. But thank you for your kind offer. And please give my regards to Lady Bewley.'

She curtseyed. He looked startled but not disapproving of their proposed destination. He lifted his hat.

'Be safe,' he said.

The footman closed the door and resumed his position, and the carriage rolled away. Bridget looked around; the last vestiges of daylight had almost subsided and there were no lamps lit on this street. It would be best to get inside quickly. She surveyed the tenement building with its vacant windows and shabby exterior. What had prompted Cormac to suggest it as their rendezvous point? They could not expect a warm welcome from Tess. But this was the place he had chosen and she was going to ensure that she would be there for him if – *when* – he arrived. Part of her wondered if he might have even reached the shelter before them.

She knew as soon as they stepped through the doorway that he had not. Marty had been sleeping and gave them a horrible reception when he woke to find strangers in his territory. Fortunately, Tess appeared from the back room and calmed him down. He retreated into a corner, muttering about 'nuisances' and 'peace and quiet'.

Tess turned with her hands on her hips, ready to deliver a cutting retort, but then her gaze travelled past Bridget to Orlaith. Her jaw dropped.

'O-Orlaith?'

For the first time since they had discovered her at Anner House – it had only been earlier that day but it seemed like a century ago – Orlaith smiled.

'Tess,' she said with warmth.

They embraced each other like long-lost sisters, and Bridget belatedly recognised Cormac's astuteness in sending them here. Tess drew back and regarded Orlaith in amazement.

'I can't believe they found you.' She looked over at Bridget and Emily and frowned. 'Where's –'

'There has been some trouble,' Bridget broke in. 'We need to stay here for a little while, but I hope not for long. Would that be acceptable?'

'What trouble?' said Tess with both confusion and suspicion.

Keeping it brief, Bridget described their predicament and explained how Cormac had promised to meet them

307

here as soon as he was able to break free from his captors.

'And you believed him?' said Tess.

'*Yes*. May we wait here until he comes?'

With a fleeting glance at Orlaith, Tess nodded. 'But, y'know, Cunningham isn't known for his mercy or his carelessness. You should start preparing yourself for the worst.'

Bridget closed her ears to the warning. 'Is there someplace where Emily could lie down? We have been walking for most of the day and she is all but asleep on her feet.'

Tess squinted at Marty, still grumbling in the corner, and said, 'Come upstairs.'

She led them through to the back room of the shelter and up a rickety staircase to the next floor. They glimpsed other ragged figures who shied away from them, slipping out of sight into the shadows. Orlaith appeared to be struggling to conceal her feelings and Bridget imagined how difficult it must be for her to return to the place where her mother and sister had died.

Tess showed Bridget a small pile of blankets in one of the upstairs rooms.

'This is my own place for sleeping. Your little girl can rest here.'

'Thank you very much,' said Bridget. She looked down at Emily, who was sagging with weariness. 'Time for bed, gooseberry.'

Emily stared around the room and then up at Bridget. 'I don't want to sleep alone.'

'I am going to be right here beside you,' Bridget replied, attempting to smile. She knelt on the floorboards next to the blankets and beckoned Emily to her. Emily lay down and Bridget arranged the blankets around her, tucking Mabel in too.

'Is Papa all right?' Emily asked in a tiny voice.

'Of course. He is going to be here when you wake up.' She prayed that Cormac would make that statement true.

'Go to sleep. You have nothing to be afraid of.'

She stroked Emily's golden curls and before long the little girl's eyelids fluttered and closed.

Orlaith and Tess were deep in conversation over by a broken window but Bridget, loath to intrude on their reunion, did not join them. She sat alone with her sleeping daughter and her own thoughts.

And what frightening thoughts they were. She could feel the grip of despair threatening to take hold of her again. The longer Cormac took to appear, the less likely it was that he would. It was so hard to keep up hope when all the evidence suggested that such expectation was folly. Cunningham and the men he led were diabolical thugs. It would take an extraordinary amount of luck for Cormac to survive an encounter with them. Was he that lucky? Or was the danger just too much this time?

She pressed her hands to her mouth to prevent her emotions from spilling over. She could not imagine how she would even breathe without Cormac. It was agony not knowing whether he was alive or dead, whether their fate had already been decided. She was in the dark – mind, body and soul.

She could not say how much time had passed – it might have been five minutes, or it might have been five hours – but gradually she became aware of a commotion downstairs. Marty was shouting in the room below and he was making no effort to be quiet.

'—tired of people walking in here!' she heard him bellow. 'Get out, I'm trying to sleep!'

Her mind was sluggish but she managed to process the fact that someone had disturbed his slumber.

There was somebody at the door.

She jumped to her feet and dashed for the staircase. Orlaith and Tess came running behind her. She took the stairs two at a time, slipped four steps from the bottom and fell to the floor on her hands and knees. Picking herself up, she tore into the front room and stopped dead.

The old man who had first told them about Tess stood in the centre of the room holding up a rushlight and pleading to Marty for some peace; the rushlight's dim glow illuminated the youth, who had taken up a hostile stance in the doorway, blocking the entrance to a figure beyond him.

'Go on, get out of here!' he roared.

'Marty, move out of the way!' Tess snapped behind Bridget.

She seemed to be the only person to whom he listened. He swore and stood back.

And there was Cormac. Bridget uttered a passionate cry of relief and rushed towards him. He leaned against the door jamb and smiled at her.

'There you are,' he rasped.

Then he fell through the doorway and onto the dusty floorboards in front of her. She gasped and dropped to her knees beside him. That was when she saw the blood soaking the sleeve of his coat and the small hole in his upper arm.

'He's been shot!'

To her surprise, Tess knelt down next to her.

'Turn him over,' she said urgently.

They rolled Cormac onto his back and Tess beckoned the old man closer with the rushlight so she could scrutinise the front of Cormac's arm.

'There's another hole here,' she said, pointing. 'That's good, means the ball came out the other side. But he's lost a lot of blood. We'll need to work fast.'

Bridget stared in shock as Tess took charge, ordering Marty to fetch a bowl and fill it from the water fountain at the end of the street. He obeyed with only a minimal amount of grousing. She began pulling Cormac's coat off him, answering Bridget's look of astonishment with a grimace.

'This isn't the first time I've seen a man shot. When you've lived on the streets as long as I have, you get to learn a thing or two about survival. Perhaps in another life I could've been a nurse.'

'And you are willing to help him?' Bridget stuttered. 'Despite what you believe about him?'

'If Cunningham tried to kill him,' said Tess, now ripping Cormac's shirt sleeve away to expose the gash in his flesh, 'then maybe he's a good man after all.'

Before Bridget could respond, Cormac murmured her name. She leaned in close to him and grasped his hand, disregarding his bloody knuckles. 'I'm here.'

'Emily? Orlaith?'

'They're safe too.'

'I ran,' he mumbled. 'They…didn't follow…knew they had got me. Dizzy…lost my bearings…but I found you.'

Even in the dimness, she could make out the marks and swelling on his face that showed how viciously the men had beaten him. She gulped.

'Yes, you did. You found me. And you must stay with me now. Don't leave me again. Do you promise?'

His eyelids flickered shut. When he opened them again, he had difficulty focusing on her.

'Some promises…hard to keep.'

She heard Tess calling to Orlaith to find some rags to bind the wound but blocked it all out, concentrating only on those disorientated blue irises.

'This one you have to keep,' she said firmly. 'Do you hear me? Promise me that you will stay with me.'

His breathing was shallow and erratic. She kissed his lips.

'Promise me.'

'I…'

His voice was so weak that she could scarcely hear him. Crouching next to his battered body while Tess staunched the bleeding from his arm and bandaged the wound, she prayed to God that he would not lose his grip on life.

'Orlaith,' she croaked and the girl bent down beside her. 'I need you to take a message to Rutland Square.'

311

It was the only possible source of aid left to her. She gave Orlaith directions for locating the square and Lord Walcott's residence.

'Please go there as quick as you can,' she entreated. 'Tell my uncle we need his help.'

Orlaith glanced down at her brother and, without another second's delay, vanished out the doorway.

Bridget stroked Cormac's hair. 'Speak to me,' she coaxed. 'Explain what happened in the alley.'

So fearful of his slurred speech and unfocused gaze, she encouraged and bullied him to keep talking. She was terrified that if she let him fall asleep, he might never wake up. The minutes stretched, distorted beyond any resemblance to the normal passage of time, and she began to feel that this was the longest day of her life.

At last, Orlaith reappeared and her look of optimism gave Bridget a shred of hope. Despite the lateness of the hour, her uncle had responded to her plea for help and had sent a carriage to the tenement to bear Cormac back to Rutland Square where Lord Walcott's own physician would treat him. Bridget, Emily, Orlaith and Tess all piled into the carriage too, Tess still applying pressure to the dressing on Cormac's arm, and they clattered towards Lord Walcott's house through the quiet city streets, where a faint gleam in the sky foretold that the dawn was about to break.

Chapter 25

Cormac winced as he stirred awake, reluctant to open his eyes lest the action add to his list of aches. He could tell he was lying on a soft surface of some sort, probably a bed, but that provided little comfort to the blinding pain in his temples or the dull throbbing in his arm or the tenderness in his jaw and limbs. His stomach roiled with nausea and he focused for several moments on not being sick. Once he was reasonably confident that the worst of it had passed, he risked opening his eyelids.

A figure sat by the bed; he blinked and Bridget swam into focus. She was gazing down into her lap.

'Bridget?'

Her head snapped up. Anxiety and hope filled her features. She stood and leaned over him. 'Yes, it's me. You know it's me?'

'Of course,' he said.

She covered her mouth and started to weep.

Mystified, he added, 'How could I not?'

She cried harder, heaving unashamed, shuddering sobs of relief. He squinted against the light and waited until her tears had subsided enough to respond.

'Yesterday you were confused,' she said with a sniff. 'And the day before was worse. Do you recall much of the past few days?'

He concentrated, even though it hurt to do so. 'I can remember sporadic headaches.' He grimaced. 'And a bout of severe vomiting, if I'm not mistaken. The rest is a bit of a blur.'

She nodded. 'Your sense of awareness was erratic at

best. We've been so worried but my uncle's physician said to give it some time. Dear God, you have no idea how happy I am to see such clarity in your eyes.'

She cupped his cheek and kissed his lips. When she sat back in her chair, he pushed aside the bedcovers.

'What are you doing?' she objected, jumping to her feet again.

'Getting up?' he tried.

'You shall do no such thing.' She pulled the bedcovers firmly back into place. 'You'll lie there until the physician says otherwise.'

This was wise advice, for the thumping in his head had intensified. He lay back against the pillows. 'Where's Emily?'

Bridget sat on the edge of the bed, perhaps to prevent further attempts at escape. 'Off shadowing her new aunties with adoration.'

'Aunties?' he repeated, worried that his confusion had returned.

'She's decided that Tess is as good as an aunt to her. Orlaith and Tess have been inseparable since they reunited.'

He was very glad to hear that for his sister's sake, even if his own standing in Tess's eyes was uncertain.

'What about Cunningham?'

Bridget's face darkened at the name. 'My uncle prevailed upon his footman, Simon, to make some cautious enquiries. It seems by all accounts that Cunningham has vanished and his men have scattered.'

She went on to tell him that the footman had heard rumours of rejoicing in the back alleys of Dublin at the disappearance of Cunningham. It would surely not be long before one of his thugs decided to take up his mantle but for now the money lender's business was in tatters. However, Simon had confirmed that Thomasina's associates remained in the lodgings that had been occupied by Cunningham's men, and perhaps it would be only a matter of time before the building turned into a brothel.

This news once more spurred a desire in Cormac to leave his bed but Bridget was unyielding on the matter. He was obliged to wait for the arrival of the physician, who chose not to make an appearance until the following morning. Upon the man's examination of him, Cormac made light of any residual aches and pains to achieve his release. In spite of Bridget's protestations that he still needed to rest, the first thing he did once he was finally permitted to rise was to go straight to Cunningham's lodgings.

When he strode into the place, the women goggled at him.

'Here, where d'you think you're going?' one of them demanded.

'Rest assured, I don't intend to stay long,' he said, his skin crawling at being under that roof again.

He hunted high and low and eventually found Henrietta hiding in a cupboard with her doll tucked under her arm. She looked dirtier than ever and ravenous with hunger. He picked her up, ignoring the pain in his injured arm, and cast an admonishing glare at the women who had followed on his heels as he searched.

'Did you forget she was here?' he accused them.

'We was looking after her, we swear!'

He carried Henrietta and the doll out of there without a backward glance.

Though it was against his better judgement, he brought her to O'Hara's on Meath Street. Mrs O'Hara's gap-toothed mouth fell open when he entered her shabby establishment and set the child down in front of her.

'She's your grandniece and you're the only family she has left,' he declared.

She didn't reproach him for neglecting his paternal obligations, so he could only assume she had been wise to Thomasina's lies. She peered down at Henrietta, who was chewing on the skin around one of her fingernails.

'Are you going to do the right thing?' Cormac asked.

Mrs O'Hara faltered for only a moment before nodding and, to his shock, a tear rolled down one of her withered cheeks.

'My dear Thomasina, bless her soul. She's gone to God too soon. Yes, I'll take care of her little girl.'

Cormac crouched on his hunkers to say goodbye to Henrietta. She didn't speak, only clasped the doll to her like she would never let it go. He felt a tug of regret behind his ribs as he walked out the door.

Afterwards, he told Bridget what had happened in a despondent voice, while she replaced the bandage on the wound in his arm which had started leaking blood again.

'I hope I've made the right decision,' he said, passing a hand over his aching forehead in doubt. 'Part of me wanted to bring Henrietta with us but Mrs O'Hara is her flesh and blood. I couldn't take her away while she still has family in Ireland.'

'Moreover, the responsibility for her doesn't fall to you,' Bridget reminded him gently, for he had imparted the details of Henry Munroe's startling revelation. 'She isn't your child.'

He let out a sigh. 'But the point is she could have been.'

Bearing that in mind, he resolved to correspond with Mrs O'Hara in the future to see how Henrietta was faring. He hoped that, notwithstanding the loss of her mother, she would lead a happier existence away from the dreadful place where her life had begun.

Bridget finished binding the wound on his arm and rolled up the used bandage. Casting a critical eye over his battered appearance, she said, 'You are going to create quite a stir at the solicitors' office.'

They had been obliged to postpone the Tuesday appointment at Webb & Brereton Solicitors until Cormac had recovered his full faculties and the swelling on his face had diminished somewhat. Even so, his lingering bruises caused Mr Croft's eyebrows to nearly vanish into his hairline upon their arrival at Baggot Street. They invented a story about an assault by a brigand on the street and succeeded in signing the contract drawn up by Mr Brereton, but they were all too aware that the circumstances of their two visits had come across as highly irregular. Any subsequent correspondence the solicitors might choose to send to Wyndham House in London, despite Cormac's instruction to write directly to the stewards at Oakleigh, would alert Garrett to their deception.

Taking that into account, Bridget opted to write to Garrett herself and explain what had transpired at Oakleigh, from Lady Courcey's despicable actions which had triggered the uprising to Bridget's decision to appoint Laurence Enright and John Corbett as joint stewards. She placed a great emphasis on the fact that the new arrangement would bring Garrett income without the slightest need for his involvement.

'I hope he will react in a reasonable way and see that it is for the best,' she said to Cormac as she sealed the letter.

He offered a one-armed shrug, avoiding any jerky movement with his injured arm – his rescue of Henrietta had impeded the healing process somewhat. 'If he chooses to make trouble and insists upon taking control of the estate, then perhaps we can encourage the tenants to revolt again.'

She laughed but he hadn't spoken entirely in jest.

Their lives became ruled by letters as they awaited responses to the enquiries Lord Walcott had sent out. When he learned of Tess's speculation that Bronagh may have travelled to America, he dispatched messages to the authorities managing the various ports around Ireland, seeking information as to whether her name had appeared on any passenger lists over the past five years. He used the power of his title to encourage the officials to adopt the utmost speed in their replies.

Cormac and Bridget were taking breakfast with him one morning in the library when Simon carried in a tray bearing a letter.

'Oho!' he exclaimed and Brutus emitted a feeble yap at the loud noise. Lord Walcott hushed the dog as he opened the letter. 'It is from the Cork Harbour Commissioners.' He scanned it quickly and repeated, 'Oho,' with a deep pitch of satisfaction.

Burning with the desire to know its contents, Cormac said calmly, 'What does it say, my lord?'

Lord Walcott beamed. 'They have a record of a Bronagh McGovern on one of their passenger lists.' He skimmed down the letter again. 'It was two years ago. The ship in question stopped at Cove on its way from Liverpool to Boston.'

Cormac's heart almost burst with exhilaration. 'That is such welcome news.'

'Do you believe it's her?' Bridget said breathlessly.

'It could very well be. She doesn't have a common name, after all.' He frowned. 'Only two years ago though. If it's our Bronagh, that means three years passed between her running away from Dublin and getting on the ship in Cork. What could she have been doing during all that time?'

'Perhaps she was earning the money to pay for her ticket?' Bridget suggested.

'Speaking of tickets,' Lord Walcott said, 'it says here that her ticket was purchased as part of a pair, according to their records, but the ink on the second name was smeared and regrettably illegible.'

This was surprising but pleasing to hear. Whomever she had travelled with, Cormac was glad she had found a companion and had not made the journey alone. While the letter was not irrefutable evidence that the Bronagh McGovern on the passenger list was his own sister, it was the closest to proof they could expect to obtain. This

Bronagh had crossed the Atlantic Ocean and so they would follow through on their decision to do the same.

Chapter 26

The breeze was cool on Bridget's cheeks. Seagulls wheeled and screeched in the air above and merry waves lapped the hull of the ship. The ocean spread out in every direction around her. It was blue and calm beneath the cloudless sky, a day of perfect weather on this lengthy sea crossing. She breathed in deeply, her palms resting on the gunwale and loose tendrils of hair tickling her face.

The sound of laughter came to her – Emily playing with Orlaith and Tess further up the deck of the ship. Waving her imaginary sword, Emily loudly proclaimed that she was already seven and a quarter years old, therefore she would be the one in charge of the treasure they would seize from the next pirate ship that came sailing by. Six had been a turbulent year for her but seven was going to be better. Much, much better. Even Orlaith and Tess had been convinced to hope for greater things across the water.

Bridget smiled as a hand drew her hair away from her neck and a pair of lips pressed a kiss to her exposed nape. She glanced back at Cormac, who gave her a boyish grin. After all the perils he had faced, he was alive and well, and she thanked God every day for it.

So much had happened since they had landed in Ireland and yet, with all their travels around the country, they had ended up back in Cove. Naturally, they had not looked for accommodation at McLoughlin's Boarding House but, while they had arranged passage on the next ship heading for Boston, they had sought out Nancy McLoughlin, who had been delighted to see them. Her children were growing like weeds and she had intimated that she had the bigoted Agnes firmly under her thumb.

When they had finally boarded the ship bound for America, it had been with no small amount of sadness for they did not know when they would return to Irish shores. But family came first – even though, by crossing the ocean to seek one family member, they had left another behind. Still, they had not left Patrick in an unhappy situation, from his own perspective at least. He was spoiled but he was neither hungry nor cold, and he would grow up with the best of everything. While the encounter on the doorstep of Anner House had ostensibly achieved nothing, it was still possible that they had sown seeds of doubt in his young mind. Perhaps when he got older he would become more curious about the family who had first raised him. All they could do was wait and see.

'I can see land!' The cry came from Emily who jumped up and down on the deck and pointed excitedly.

Everyone stared at the horizon. There was a faint smudge far out in the distance where the water met the sky – could it be land? Was America in sight? Emily came running towards Bridget and Cormac, leaping into Cormac's arms with a squeal. His injury was now fully healed and he swung Emily around, causing her to shriek with glee. Bridget was glad to see her enthusiasm. The poor child had struggled with seasickness early in the voyage so it was cheering to see her in high spirits once again.

'We're nearly there!' Emily said happily.

'Thanks be to God,' Cormac replied.

Emily responded by blessing herself. She had taken to doing this at any mention of God since Cormac had shown her how to do it. He had also been teaching her Catholic prayers for he and Bridget had decided that they would baptise Emily in the Catholic faith once they reached America. Bridget intended to convert as well, and the prospect of it brought her joy.

Emily looked out across the water again. 'Do I have time

to make a painting of it?' she begged. 'I still have two sheets of paper left.'

Once she had recovered from her seasickness, her painting had kept her entertained during the long, monotonous days at sea. Her watercolour box remained safe in her possession, for Simon had gone to the inn to retrieve their valises from the innkeeper when Bridget had been too anxious to stir from Cormac's side.

'I don't see why not,' Cormac said to Emily. 'It will be quite a while yet before we get to dock.'

Beaming, she slid down out of his grasp and called, 'Come on, Auntie Orlaith, Auntie Tess! Let's go painting.'

Orlaith followed her niece at once, accompanying her in the direction of their cabin. Throughout the voyage, Bridget had continually felt gratitude towards her uncle who had both insisted upon them travelling as cabin passengers and provided them with enough funds to do so. Having witnessed the deplorable conditions that the steerage passengers had been forced to endure these past weeks at sea, Bridget could only shudder at the thought of their suffering. She had made a habit of slipping biscuits into her pocket so that if any of the young children from steerage came near her on deck she could give them a bite to eat to fill their constantly rumbling stomachs.

Tess trailed after Orlaith and Emily but came to a stop in front of Bridget and Cormac. She glanced out at the distant smudge, her red hair fluttering in the breeze.

'Who would've thought Teresa O'Leary would ever clap eyes on the coastline of America?' She shook her head. 'If only my ma could see me now.'

When she looked at them again, her gaze focused solely on Cormac, freezing Bridget out of the conversation.

'I want to apologise,' Tess said. 'I was wrong about you. I made some nasty accusations that evening at the inn and I'd like to take them back because it's plain as day the person you are doesn't match the reputation of the brute McGovern. Maybe you did some bad things in your time, but sure haven't we all?' She peered down at the deck. 'And I'm sorry for telling those men where to find you. You didn't deserve that, 'specially not with all the trouble it brought.'

'You don't need to say any of this,' Cormac interjected. 'Honestly, I don't hold it against you.'

'I *do* need to say it.' Her tone was almost angry. 'You're the reason I'm about to set foot on American soil instead of heading out onto the streets in search of another man who'll pay me if I satisfy him.' Her cheeks had gone as red as her hair. 'I have a whole new life ahead of me. You're my guardian angel all over again.'

When she peeked up at him once more, there was an unmistakable glow in her eyes. She reached out with both of her hands and he automatically took them.

'Thank you,' she said fervently, 'for saving me.'

She dropped his hands and hurried away after Orlaith and Emily. He turned to Bridget, looking embarrassed at Tess's praise.

'That was more demonstrative than we are used to seeing from her,' he said, for Tess had kept to herself or Orlaith's company for most of the voyage. 'I'm glad we've been able to make her life better. She is as much a part of the McGovern family now as any of us.'

Bridget didn't think Tess viewed him as a brother but she kept her observations to herself. 'Here's hoping we can add another sister in due course.'

His expression grew sombre. Would they find Bronagh? What lay ahead of them in this unknown country?

'Here's hoping,' he echoed.

Moving to stand behind her, he encircled his arms around her waist. He kissed her temple and together they looked out to the horizon again. His chest expanded against her back in a deep breath. Then his hands tightened on her belly, feeling the roundness that had not been there before.

She smiled. 'Yes,' she said in answer to his unspoken

question. 'Another impending addition to the McGovern family. Are you happy?'

'I don't think I have the words to express how I feel,' he said, but the strength of his embrace told her enough.

What's Next

Thank you for reading! Would you like to spend more time in Bridget and Cormac's world? Join the **Susie Murphy Readers' Club** on www.susiemurphywrites.com, where you will receive a collection of five free short stories which are prequels to the whole series. You will see exactly how Bridget and Cormac became friends, how they were first torn asunder, and the tumultuous events that brought about their transition from childhood to adulthood.

By joining, you will also be the first to get updates about A Matter of Class, including book release details, bonus content, and a chance to read future books in the series before they're published!

Did you enjoy this book? If you did, please help other readers discover Bridget and Cormac's story by leaving an honest review about A Class Forsaken on Amazon and/or Goodreads. A short review will make a huge difference in spreading the word about A Matter of Class.

The next novel in the series will be A Class Coveted.

Acknowledgements

My heartfelt thanks to Averill Buchanan for her keen editorial eye and to Andrew Brown at Design for Writers for creating such a stunning cover for this book.

My husband, Bob, deserves high billing for his unending patience. I can recall the night I came to bed at 2am after working on a particular scene and proceeded to discuss the intricacies of 19th century inheritance law with him. Happily, I teased out the plot line that was giving me trouble, but I'm sure Bob would have much preferred to be asleep.

I owe a debt of gratitude to my first readers of this book: Bob Murphy, Miriam Bourke, Grace Noon, Miriam Lanigan, Noreen Uí Ghríofa, and Claire Moloney. They offered feedback on the manuscript with a tremendous generosity of both time and thought.

Huge thanks next to my advance reader team who agreed to read this book before it was released. Their passion for Bridget and Cormac's story has been an absolute joy to behold.

A very special mention goes to Michele Quirke who has done so much to spread the word about this series that I need to start paying her a commission. She is a superstar in the Twitter writing community.

Elizabeth Bell also merits particular recognition for her timely advice, astute observations and empathetic support.

Words cannot express how grateful I am to the authors, bloggers and book reviewers who have been so willing to shine a light on my little corner of the book world. Thank you especially to Claire Bridle, Lisa Redmond, Trish Hannon, Valerie Whitford, Ashley O'Melia, Anne Mendez, Stacie Tyson, Tony Riches, Kelsey Gietl, Nicola Cassidy, and Niamh Boyce.

I greatly appreciate the kindness of Anne O'Grady at the Tipperary Star and Fran Curry at Tipp FM.

Thanks, as always, to my fantastic family and friends for their enthusiasm and support.

Finally, I acknowledge YOU, my wonderful readers. Thank you so much for reading and for continuing to follow Bridget and Cormac's journey. Your lovely messages, reviews and comments mean more to me than I could ever say.

Get in Touch

www.susiemurphywrites.com
www.facebook.com/susiemurphywrites
www.twitter.com/susiemwrites
www.instagram.com/susiemurphywrites

Made in the USA
Coppell, TX
05 January 2021